MARK'S POWER PEEK

2007

HAY HOUSE TITLES OF RELATED INTEREST

Astrology Through a Psychic's Eyes, by Sylvia Browne

Astrology—Your Quantum Key to Co-creation,
by Robert Ohotto (available May 2007)

BY WILLIAM R. LEVACY:
Beneath a Vedic Sky:
A Beginner's Guide to the Astrology of Ancient India;

Beneath a Vedic Sun:
Discover Your Life Purpose with Vedic Astrology; and

Vedic Astrology Simply Put:
An Illustrated Guide to the Astrology of Ancient India,

○◑◐●

Born to Be Together: *Love Relationships, Astrology, and the Soul,* by Terry Lamb

Colors & Numbers: *Your Personal Guide to Positive Vibrations in Daily Life,* by Louise L. Hay

The Complete Book of Numerology: *Discovering the Inner Self,* by David A. Phillips, Ph.D.

Discover Yourself: *Understand Your Mind, Know Your Body, Nurture Your Spirit, Realize Your Potential,* by Lillian Too

The Ultimate Astrologer: *A Simple Guide to Calculating and Interpreting Birth Charts for Effective Application in Daily Life,* by Nicholas Campion

○◑◐●

MARK'S POWER PEEK 2007

A DAILY ASTROLOGICAL COMPANION

MARK S. HUSSON

HAY HOUSE

Hay House, Inc.
Carlsbad, California
London • Sydney • Johannesburg
Vancouver • Hong Kong • New Delhi

Published and distributed in the United States by: Hay House, Inc.: www.hayhouse.com • ***Published and distributed in Australia by:*** Hay House Australia Pty. Ltd.: www.hayhouse.com.au • ***Published and distributed in the United Kingdom by:*** Hay House UK, Ltd.: www.hayhouse.co.uk • ***Published and distributed in the Republic of South Africa by:*** Hay House SA (Pty), Ltd.: orders@psdprom.co.za • ***Distributed in Canada by:*** Raincoast: www.raincoast.com • ***Published in India by:*** Hay House Publications (India) Pvt. Ltd.: www.hayhouseindia.co.in • ***Distributed in India by:*** Media Star: booksdivision@mediastar.co.in

Editorial supervision: Jill Kramer • *Design:* Tricia Breidenthal

Library of Congress Cataloging-in-Publication Data

Husson, Mark S.
Mark's power peek 2007 : a daily astrological companion / Mark S. Husson.
p. cm.
ISBN-13: 978-1-4019-1156-0 (tradepaper)
ISBN-10: 1-4019-1156-0 (tradepaper)
1. Astrology. I. Title: Power peek 2007. II. Title.
BF1708.1.H87 2006
133.5'4042--dc22

2006000363

ISBN 13: 978-1-4019-1156-0
ISBN 10: 1-4019-1156-0

09 08 07 06 4 3 2 1
1st printing, August 2006

Printed in the United States of America

To the Bean

♎

CONTENTS

PART III: APPENDICES

FOREWORD

It's been said about the ancient and fascinating art of astrology that "a wise man rules his stars; a fool is ruled by them." Well, I know Mark Husson, and he's anything but a fool. In his newsletter, time and time again I've seen him empower his readers as opposed to just telling them what to do, educate people rather than just selling them something, and foster real spiritual growth instead of simply playing on their hopes. Mark is not only one of the best astrologers in the world . . . he's a great guy.

You may ask why a teacher of *A Course in Miracles,* which explains the dreamlike, illusory nature of the Universe and a way to end the cycle of being born into it, would want to write about Mark and his work. The answer is simple: Astrology, when done well, is fascinating—illusory Universe or not. Plus, I'm proud to call Mark a friend of mine, and when he asked me to write this Foreword, it didn't take me more than ten seconds to say yes.

So, why has this art always been so fascinating to people? Certainly, when it was first developed, astrology was practiced by people who were closer to nature and the beauty of the cosmos. After all, without city lights to interfere, the heavens are a wonder to behold at night. I was recently in Florida after a bad hurricane, and people were in awe of the spectacle of stars they'd seen when the electricity was lost for over a week and there were no lights to obstruct their view—they simply couldn't believe how beautiful the sky was. But that connection to the stars was a normal way of life for people before the 20th century.

Everything is one . . . thus, everything is connected. My teachers in the books *The Disappearance of the Universe* and *Your Immortal Reality* speak of how electromagnetic energy swirling through the Universe regulates everything about us, and how this power is controlled by the total movements of the stars, suns, moons, and planets. Just as this electromagnetic energy corresponds to all events, astrology relates to the "script" of time and space that we agreed to participate in before we ever appeared here.

Of course, that doesn't mean that astrology is perfect. Indeed, nothing can ever be totally predictable because, paradoxically, the Universe is set up through strange attractors and multiple other features *not* to be completely foreseeable. If it were, then it wouldn't be any fun . . . and it also wouldn't be full of fear. It's this very duality that makes a Universe apart from our Source seem possible.

If all is connected, then whatever happens anywhere in the Universe is one with anything else that happens, ever has happened, or ever will. Thus, there can be no accidents. The force of the beginning of the Universe—the so-called big bang—was so huge that it set a history of events into motion that would, by definition, have to happen, and couldn't do so in any other way. Within that history are patterns, which astrology maps, along with the resulting energy, revealing the influences that are at play in our lives and those of others. It can be fun to use this knowledge in the quantum (that is, oneness and no separation) rather than the Newtonian (subject and object) sense, keeping in mind that the real purpose of everything is forgiveness. It's this kind of forgiveness that empowers us to be peaceful *regardless* of what appears to be taking place in the world.

Mark has a tremendous talent for explaining the astrological influences that are present in our lives and for coaching us on how to best make use of them. I've asked him for his advice on several occasions and have always been blessed by his responses, which are consistently empowering and educational.

The great industrialist J. P. Morgan once said, "Millionaires don't use astrology; billionaires do." Morgan was the only billionaire at the time that he made this statement. (He also declined an invitation to sail on the maiden voyage of the *Titanic*.) I don't promise that if you follow Mark's advice, you'll become a billionaire. J. P. Morgan's success, like anyone else's, was preordained . . . we all live extremely rich lifetimes at one point or another, and in his next one, he probably didn't have it so good. What I *can* promise you is that if you're wise enough to rule your stars and not be ruled by them, Mark's work is the best you can turn to for a masterly understanding of a great and durable art.

— Gary R. Renard

○☽☾●

PART I

INTRODUCTION

HOW AND WHY THIS BOOK WILL ENHANCE YOUR LIFE

I know what you're thinking: *Not another horoscope book!* Well, it's not . . . but let me explain why.

I spent all of my early life looking for something that could help me understand who I was and why I felt so different. I did all the things a confused young man would do with such an aim: When I was 10, I opened my first Freudian psychology book, one that my father had from his school days; I sought psychotherapy starting at the age of 16; and then I majored in psychology in college, eventually acquiring a master's degree in counseling. Everything I did up to age 30 was devoted to trying to understand myself.

Most of my undergraduate years found me firmly embedded in the self-help section of the local bookstore, where I would spend hours looking for titles that had my answers. The late 1970s (God bless them!) were spawning new pop-psych books faster than you could say, "I'm okay, you're an idiot," and I'm sure that I read most of them—always seeking, never finding. Then it happened . . . meandering in the New Age section brought me to my first astrology book—and my life changed.

My early Gestalt training, combined with the wisdom of astrology, taught me that everything we see is a reflection of something we believe about ourselves. So if I fear the planets in some way, it's a metaphor for something that I fear about myself. My astrology chart explained so much to me: my shyness, my need for answers, my deep spirituality—*everything*. At last, not only was I able to accept myself completely, but I was also able to accept everyone I knew. I now understood why my Virgo mother abhorred having company, and why my Cancer father was always cooking for us. The knowledge poured in, and my brain was a willing sponge. My therapist was so impressed with my growth and self-discovery that he began studying astrology, too.

In 1982, I took what I knew of astrology out into the world (Denver, to be exact), and I had a startling realization: Horoscope writers had corrupted the meaning of astrology. It seemed that the very mention of myself as an astrologer led the majority of the new friends I'd met to dismiss me. One of my counseling colleagues summed it up: "Astrology is a silly opiate that preys upon the weak." He didn't know that he was really talking about commonplace, garden-variety horoscopes, which don't apply to true astrology. The poor guy had no idea that he could have been a much better counselor knowing even just a little about the gifts inherent in an astrological chart. But it was clear that, according to most of the world around me, only a fool would make a career out of astrology.

In a way, I couldn't blame people. The only powerful books on the subject then in existence were written for a small audience who were already astrologers, and inane horoscopes were to be found everywhere—in every magazine, every newspaper, and later, on millions of Websites—usually written by non-astrologers who were adept at offering random warnings (at best) without any genuine astrological foundation.

My task seemed daunting, but my passion to bring astrology to a newer and wider audience was fueled. My weekly newsletter, the "Power Peek," came to life as a way to speak to the masses about the wonders of astrology, in a format that everyone was familiar with. I had to assume that horoscopes remained attractive to people because they wanted validation for their experiences in life, especially in difficult times. It's an idea that rides at the fringes of the phrase "Misery loves company," but goes beyond that. I think it would be more accurate (though perhaps less poetic) to say, "Misery is simply less miserable when we don't feel alone." If a horoscope sounded remotely familiar within the reader's set of circumstances, there was some relief . . . even if only for a second.

The premise of "Power Peek" is that we all live under the same astrological influences, regardless of our individual signs. It's like a weather forecast, but it's based on the actual relationships that the planets form with each other. I like to think of it as if we each were a different type of automobile: Some of us are SUVs, others are sports cars, and the rest of us are the various other kinds of motor vehicles in-between. Now imagine that I see snow in the forecast. When that snow shows up on the roads, each vehicle is equipped to react differently (sports cars will likely be left in a spray of slush as the SUVs pummel forward, and so on), but one thing is certain to all: It definitely snowed.

I launched **www.12house.com** in 1996 and posted the first edition of the weekly "Power Peek," whose name I'd hoped would subtly imply that the content was empowerment, not fear. I outlined the basic astrological trends without sounding too technical, and whenever I could, I reminded my audience that the planets were their "friends." Each week, the "Power Peek" became more bold and honest. As I grew, it did, too, and my readers watched me struggle through a battery of issues, some that I could resolve with astrology, and some that I'd have to figure out as my own maturation process evolved. My site's members were unbelievably kind and supportive, writing to encourage me with their wisdom and their own experiences. The "Power Peek" had found its audience, and *I* had found an entire family of allies.

It's been heartwarming to watch the membership of **12house.com** consistently increase each month, mostly through word of mouth. My mission to share the wisdom and gifts of astrology continues to inspire my weekly message, and with the publication of this book, it's my hope that many more readers will feel empowered to recognize the choices they can make to accept themselves and those around them for who they are: perfect reflections of a Divine spark.

This book carries on the tradition of the weekly "Power Peek," but with daily horoscopes describing what you can expect. There's a monthly summary to give you a hint of what's to come, as well as my "Thought for the Month" for a slice of encouragement. Look to the "Success Rating" each day to show you at a glance what the day has in store for you. While I don't want to pull the curtain *too* far back from the wizard, the Success Rating is based on the major astrological aspects (which are the focus in the "Big Spins of the Day" sections), as well as less commonly known aspects (inconjuncts, parallels, contra-parallels, and so forth) that I use to scrutinize the subtler nuances of a particular day.

The next three chapters will give you some basic explanations of the astrological terms that I employ throughout these pages in order to make the interpretations more practical. Use this book in the way it was intended, as a companion and guide, but not as a bible. I hope that you find it as much of a joy to use as I found it to write.

And, as always, I'm with you on the quest. . . .

— **Mark**

YOUR SPECIAL RELATIONSHIP WITH THE MOON

The Cycles of the Moon

The Moon moves through your life in a constant ebb and flow, just like the ocean's tides that it so visibly affects. The Moon passes through all 12 Zodiac signs during the 29-day lunar month, and there are certain times when those influences become stronger and more specific in the types of experiences that they bring. Noting how the Moon makes you feel throughout the month can be fun and insightful. I'll now summarize the major phases of the Moon so that you can more deeply understand these time periods when you read about them in Part II: Your Daily Guide.

New Moon (Sun and Moon Conjunct): When the Sun and Moon renew their acquaintance, they're at the same degree, in the same sign, and they signal a new beginning. Since the Moon is covering the Sun, we only see a dark orb, which is why this Moon is also referred to as the Dark Moon. This darkness starts the "waxing" moon, and as the light increases, so do the opportunities to plant new seeds, ideas, and projects that will expand your life experiences. It's a great time to think about what you'd like to "grow" over the next two weeks. Sometimes I'll recommend that you light a candle and make a list, and although it certainly isn't necessary, doing so can help you focus on your desires—and that's a good thing!

First Quarter Moon (Sun and Moon Squared): The Sun and Moon meet in some tension as they square off in this second phase of the lunar cycle. Obstacles to the ideas or changes initiated at the New Moon may become more apparent to you, which means that they can now be overcome. These challenges are often remnants of the past, which is reflected by the signs involved. Now is the time to be willing to look consciously at these past issues and make new choices if you want things to be different. Remember, if you see an obstacle, you're also seeing something that's encouraging you to get "back on track."

Full Moon (Sun and Moon in Opposition): The Moon is now opposite the Sun, with the Earth in the middle, allowing us to see the Moon's full glory. This bright Moon has traditionally been seen as a time of completion and clarification of whatever's been started during the last New Moon cycle. This begins the "waning" phase of the Moon, in which the emotional forces of our unconscious show up. The Moon will lose light from this day on, making it a powerful time to release and renew.

Last Quarter (Sun and Moon Squared): As the light of the Moon diminishes, your experiences may culminate in a feeling of crisis as you move toward the final point of understanding for the entire lunar cycle. Whatever previously went unrecognized or unresolved can now be seen in this last opportunity for clarity and release before the new cycle begins.

Moon Void of Course: The Moon travels through all 12 signs of the Zodiac each lunar month. As it reaches the end of one sign and is getting ready to enter the next one, there's a period of time in which it has no aspect relationship to any of the planets or to the Sun. The Moon is considered "Void of Course" during this interval, which could last anywhere from seconds to days. Since the Moon helps you feel your way through life, during this rather disconnected phase you may experience a sense of distance or confusion with what's going on outwardly in your environment. It's as if all the lights are on, but nobody's answering the front door.

This is a good time to go inward and be centered, knowing that you and the world are feeling fuzzy and distracted. During this lack of focus, it's not a particularly helpful time to make important decisions—especially those that will create long-term commitments in the world. You will, however, have access to incredible spiritual, emotional, and creative insights if you're willing to pull your attention inward. The Void of Course ends when the Moon enters the next sign.

Solar Eclipse (Sun and Moon Conjunct): The definition of a Solar Eclipse is almost identical to a New Moon. It's true that the Sun and Moon are located at the same sign and degree, but this time, they're also at the same height such that the Moon literally blocks the light of the Sun and casts a shadow on the Earth. This Moon holds the same meaning as a New Moon, but has a stronger impact and tends to last longer. Since the Moon's energies are amplified, we tend to feel a bigger emotional reaction during Eclipses.

Lunar Eclipse (Sun and Moon in Opposition): Like a Full Moon, the Lunar Eclipse occurs when the Sun and Moon are in opposite signs with the Earth in the middle, aligned in such an exact position that it causes the Earth to cast a shadow on the Moon. The more exactly the shadow of the Earth is on the Moon, the more total the Eclipse is. This Moon has the same meaning as a Full Moon, but we tend to feel it more intensely. This is still a time of completion and clarification, but our issues get magnified. Eclipses can be tracked on 19-year cycles, so you can actually look back to see how the last exact one affected you.

○◑◐●

UNDERSTANDING THE RELATIONSHIPS BETWEEN THE PLANETS

Aspects and Angles

Everything in astrology is based on how things appear from our perspective on Earth. For example, we know that Earth really revolves around the Sun, but from our vantage point, the Sun appears to rise in the east and set in the west, so it's actually considered a planet. From this *geocentric* (Earth-centered) viewpoint, the entire solar system is spinning around us in a contained area that easily allows us to view the relationships of the planets to each other. Sometimes Mars will look as if it's 90 degrees away from Pluto, or maybe Jupiter will appear to be in the same location as Venus. The combinations are endless and could make your head spin right along with the planets if it weren't for the help of computers.

These combinations of planetary relationships are called *aspects,* and they're based on the angle of relationship between the planets. Since astrology is a metaphorical map, as the planets interact with each other, they also reflect that same interaction in our lives. There are certain relationships that make a more definite impact—namely, when the planets are at the same point in space, or at various 30-degree increments. The following are the most significant aspects I'll be using in this guide:

Conjunction (0°): When planets are at the same degree in the sky, their energies strongly affect each other. They become blended, and depending on the planets involved and which sign they're in, an easy or a challenging experience could be created. We can feel this aspect in powerful and profound ways. The planet that's actually farthest out in the solar system often carries the greatest influence. For example, someone with Venus in Gemini enjoys light and frivolous dialogue, whereas a person with Venus in Gemini conjunct Pluto enjoys talks that are deep and forthright, dismissing idle chitchat as mere gossip. I consider the Conjunction to be one of the most potent of all the aspects.

Sextile (60°): Sextiles are your friends. In lay terms, this is the "every-other-sign" aspect because in the Zodiac wheel, every other sign is composed of compatible elements (Water and Earth, Fire and Air). For example, Aries is a Fire sign. Two signs ahead is Gemini, an air sign; and two signs behind is Aquarius, which is also an Air sign. If you have a planet in one sign and another planet positioned two signs away, you have a Sextile. It's a harmonious connection that requires effort to initiate. So if you take action while a Sextile is engaged, chances are good that your endeavor will be supported.

Square (90°): Considered one of the more challenging relationships in the Zodiac, Squares give both planets similar dispositions—so they compete to act at the same time, but each with different goals. Squares are approximately three signs apart on the Zodiac wheel. For example, Aries is *square* to Cancer (three signs ahead) and Capricorn (three signs behind). Aries, Cancer, Capricorn, and Libra are all considered aggressive ("Cardinal") signs, which means that they all want to take the lead. For example, let's say you have your Moon in Cancer and your Sun in Aries. The Cancer Moon wants to nurture, but the Sun in Aries would like to feel unattached. You can't take someone under your wing while simultaneously demanding your independence—so you have to compromise and engage each desire separately. Squares *can* be your friend if you use them consciously—plus, they're a great source of energy.

Trine (120°): This aspect is considered to be a very "easy" influence with beneficial results. The signs involved are readily compatible; therefore, they move and blend smoothly. Trines involve signs of the same element and allow the planets in them to "communicate" effortlessly with each other. The upside of Trines is that they tend to ensure success when the person uses them. The downside of this aspect is that it can induce laziness and lethargy. When no effort is put into a Trine, then no results can be realized. Conversely, efforts applied during a Trine will usually yield supportive results.

Opposition (180°): At 180 degrees, the planets are farthest away from each other, which can create some tension. Because they're in opposite signs, this relationship brings us awareness of our experience with each of these planets in our lives as they push and pull at one another. Oppositions usually involve elements that are compatible. For example, Taurus is opposite Scorpio. Taurus is Earth and Scorpio is Water, suggesting that the two signs can work together to find resolution. There's some common ground in opposing signs, which can help us understand our comfort level with the energies involved. If we pay attention, an opportunity for growth is always provided.

○◑◐●

UNDERSTANDING THE MEANING OF RETROGRADE

Planets Moving Retrograde

With the exception of the luminaries (the Sun and the Moon), all planets go into what's called a "retrograde phase" at some point. Some of them go retrograde every year, while others may only do so every few years. *Retrograde* means that from the Earth's viewpoint, the planet in question visually appears to pause and then begins to move backward through its normal path across the sky. Of course the planets don't actually change direction, but since the Earth is considered to be the center of the Universe in geocentric astrology (which is what we use in this guide), we only care about *our* perspective.

When a planet goes retrograde, the issues it reflects as it travels back through the sign (or signs) tend to have you revisiting the experiences that you had when it moved across that point in its original forward movement. You see, prior to moving backward, a planet must first pass through the retrograde territory in direct motion. Because it will return to this point during the retrograde phase, this is called the "pre-retrograde zone," as it allows you to take note of issues that may emerge before the actual retrograde. After the planet has gone through its retrograde, it then moves forward, traversing once again the same course it did while traveling backward. This is the "post-retrograde zone," and since it occurs afterward, it often brings closure and clarity to those issues experienced throughout the earlier phases. (Please see the section "Being Prepared: The Pre- and Post-Retrograde Zones" in Part III for more details.)

The Myth of the Mercury Retrograde

Feared, disparaged, and despised, the Mercury Retrograde is rapidly becoming the most maligned phenomenon in popular astrology. Without justification, this event stands among infamous superstitions such as stepping on cracks, breaking mirrors, and opening umbrellas indoors. The purveyors of astrological fear have successfully managed to give the world a reason for all its woes, but who can blame us for accepting a ready-made scapegoat? Now broken cars, miscommunications, and botched performances are no longer the fault of human error—rather, they're just a few of the many ills that belong to the irresponsible antics of Mercury.

The hardest mountain I have to climb is changing the minds of the millions of people who fall prey to this sort of erroneous belief. This is the kind of thinking that takes astrology back 100 years, when the planets were seen as evil forces that bore ominous warnings. Astrologers were powerful advisors in the days of old; the more foreboding their predictions, the more power they were given.

Many current practitioners in my field still echo the voice of the old soothsayers. They proclaim that Mercury, the planet of communication, is moving backward, and then they warn you not to sign or buy anything because of the harm it will do later. If you've been around astrological circles, it's likely that you've heard that warning more than once—which is why you can't get rid of the gnawing sense of caution every time you hear about the Mercury Retrograde. The biggest problem with this planetary event is fear, and that's no small problem to overcome.

What makes this myth about Mercury so difficult is that we *like* having something to blame. A car accident is much easier to justify if Mercury is retrograde. Inappropriate comments, plane delays, mechanical breakdowns, and broken contracts all become much more palatable if we can point a finger at the little planet of communication.

When using astrology as a tool to guide our lives, it's important to recognize the issue of self-fulfilling prophecy, that unconscious desire to ensure that we get the outcome we believe we will. In other words, if we proclaim that since Mercury is going to be moving retrograde, bad things will happen, then there's a good chance that they indeed will.

A New Perspective on Mercury Retrograde

In truth, Mercury Retrogrades allow us to tune in more closely to our intuition, heighten our senses, and gain a larger overview of our lives. Rarely has there been a Mercury Retrograde that didn't assist in uncovering mistakes that would have otherwise gone unnoticed. This opportunity for reappraisal may account for why so many successful businesses were launched during the retrograde cycle.

Let's try thinking of the Mercury Retrograde period as a big contemplation cycle. Contemplation is how we connect to our higher mind—and *disconnect* from our daily distractions—in order to look at life from a broader perspective. Certainly decisions made while in such a state are bound to be supported. It's a time of review, and an opportunity to enhance decisions that we've already made. What other period of our lives do we get not just two, but *three* chances to make something work? This is the best time to look at our relationships and speak what's on our mind. Mercury embraces communication—it encourages it. It's time to take charge of our life and learn to live it fearlessly. Let's move to make the Mercury Retrograde our comrade in wisdom: Change those old beliefs that keep us in fear.

I've made the following list of ideas to help you navigate Mercury Retrograde, so the next time you hear that one's coming, return here and review the list.

Mercury Retrograde Help List

More than 50 percent of the top 100 Fortune 500 businesses were started under the Mercury Retrograde. Imagine what *you* could do:

- Now, thoughts that have been lost to you can come back renewed and ready for consideration.

- Finally, you can slow your obsessive mind down and start feeling your life.

- You can now meet with [insert name of boss, friend, co-worker, sibling, parent, child, or what have you] and clear up that misunderstanding.

- You can abandon your routine in favor of spontaneity.
- This is a great time to relook at that important decision.
- Your mind is less attached to things—now you can release that "bad" habit without fear.
- It's time to give attention to your car, that toothache, or the new computer.
- And if you're tired of the same boring vacations, Mercury Retrograde is ready to show you a good time!

Remember, this could be a time of celebration and grandeur, or of fear and isolation . . . you get to *choose.* (*Hint:* One choice is a lot more fun than the other!)

○◑◐●

PART II

YOUR DAILY GUIDE

Author's Note: The times of day listed for astrological events are based on when they occur from the perspective of North America, and are expressed in Pacific Standard Time (PST)/Pacific Daylight Time (PDT) and Eastern Standard Time (EST)/Eastern Daylight Time (EDT). You will have to make appropriate adjustments based on your regional time zones.

On August 8, 2005, President George W. Bush signed the Energy Policy Act of 2005. This Act changed the time-change dates in the U.S. Beginning in 2007, daylight savings time (DST) will begin on the second Sunday of March and end the first Sunday of November. At the time of this writing, Congress is awaiting the report from the Cabinet as to the impact of this revision and retains the right to change it back. This calendar, therefore, is reflecting the change as if it's in effect. However, should Congress rescind the bill, please be aware that the dates DST is effective will be different from those listed.

JANUARY 2007

SUMMARY

The month of January is a fascinating blend of energies, moving you as if on a giant swing from frivolity to duty and back again! Starting with an early Full Moon in Cancer on the 3rd, your attention will be brought to your family and essential security needs. You'll make plans and devise, scheme, and invent dramatic ways to navigate this month . . . and you'll be given loads of assistance. You'll see a collection of the most successful planetary alignments peeking through this active month, and a couple that may have you holding your breath. Venus, Mercury, and Mars will all be changing signs—a clear indication that you'll be making some changes in your own course.

January is the month where you move from the stoic missions of Capricorn toward the idealistic ones of Aquarius. This year you'll see more of the Aquarian ideals coming to light than you have in a long while. In fact, Mercury will be moving backward in Aquarius, and that's a significant indication of real mental change—especially in your attitudes.

Watch for philosophical as well as literal changes confronting you this month. From making devout resolutions (such as becoming more diplomatic) to experiencing natural phenomena (such as going through an earthquake), you'll meet challenges that will be reflected in your own psyche as well as outwardly in life.

For those of you who are familiar with astrological terms, the following are the big events occurring in January. If you're new to astrology and its lingo, each of these will be further described throughout the month.

Main Events:

January 3:	Full Moon at 13° Cancer; Venus enters Aquarius
January 9:	Jupiter returns to this point during the retrograde phase later
January 15:	Mercury enters Aquarius
January 16:	Mars enters Aquarius
January 18:	New Moon at 29° Capricorn
January 20:	Sun enters Aquarius
January 27:	Venus enters Pisces
January 30:	Mercury returns to this point during the retrograde phase later

Whew! That's a lot of activity, and there's so much more. . . . Let's dive into each day to get a better handle on its motions. Remember: *You control the planets; they don't control you.* Fear is your worst enemy. There isn't a single planet that can do anything you don't want it to do, regardless of what I say about it.

At the end of the month, make a list of things for which you're grateful, including difficult events that occurred and the ways that they could become gifts in your life. Trust me, doing so gets you in the right mind-set—in particular, the one that says, *I am not the victim of any circumstance!*

◐

○◑◐●

MONDAY

January 1

MOON IN GEMINI
SUCCESS RATING: ★★★

New Year's Day is introduced by a Gemini Moon, which activates your brain and gives power to your thoughts. It's a perfect way to remind yourself to make resolutions concerning how you think, not what you do. If you like making New Year's resolutions, consider committing to ones that improve your outlook by changing your perspective (see the affirmation below).

There's a Full Moon coming in only two days, and you'll want to have your mind clear enough to make a wish list of the changes you'd like to see in your life. Use the playful Gemini Moon to make a game of clearing out some clutter in your home or office. Toss out those old magazines from last year, and create an environment that encourages you to start anew. Of course you'll first have to make all the right phone calls to family, friends, and colleagues so that you can communicate (a favorite Gemini Moon activity) your wishes for the New Year.

There's a surreal quality in the air. You may notice that you tire quickly today, and that should be your signal to slow down. Isn't it great? You get to wake up, make some calls, and then lie back down. I'm sure that there are some fabulous New Year's shows to watch on TV. Tomorrow a complete shift occurs, so get to bed early—you're going to need the rest.

AFFIRMATION FOR THE DAY:
I resolve to find gratitude in each day.

BIG SPINS OF THE DAY:
None

○◑◐●

TUESDAY

January 2

MOON IN GEMINI/CANCER
SUCCESS RATING: ★★★

Your sluggish feelings this morning will begin to dissolve as the Moon enters the homebody sign of Cancer. Moodiness is also part of the Cancer Moon experience as your sensitivity turns from your mind to your emotions. Under this Moon, you'll often be the last to know what your feelings are responding to, but friends will usually waste no time in giving you feedback. (Pack some aspirin just in case this gets annoying.)

Don't worry about your changing moods—they're going to be especially erratic thanks to a quirky Uranus aspect. Don't overdo making commitments today, because this is the kind of aspect that makes for impulsive choices that can often lead to regrets later. Since everything is complicated by the fact that your moods are dominating you, it's best to wait on all important decisions. Focus your attention on a loved one instead—the Moon is insisting upon it.

Since tomorrow's Full Moon is early, you may want to prepare a little ritual tonight that will help you bring desired changes into your life. Start with a candle, add your deepest wishes, light it, and send out your intentions. If you have a partner, encourage him or her to participate with you. Cancer Moons are powerful, especially when they're full!

AFFIRMATION FOR THE DAY:
I deserve all that I desire and more!

BIG SPINS OF THE DAY:
Moon Void of Course: 2:07 A.M. PST / 5:07 A.M. EST until
Moon enters Cancer: 7:15 A.M. PST / 10:15 A.M. EST
Sun sextiles Uranus: 1:16 A.M. PST /4:16 A.M. EST

○◑◐●

WEDNESDAY

January 3

FULL MOON IN CANCER
SUCCESS RATING: ★★

Happy Full Moon! It's also called the "Wolf Moon" because Native Americans noticed many wolves howling at this big winter orb. The Cancer Full Moon beckons you to pay attention to your immediate family and other loved ones. The sign's worrisome nature can emerge today—if not in you, then in those around you. Worry is a very normal response during this Moon, but it won't linger too long if you refrain from overreacting to it.

This Moon activates your desire for security. You may feel less confident during the first few hours of the day as you note all of the places in your life where security is lacking. However, it may help that there's a particularly long Void of Course Moon in your midst, which can mitigate fear and tone down any potential emotional upheavals.

Your mind takes the high ground today, giving you the opportunity to see things from a broader perspective. Use this objectivity to relook at problems that you've been facing—the clarity you have will amaze you. Venus enters Aquarius tonight . . . get ready to appreciate all that's not your normal course!

Also, keep in mind that this isn't your best day to sign important papers.

AFFIRMATION FOR THE DAY:
I completely trust the unfolding of my life!

BIG SPINS OF THE DAY:
Full Moon at 13° Cancer: 5:58 A.M. PST / 8:58 A.M. EST
Moon Void of Course: 5:58 A.M. PST / 8:58 A.M. EST until tomorrow
Venus enters Aquarius: 7:32 P.M. PST / 10:32 P.M. EST
Mercury sextiles Uranus: 9:20 P.M. PST / 12:20 A.M. EST

○◑◐●

THURSDAY

January 4

MOON IN CANCER/LEO
SUCCESS RATING: ★★

It's time to complete your leftover workload and any other unfinished business that you may have lying dormant. You're likely still reeling from the effects of the Full Moon, but by early afternoon you'll be ready to release the past and move into a more optimistic perspective. Whenever the Moon changes signs, you have to move a bit cautiously so that you have time to adjust to the shift in lunar climate. Symptoms of this include lethargy, depression, and general malaise—but remember, it's only temporary. The Leo Moon will help you perceive the light at the end of the tunnel.

Mercury is still being mischievous, so you're encouraged to mind your thoughts and words. If you feel that someone's trying to manipulate you, you could be right . . . but it's best to use awareness as your defense and *not* for confrontation. It may take a day or two, but careless words have a way of coming back around to bite their owners!

AFFIRMATION FOR THE DAY:
I connect with the love inside of me
and then extend it outward.

BIG SPINS OF THE DAY:
Moon Void of Course: until 1:15 P.M. PST / 4:15 P.M. EST
Moon enters Leo: 1:15 P.M. PST / 4:15 P.M. EST

○◑◐●

FRIDAY

January 5

MOON IN LEO
SUCCESS RATING: ★★★★

The Leo Moon is being supported by some fabulous planetary energy, sending you the signal that this may be your day to move forward in your personal goals. Admittedly, there could be some hurdles in your path, and an irritating display of ignorance by certain people may make you doubt your momentum—but if you're feeling it, trust that first!

If you so choose, you have the ability and planetary support to appear extra positive in the eyes of others. Need a raise? Maybe now is the time to ask for one. Had your eye on someone at school or the office? Perhaps this is the day to state your case.

Make great strides today. You're ending a cycle that began awhile ago (November 2006), so make the best of it. Of course, I must reiterate that your personal chart may be activated in such a way that you feel hesitant to take action. Trust that feeling first—your opportunity could be off by a day or two.

AFFIRMATION FOR THE DAY:
Just as rushing water knows where to flow, my life is on course and needs little tampering from me.

BIG SPINS OF THE DAY:
None

○◑◐●

SATURDAY

January 6

MOON IN LEO/VIRGO
SUCCESS RATING: ★★★

Yet another powerful day is in store for you as the Moon completes its journey through Leo. You may be confronted with a duty or responsibility that must be attended to. The Moon is holding hands with Saturn and imbues you with a serious need for productivity. Luckily, this serious tone doesn't last for the whole day—just long enough for you to get that garage in order or perform some other organizational act that will satisfy those responsible urges.

When you're done, take a shower to rinse off the day and prepare yourself for the entrance of the Virgo Moon. Tonight it aligns with Pluto and invokes the desire to accomplish anything that you're passionate about. Try diving into a mystery novel or cracking open that spiritual book you've wanted to revisit—this evening insights abound and pleasure seeking takes a front seat!

AFFIRMATION FOR THE DAY:
What I desire matters.

BIG SPINS OF THE DAY:
Sun conjuncts Mercury: 10:05 P.M. PST / 1:05 A.M. EST (Sunday)
Moon Void of Course: 4:56 P.M. PST / 7:56 P.M. EST until
Moon enters Virgo: 10:19 P.M. PST / 1:19 A.M. EST (Sunday)

○◑◐●

SUNDAY

January 7

MOON IN VIRGO
SUCCESS RATING: ★★★

Put on your thinking cap . . . or better yet, take it off. The Sun and Mercury are so close together that they could cause you to overanalyze just about everything. It's fine to aim your focus on those dirty baseboards and kitchen cabinets, but if you start picking on the people around you, you may have gone too far.

Take some time to respect the Virgo need for solace, for it's how you can regain your footing without hurting anyone's feelings. Use your steel-trap mind to figure out your next plan of action, especially in the area of personal success. Today you're a wizard, a mental giant, so be sure to act with compassion and respect, and let your insights bring you the gifts that you desire.

If you have to make a big purchase or sign a contract, it's best to bring someone with you. Any diagnosis that you receive today warrants a second opinion.

AFFIRMATION FOR THE DAY:
I don't have to be careful what I wish for—
the Universe knows what I mean.

BIG SPINS OF THE DAY:
None

○◑◐●

MONDAY

January 8

MOON IN VIRGO
SUCCESS RATING: ★★★★

Mars is making a wonderful connection to Saturn that allows us a new spin on an old idea. Perhaps with the Virgo Moon's help you'll get the urge to clean or remodel something that's grown "blah." Today gets high ratings in both the romance and finance departments as well. Someone you meet today could prove to be a valuable asset in your life, but you may have to leave your house to meet him or her.

Why not invite a colleague to lunch or even dinner? You'll want to look your best, so stash a lint brush in the car and keep your hands clean—people notice tiny details under this Moon.

Today holds the guarantee of progress, but be careful: Making mountains out of molehills doesn't count as successful building! By the way, if someone's lagging behind or feeling a little under the weather, a bit of support on your part will have far-reaching effects!

AFFIRMATION FOR THE DAY:
Today I seek joy, one "peace" at a time!

BIG SPINS OF THE DAY:
Mars trines Saturn: 10:06 A.M. PST / 1:06 P.M. EST

○◑◐●

TUESDAY

January 9

MOON IN VIRGO/LIBRA
SUCCESS RATING: ★★★

Cool your jets until you're past the early-morning Void of Course Moon, then go on a social rampage! Libra loves a party, and nothing stands in the way of your having one on a day like today (as long as you give yourself some time to adjust to the Moon's change of signs). There's also more romantic success in the air. However, if romance isn't your thing, perhaps it's time for a new gadget—something that makes your life a little easier (a sports car may be stretching it a bit).

Plan an evening where you get the pleasure of dressing up and having everyone tell you how gorgeous you look. I call it the Libra Moon's "prerogative to be prissy," so have at it! You may need to get a tad serious tomorrow, so throw caution to the wind tonight.

(**Special note:** Jupiter will be moving retrograde in April and will return to this point. Pay attention to the opportunities that you're presented with today because they'll be back in the spring.)

AFFIRMATION FOR THE DAY:
I have everything I need.

BIG SPINS OF THE DAY:
Moon Void of Course: 4:51 A.M. PST / 7:51 A.M. EST until
Moon enters Libra: 10:15 A.M. PST / 1:15 P.M. EST
Jupiter returns to this point. Pay attention!

○◑◐●

WEDNESDAY

January 10

MOON IN LIBRA
SUCCESS RATING: ★★

The lower Success Rating today is simply to slow you down a bit before taking a leap. There's certainly a lot going on today, and you may find out some answers to an investigation that you undertook.

Although you could be feeling more emotionally agile today, you may need to put some tape over your mouth so that you don't just spew out every thought that comes into your head. If you can, show discretion, as your words could ignite a battle that you don't need right now. This is particularly important under a Libra Moon, where propriety plays a bigger role than righteousness.

Someone could try to control your natural movements today. Remain focused but pleasant, since the Libra Moon *loves* everything pleasant.

Amazing dreams await you tonight—try to get to bed at a decent hour so you can capture them. Tomorrow will help you gain a few of the missing puzzle pieces, so be patient and don't make a drama out of something that otherwise might go unnoticed!

AFFIRMATION FOR THE DAY:
I breathe in the support that is all around me and exhale the kindness that ensues.

BIG SPINS OF THE DAY:
None

○◑◐●

THURSDAY

January 11

LAST QUARTER MOON IN LIBRA
SUCCESS RATING: ★★

This is called the Last Quarter Moon because it's the final, tense connection between the Sun and Moon before they become the New Moon. In plain English, it's the time when you'll be shown any obstacles that are in your path, ones that are preventing you from achieving your personal goals.

I know it sounds like a cliché to think that obstacles are really supporting you, but you do have the choice of seeing them that way. Yet I know that under the Libra Moon, there's a tendency to avoid conflicts and responsibility, so confronting them directly isn't so easy.

Remember that wherever there's a problem, you're given a chance to fix it . . . regardless of whose fault it is. Verbal confrontations are possible, so bite your tongue, even if other people are lashing theirs at you! Discipline is key, and follow what you know to be true for you.

AFFIRMATION FOR THE DAY:
I move in accordance with the
universal flow, which is never wrong.

BIG SPINS OF THE DAY:
Last Quarter Moon at 21° Libra: 4:45 A.M. PST / 7:45 A.M. EST
Moon Void of Course: 5:56 P.M. PST / 8:56 P.M. EST until
Moon enters Scorpio: 11:08 P.M. PST / 2:08 A.M. EST

○◑◐●

FRIDAY

January 12

MOON IN SCORPIO
SUCCESS RATING: ★★

Put on your reflective gear because things are heating up! The Moon has entered the Scorpion's lair, and it encourages you to go within and explore. That's great advice if you live in a cave, but you probably have to go out and mingle with the world, so practice putting on your happy face and get out there.

The day holds the promise of moderate accomplishment due to the union of several planetary players (Mars and Pluto, Saturn and the Sun), but it's easy to lose interest in anything that you don't have a passion for. Today the Moon insists that you follow your heart, with only some minor restrictions (that is, serial killers may ignore it, but the rest of you must do what feeds you). Look to world news for big happenings, because issues of power are likely to be revving up!

If you're in a job that lacks spark, today may be the day to quit being the victim and start doing something about your complaints. Look below the surface for answers and take time to listen . . . sometimes the voice of reason speaks very softly.

AFFIRMATION FOR THE DAY:
My life is always filled with more splendors than my eyes can see.

BIG SPINS OF THE DAY:
Venus sextiles Jupiter: 4:45 A.M. PST / 7:45 A.M. EST

○◑◐●

SATURDAY

January 13

MOON IN SCORPIO
SUCCESS RATING: ★★★★

With the Moon planted firmly in the sign of Scorpio, you may feel more comfortable and centered. You're getting lots of help focusing, thanks to a connection between Mars and Pluto. Sexual energy is high, and that can translate into manifesting your desires quite easily (provided that you have a few tucked away). This combination of Mars and Pluto is basically saying that you can have anything you want, but be warned—it borders on obsession.

There's nothing wrong with a good, healthy passion here and there, but it's difficult to recognize when it starts consuming you. Make a note to check in with yourself and be sure that at least 50 percent of your time is being given to other areas in your life (eating, for example).

If you're engaged in a legal battle, success is almost guaranteed—provided that you've told the truth and stayed true to your course. It doesn't hurt that Jupiter and the Sun are connecting, bringing much luck to any situation.

Be careful not to overindulge in *anything,* including bragging and spending money. Also, pay attention: World events could spark big news stories.

AFFIRMATION FOR THE DAY:
I have come a long way, and
I deserve the gifts awaiting me.

BIG SPINS OF THE DAY:
Mars conjuncts Pluto: 1:58 A.M. PST / 4:58 A.M. EST

○◑◐●

SUNDAY

January 14

MOON IN SCORPIO/SAGITTARIUS
SUCCESS RATING: ★★★

It's hard not to feel some excitement when the Moon leaves Scorpio for Sagittarius. The inspiring sign of the Archer wants to take you on a journey that lifts your head up—a direction that you haven't looked in for several days.

Although luck is filling the air, you're cautioned to let the morning pass before leaping blindly forward. You'll probably feel a lucky breeze entering your awareness and the blessing of good fortune bearing fruit around you—but it's not quite ripe enough to pick. Let today guide you to your perfect timing. Taking risks now could cost you in a big way if you're not sufficiently prepared. Those of you who have set this date to launch a new project can easily move forward, as long as you've laid the necessary groundwork.

An early bedtime is encouraged so that your mind can have a little extra time to wind down. A good rest will bring you the energy you'll want to have for tomorrow.

AFFIRMATION FOR THE DAY:
I am whole, complete, and fulfilled just being who I am!

BIG SPINS OF THE DAY:
Moon Void of Course: 7:50 A.M. PST / 10:50 A.M. EST until
Moon enters Sagittarius: 10:12 A.M. PST / 1:12 P.M. EST

○◑◐●

MONDAY

January 15

MOON IN SAGITTARIUS
SUCCESS RATING: ★★★★

In the wee hours of the morning, Mercury leaves Capricorn and enters the lofty sign of Aquarius (*lofty* because it holds grand ideas). The driven mind that you've carried since the beginning of the year is being replaced by an idealized one that's ready to break any rules that prevent creative new solutions.

A surprisingly delightful day is in the mix, starting with an early revelation and evolving into a pretty nice time for relating to other people. For many of you, this is a holiday celebrating the ideals of a man (Martin Luther King, Jr.) who sought to bring equality and peace to everyone, and today's alignments echo the same sentiment. Certainly nothing stands in the way of your having a spectacular time.

AFFIRMATION FOR THE DAY:
Today I see only opportunities
for my advancement into joy.

BIG SPINS OF THE DAY:
Mercury enters Aquarius: 1:25 A.M. PST / 4:25 A.M. EST

○◑◐●

TUESDAY

January 16

MOON IN SAGITTARIUS/CAPRICORN
SUCCESS RATING: ★★

You may not care if you get any work done this morning, and it won't matter since both the Moon and Mars are entering the serious sign of Capricorn this afternoon. You might as well play while you're in the mood, because the tide is soon going to change, and your attention will naturally turn toward your work.

For the past month and a half, Mars has been inspiring us to learn new philosophies, to travel, and to boldly go where no one has gone before. Now it joins the Moon, and to put it bluntly, the party's over. It's time to put your nose to the grindstone and make plans for your success. But there's no hurry . . . you can start tomorrow, as Mars is going to be in Capricorn for about five weeks.

Get plenty of sleep tonight—you have dreams waiting!

AFFIRMATION FOR THE DAY:
I accept and love my life, every morsel of it.

BIG SPINS OF THE DAY:
Mars enters Capricorn: 12:54 P.M. PST / 3:54 P.M. EST
Moon Void of Course: 1:29 P.M. PST / 4:29 P.M. EST until
Moon enters Capricorn: 5:50 P.M. PST / 8:50 P.M. EST

○◑◐●

WEDNESDAY

January 17

MOON IN CAPRICORN
SUCCESS RATING: ★★★★

An all-day Capricorn Moon means that there's nothing in the way of pushing forward toward your goals and objectives. (Capricorns love the phrase *goals and objectives.*) You'll probably find that you have tireless energy for most projects, and staying on task seems like the natural course.

Keep in mind that it's the day before the New Moon, a time when the Moon blocks the Sun in such a way that it appears to go dark. Sometimes things feel hopeless and bleak just prior to the New Moon, but don't let that stop you from creating a list of desires that you'd like to see manifest. Acknowledge any fears that emerge, and watch how quickly they fizzle out. This isn't the day to take your thoughts too seriously, but it *is* the day to direct them toward your new goals. A New Moon is like a blank slate waiting to be filled, so pick things that are perky and supportive!

Tomorrow is another active day . . . a good night's sleep isn't a bad idea.

AFFIRMATION FOR THE DAY:
My home is always safe and secure,
for my home is always inside of me.

BIG SPINS OF THE DAY:
None

○◑◐●

THURSDAY

January 18

NEW MOON IN CAPRICORN
MOON IN CAPRICORN/AQUARIUS
SUCCESS RATING: ★★★★

Intentions under this Capricorn New Moon will most likely be serious and filled with specifics. That's fine if they support you, but I like to think that the Universe around us is far wiser than we give it credit for . . . after all, it does represent the *Big Picture.* Try setting goals that have a general tone to them, ones that seek contentment or success without detailed descriptions that are limiting. Too often we're quoted fear-based nonsense such as "Be careful what you wish for—you just might get it." Rubbish!

Believe it or not, the wisdom of the Universe is much better at lovingly handling our course than we are, so step aside and let magic happen. Candles are great support devices that can be used to anchor in New Moon aims—light 'em up, and send out your intentions with power and authority. And remember: You deserve to get what you want.

AFFIRMATION FOR THE DAY:
I accept all the riches that come my way.

BIG SPINS OF THE DAY:
Venus conjuncts Neptune: 6:48 P.M. PST / 9:48 P.M. EST
New Moon at 29° Capricorn: 8:02 P.M. PST / 11:02 P.M. EST
Moon Void of Course: 8:02 P.M. PST / 11:02 P.M. EST until
Moon enters Aquarius: 10:16 P.M. PST / 1:16 A.M. EST (Friday)

○◑◐●

FRIDAY

January 19

MOON IN AQUARIUS
SUCCESS RATING: ★★★★★

What a wonderful post–New Moon day! As the Moon slowly starts to regain its light, you'll begin to see a new horizon in front of you. The Aquarius Moon activates your desire for freedom, and you may have to rebel against something just to flex a muscle that hasn't been used in a while (due to all that Capricorn conformity).

If you'd like to launch a new project or business, this is a perfect day to do so, and wedding plans for this weekend are also given the green light—all thanks to some wonderful Venus alignments. Go ahead, ask for that raise or to get engaged. It doesn't matter what the outcome is . . . what counts is that you get that energy in motion. Onward ho!

AFFIRMATION FOR THE DAY:
I am always at the center of peace and joy, regardless of what my mind believes in the moment.

BIG SPINS OF THE DAY:
None

Happy Birthday, Aquarius!

JANUARY 20–FEBRUARY 18

Unconventional Aquarius is almost completely opposite in nature to the traditional Capricorn, the sign it follows in the Zodiac. Aquarians *hate* authority, constantly bursting through with new ideas and shattering thoughts and beliefs that they feel are antiquated and unsupportive. The roots of this sign's rebellion can be found in the myth of Prometheus, the Titan who stole fire from Zeus and gave it to humankind. Clearly humanitarians, Aquarians live in a world of strong mental pictures and ideals, and unless you can match the brilliance of their minds, you'll rarely be able to change them.

Aquarians' gift is in their genius—their intellects have been refined to work with precision, and their ideals are usually focused on the underdogs: the oppressed masses, the hungry, the homeless, or the sick. Once an Aquarian has championed your cause, there's little you can do to break that allegiance.

Often shocking in appearance, people with this sign love living outside of society's "box" of rules. They're the rebels who understand that hearing their own drummer is far more important than marching to the established beat. Because of their strong minds, Aquarians can be prone to obsessive thinking and are often burdened with a symbolic bag of "shoulds."

Aquarians are the inventors and forgers of the Zodiac, using their rebellious minds to create alternatives to what's already established—exemplified by Thomas Edison, Wolfgang Amadeus Mozart, Gypsy Rose Lee, and Helen Gurley Brown. Each of these individuals wrote his or her own script and followed his or her own inner spirit.

AFFIRMATIONS FOR AQUARIUS:

My feelings are a source of strength.
I have the power to change my ideas anytime I choose.
I honor wisdom from all sources.

○◑◐●

SATURDAY

January 20

SUN IN AQUARIUS
MOON IN AQUARIUS
SUCCESS RATING: ★★★★

Good news for Aquarians everywhere: For the next 30 days, the Sun will be in your sign, and the rest of us will fully understand you . . . or not! Being fully understood isn't something that you're going to *want* under the Aquarius Sun. In fact, you're probably going to walk outside the boundaries of your normal routine just to shake things up. There are five—count 'em, *five*—planets in Aquarius today, and that could spell freedom for a lot of the world, so keep an eye on what's happening. Traditional astrology may use this influx of Air as a sign to watch out for airborne viruses. This could be a strong flu season, so act with prevention.

Today the Moon will end its run through Aquarius, but not until it's imbued you with the true rebel spirit for which the sign is known. Be ready to say no to any demands to conform.

The sky's filled with lovely energies that should make for some real fun, so get out there and enjoy it. The Moon doesn't go Void of Course until much later this evening, so cut loose! It's also a wonderful night for breakthrough conversations.

AFFIRMATION FOR THE DAY:
I am inextricably entwined in the perfection of the Universe.

BIG SPINS OF THE DAY:
Sun enters Aquarius: 3:01 A.M. PST / 6:01 A.M. EST
Moon Void of Course: 9:01 P.M. PST / 12:01 A.M. EST (Sunday) until tomorrow

○◑◐●

SUNDAY

January 21

MOON IN AQUARIUS/PISCES
SUCCESS RATING: ★★★★

The past isn't real. It can't hurt you. It's made up of memory cells that exist in the brain. Even though all these statements are true, that doesn't change the fact that you often let the past haunt you in myriad ways. Friends from long ago can emerge out of nowhere, inadvertently reminding you of how much weight you've gained . . . or perhaps their behavior forces you to wonder what it was you saw in them. The Pisces Moon has a way of bringing back the past as though it never left, perhaps giving you an opportunity to take that stand you once wished you'd taken. You may wander around dazed by all the fantasies and metaphors that seem to play out right in front of you.

Certainly this is a surreal day and therefore *not* a great one for making big decisions (especially the kind that may cost a fortune). When you get a chance, rest your eyes and let your mind take flight. Get to bed early tonight—you'll want some energy for tomorrow's big day.

AFFIRMATION FOR THE DAY:
I am not my mind, and I am not what I think—I am a light that never dims and a boat that never sinks.

BIG SPINS OF THE DAY:
Moon Void of Course: until 12:49 A.M. PST / 3:49 A.M. EST
Moon enters Pisces: 12:49 A.M. PST / 3:49 A.M. EST

○◑◐●

MONDAY

January 22

MOON IN PISCES
SUCCESS RATING: ★★

More Pisces Moon adventures await you, but this time you're used to them and can navigate the terrain with a tad more sanity than you did yesterday. (Yes, I saw everything.) Now Venus is supporting getting your boundaries back as well as your focus, and you'll appreciate the help because the day is filled with potential distractions.

Today's Jupiter-Uranus clash isn't horrible because of how it makes you feel; it's just not an aspect that likes discipline—in fact, it abhors it. You may find that your inner rebel is making a comeback, using anything in sight as a distraction from doing work. Social gatherings at the watercooler seem a lot more appealing today, so if you can't complete a project, don't fret . . . just go with the flow.

You're cautioned to drive with awareness, though, since these aspects can make staying within the speed limit quite difficult.

AFFIRMATION FOR THE DAY:
My mind is at peace, my thoughts are still, and my voice of guidance is loud and clear.

BIG SPINS OF THE DAY:

Venus opposes Saturn: 6:38 A.M. PST / 9:38 A.M. EST
Mercury sextiles Jupiter: 8:13 A.M. PST / 11:13 A.M. EST
Jupiter squares Uranus: 1:44 P.M. PST / 4:44 P.M. EST
Moon Void of Course: 11:12 P.M. PST / 2:12 A.M. (Tuesday) EST until tomorrow

○◑◐●

TUESDAY

January 23

MOON IN PISCES/ARIES
SUCCESS RATING: ★★

The Moon enters Aries in the wee hours of the morning, making most of this day all about awakening our inner Ram. Shake off the Pisces doldrums and come into the fiery Aries domain. If you feel agitated, this indicates that you went excessively soft during the Pisces Moon and need to stir up the energy within to help toughen you up! Just be careful not to take any unnecessary anger out on the people around you. The Aries Moon loves to get us engaged in intense arguments, heated competitions, and, well, anything that's over the top. Be careful not to burn bridges . . . with this kind of fiery energy in the air, you'll want to guard against speaking without thinking. Remember: You're not the only one feeling feisty.

Please use caution when operating any machinery—there's still a lot of ungrounded energy floating around.

And did I mention romance? Well, that's another form of heat, and it's in the air today. . . . Go get 'em, tigers and tigresses!

AFFIRMATION FOR THE DAY:
I am fearless and full of love.

BIG SPINS OF THE DAY:

Moon Void of Course: until 2:53 A.M. PST / 5:53 A.M. EST
Moon enters Aries: 2:53 A.M. PST / 5:53 A.M. EST

○◑◐●

WEDNESDAY

January 24

MOON IN ARIES
SUCCESS RATING: ★★★★

An all-day Aries Moon fires you up today, with a lot of support from the neighboring planets. The morning mood is tinged with insights and ideas that inspire you to take solid action.

Inspiration is the magic word for today, and there's plenty of it surrounding you. You aren't a pinball, so don't bounce around aimlessly—pick a goal, and point your newfound inspiration in that direction. In doing so, you'll stay on the higher side of the Aries Moon and will be able to accomplish almost anything with great speed and ease. In addition, a visit to the gym may help you work out the excess stress and assist you in staying focused.

The lower side of the Aries Moon shows itself in the need to agitate, rather than inspire. If you find yourself picking on someone, you're practicing the art of distraction (not to mention cruelty) and should regroup to find out which area of life you're avoiding. Use today to your benefit . . . you'll be getting a report card tomorrow.

AFFIRMATION FOR THE DAY:
Peaceful is what I am—always!

BIG SPINS OF THE DAY:
None

○◑◐●

THURSDAY

January 25

FIRST QUARTER MOON IN TAURUS
SUCCESS RATING: ★

The First Quarter Moon is a nice way of saying that the Moon and Sun are fighting, and you're going to catch the brunt of it. I'm kidding (sort of), but what happens on a day like this is that something unfinished from the past tends to emerge, screaming for your attention. Perhaps the issue is related to work, a person from your past, or a bill you forgot to pay . . . whatever it is, its purpose is to get you focused. The best way to handle today is to accept what comes with an open mind and fix anything that's broken.

The Moon is in the earthy sign of Taurus and won't let you take any shortcuts. Focus your attention on your body and how you're feeling. Since this is a sensual moon, taking care of yourself physically is of the utmost importance. Listen to what your body wants, and use Taurus's steadfast and patient manner to get you through the day. No Bull can resist the promise of a good meal, so if you feel that you've accomplished a goal, treat yourself to something decadent. Oh, and if someone deserves a compliment today, go out of your way to give it to him or her.

AFFIRMATION FOR THE DAY:
There is no wrong way for me to live my life.

BIG SPINS OF THE DAY:
Moon Void of Course: 1:51 A.M. PST / 4:51 A.M. EST until
Moon enters Taurus: 5:29 A.M. PST / 8:29 A.M. EST
First Quarter Moon at 6° Taurus: 3:02 P.M. PST / 6:02 P.M. EST

○◑◐●

FRIDAY

January 26

MOON IN TAURUS
SUCCESS RATING: ★★

It's an all-day Taurus Moon, a placement that allows you to remember that your body responds to being pampered. Once you're clear on this fact, make your list of things to do for the day.

Here's *my* list:

1. Eat a solid breakfast.
2. Munch on a nourishing snack.
3. Have a filling lunch.
4. Go to the sauna.
5. Enjoy a hearty dinner.
6. Soak in the tub.

That's what I call working with the Moon! But seriously, if you do need to accomplish something today, don't make it an undertaking that requires your signature or much intensive thought . . . you're just not going to be up to the task. It's not your fault—blame Mercury. The little brat is chumming up to Neptune and stripping you of sane thought, which makes it a great day for fantasies, movies, music, and phone calls from people you haven't talked to for a long, long time.

AFFIRMATION FOR THE DAY:
My body is beautiful and supports me fully.

BIG SPINS OF THE DAY:
Venus sextiles Pluto: 2:57 A.M. PST / 5:57 A.M. EST
Mercury conjuncts Neptune: 5:20 A.M. PST / 8:20 A.M. EST

○◑◐●

SATURDAY

January 27

MOON IN TAURUS/GEMINI
SUCCESS RATING: ★★★

You may find it tough to get out of bed due to an early Void of Course Moon, but once your engine is revved, you'll find lots of productive power at your disposal. The day is mostly filled with energy from the Gemini Moon, which will activate your curiosity and need for verbal exchange. This is a great day for a good book or magazine (if you can find the time to read), and it gets sweeter as it moves forward, so don't worry about an unproductive morning.

Get your errands done in time to enjoy a warm evening at home as Venus makes her way into Pisces, an alignment that sends you on a quest for a mystical experience. Notice how your taste for music increases, and how you suddenly take an interest in the personal well-being of everyone you know. There's no need to push too hard in any one direction . . . there's plenty of time during this cycle to get all of your needs met. This is a great evening for romance and a glass of wine (okay, two glasses—but don't overdo it!).

AFFIRMATION FOR THE DAY:
All is well.

BIG SPINS OF THE DAY:
Moon Void of Course: 8:09 A.M. PST / 11:09 A.M. EST until
Moon enters Gemini: 9:10 A.M. PST / 12:10 P.M. EST
Venus enters Pisces: 7:32 P.M. PST / 10:32 P.M. EST

○◑◐●

SUNDAY

January 28

MOON IN GEMINI
SUCCESS RATING: ★★

Sometimes our minds act like little children who are very tired but just can't sleep: We threaten them, get them to lie down, turn out the light, and close the door . . . only to find out a few minutes later that they're using the bed as a trampoline.

Today your mind may have hit the overtired zone. Symptoms include feeling overwhelmed, lethargy, jumping-into-bed urges, or just plain zombie-dom (where your eyes are open and nobody's home). Not to worry—Mercury, the planet of thinking, is having a quarrel with Saturn, the stern taskmaster, and like a kid, Mercury often rebels against any form of authority. But heck, it's Sunday, so why not give in and sprout some roots on your couch, keep the remote close by, and vegetate. Someone in the vicinity is likely to notice your absence sooner or later (unless they've found their own couch to "chill" on). The good news is that after all your finger exercises with the remote, you'll sleep well.

AFFIRMATION FOR THE DAY:
I am *more* than what I *do!*

BIG SPINS OF THE DAY:
Mercury opposes Saturn: 10:07 A.M. PST / 1:07 P.M. EST

○◑◐●

MONDAY

January 29

MOON IN GEMINI/CANCER
SUCCESS RATING: ★★

You may need an extra shot of caffeine to start the day as the Moon ends its run through Gemini. There are plenty of items to organize, and you need to remind yourself that things aren't as serious as they seem or you may risk falling into an unnecessary panic. Use today to make a list of things that you'd like to accomplish for the week, and be reasonable but not rigid with your goals. The coming days unveil many opportunities for success, so relax, get out your "things-to-do" list, and start writing down your intentions.

A minor power struggle today will stay minor if you don't make it more than it is. The entrance of the Moon into Cancer this afternoon may find you yearning to go home early. Go ahead and do so if it won't get you into trouble. Otherwise, stay the course—you don't need anything else to worry about tonight.

AFFIRMATION FOR THE DAY:
I release everything that limits my life.

BIG SPINS OF THE DAY:
Moon Void of Course: 10:41 A.M. PST / 1:41 P.M. EST until
Moon enters Cancer: 2:17 P.M. PST / 5:17 P.M. EST

○◑◐●

TUESDAY

January 30

MOON IN CANCER
SUCCESS RATING: ★★★

The all-day Cancer Moon may create some worry just below the surface of your mind, but it also encourages you to find the source of anxiety. Take a fearless look at what you believe is holding you back, give it some light, and then release it. The gift of the Cancer Moon is that it offers safety where it doesn't seem to exist. (Crabs don't have indestructible shells just for looks.)

You can confidently take risks and push the envelope today, but a very long Void of Course Moon will encourage you to let things stew for a while. Allow the afternoon to take you where it may—don't worry about catching up on everything right now. Think of yourself as a chef who's mixing up batter, putting it in the oven, and setting the timer for Thursday. Also, don't schedule any meetings this afternoon unless you just want to kill some time, because not much is going to stick.

(**Special note:** Mercury-zone alert! Mercury will be going retrograde later [February 13], and it will return to this point. Start a journal now to log all events so that you'll have a better clue about which issues you can expect to be working on during the retrograde.)

AFFIRMATION FOR THE DAY:
My timing is always perfect.

BIG SPINS OF THE DAY:
Moon Void of Course: 1:31P.M. PST / 4:31 P.M. EST until tomorrow
Mercury returns to this point. Take notes!

○◑◐●

WEDNESDAY

January 31

MOON IN CANCER/LEO
SUCCESS RATING: ★★

We've got ourselves a long Void of Course Moon today. Don't misunderstand: Much *can* get done under the Void of Course Moon—but it's erratic. Since you know your feelings and intuition better than anyone, trust what you're perceiving and act accordingly.

In general, if there's nothing else pressing, use today to get your goals in order for tomorrow's Full Moon. The Full Moon is when you get to see the results of your hard work (yes, even if you spent much of your time on the couch, you still worked hard). A candle can be useful in helping you focus your intentions, so get a special one ready for tomorrow.

This is the end of January, so make a list of your successes, and only note things to be grateful for. This helps you get in the right frame of mind so you can be in charge of your life.

AFFIRMATION FOR THE DAY:
I spread my arms wide, ready
to receive all that I desire and more!

BIG SPINS OF THE DAY:
Mercury sextiles Pluto: 6:31 P.M. PST / 9:31 P.M. EST
Moon Void of Course: until 9:15 P.M. PST / 12:15 A.M. EST (Thursday)
Moon enters Leo: 9:15 P.M. PST / 12:15 A.M. EST (Thursday)

Thought for the Month

The Unlovables

One of my friends is like an alien to me because he can talk to anybody about anything with genuine interest. I make fun of his charming openness, but he never turns down a request for help. He feeds the alley cats regularly and keeps a place in his car filled with empty dishes and cat food. . . . Yes, I do think he's from outer space.

As you can imagine, I don't like his friends. They're quirky and self-important, talk about themselves incessantly, and revel in their special connection to my "alien" friend. I tell people around me that he "loves the unlovable," and it's true: He cares for those who would otherwise find their love on *The Jerry Springer Show.*

Once I was riding in the car with him, and a toothless woman carrying a sign ran up to us. She screamed his name, he smiled and said hers, and I was appalled. He asked if she needed a ride, but she was only one street corner away from her home (next to a Dumpster), so he gave her $40 and wished her well. *I* rolled my eyes and reached for the air freshener.

A few weeks ago, while recounting yet another "saint story" about my friend, I went down the list of the weirdos whom he cared for: the nut in Taos who gets evicted every other week and asks for his help, the homeless woman from our car ride, the therapist in town who should be *in* therapy, and the student who's only able to come to my friend's free tutoring classes at midnight—the list was endless. I laughed and said, "If this guy cares for you, you can pretty much bet that you're one of 'the unlovables'!" I had everyone in stitches . . . and then the realization hit. He cared for *me,* too!

So, here's the Thought for the Month, which has perhaps already been expressed in a million different ways:

The world is, and will always be, nothing more than a shattered mirror reflecting back the myriad judgments we hold against ourselves.

FEBRUARY 2007
SUMMARY

Maybe it's my natural paranoia, but I've always suspected that there's something weird about February. Let's start with the fact that it only has 28 days . . . until it has 29. And what about the fact that its name comes from a Roman holiday celebrating purification—as in purity, virginity, and celibacy—while at the same time it has a romantic holiday for lovers planted right in the middle of it like a bad joke? Or how about the fact that it's the only month that has two *r*'s in its name? . . . I'm starting to get the creeps! But regardless of all its inherent strangeness, February is also a month of adjustments due to a lot of planetary activity.

The biggest event hosted by the month is the Saturn and Neptune opposition. This is the second time these planets have met since August 2006, and this cycle could bring problems to anyone in authority who hasn't been up-front: From movie stars to politicians, if you're powerful, you're going to be exposed.

Although I like to present February as a mischievous month, in truth it's not. No one can say exactly how the planetary alignments are going to play out, but we *do* know that every sign holds great potential for remarkable results. We owe it to ourselves to hold this frame of mind and wait to cast our judgments until all the evidence has been presented.

Any month sponsoring a Leo Full Moon just can't be that bad, and if you fear the Mercury Retrograde, then you simply aren't listening to a word I'm saying!

Here are some of the February highlights:

February 1: Full Moon 13° Leo
February 2: Mercury enters Pisces
February 13: Mercury Retrograde 10° Pisces

February 17: New Moon 29° Aquarius
February 18: Sun enters Pisces
February 21: Venus enters Aries
February 25: Mars enters Aquarius
February 26: Mercury reenters Aquarius
February 28: Saturn opposes Neptune (second time)

◐

○◑◐●

THURSDAY

February 1

FULL MOON IN LEO
SUCCESS RATING: ★★

(**Note:** Some of your calendars [U.S. East Coast and U.K.] will say that the Full Moon is tomorrow because it hits at 12:45 A.M. in your time zone.)

This is called the "Snow Moon," and for many of you, 'tis the season when snow is pretty prevalent. Native Americans, who named most of the Moons for us, considered this an important night for gathering food under the brightly lit orb. Since the Full Moon is in Leo, it's spreading rays of hope (because that's what Leos do on their good days), which you should soon be experiencing.

Today doesn't get a spectacular Success Rating, mostly due to a relationship that's developing between stodgy Saturn and evasive Neptune. Together, these planets can confuse you a bit, making otherwise fleeting feelings of worry and concern now seem more serious. Don't worry, as this, too, shall pass.

It's best to start new projects a bit later in the week and use today to light your candle of intention. Remember that you don't have to be careful what you wish for, since you're surrounded by a pretty smart Divine Spirit!

AFFIRMATION FOR THE DAY:
I see myriad things that I am grateful for.

BIG SPINS OF THE DAY:
Full Moon at 13° Leo: 9:45 P.M. PST / 12:45 A.M. EST (Friday)

○◐◑●

FRIDAY

February 2

FEBRUARY

MOON IN LEO
SUCCESS RATING: ★★

An entire day in Leo following the Full Moon in that sign should feel *refreshing!*

While you were sleeping, Mercury snuck into the dream-inducing sign of Pisces, so if you noticed some rich images emerging while you were in your REM state, you now have a reason for them. Gone are the intensely analytical days of the very thoughtful Mercury-in-Aquarius mind, during which you contemplated the validity of world peace while complaining about your lack of control over your office staff. Go ahead and postulate those theories of relativity (à la Einstein) and other abstractly profound ideas, but know that you'll likely make a mess of everything you touch, thanks to the completely nonsensical, outside-the-box, "Who am I? . . . Oh, I'm you" mind of Mercury in Pisces.

This alignment has a way of bringing people from your past to the forefront and of allowing you more freedom to carve out your reality. Of course, this fluid kind of thinking doesn't fully support the idea of your signing big contracts or making large purchases, at least not today. Give yourself a bit of time to get used to the "flow."

AFFIRMATION FOR THE DAY:
I accept that I am dreaming
and not yet ready to awaken.

BIG SPINS OF THE DAY:
Mercury enters Pisces: 1:20 A.M. PST / 4:20 A.M. EST

○◑◐●

S A T U R D A Y

February 3

MOON IN LEO/VIRGO
SUCCESS RATING: ★★★

Mister Rogers would say, "It's a beautiful day in this neighborhood," and I'd have to agree with him. The Moon enters Virgo early this morning and sets your mind in harmony with the voice of your mother gently screaming, "Get your bottom out of bed, and pick up this godforsaken room!"

Aside from inspiring us to get some semblance of organization, the Virgo Moon also encourages us to be of service. Perhaps someone at the office could use an extra set of hands to get a project done, or maybe a family member needs your counsel. Whatever the situation, it would certainly be to your benefit to follow Virgo's guidance and offer your support. Being giving is not only nice, but—due to some wonderful planetary aspects—your kindness could also have positive repercussions in the future.

You're cautioned to move with awareness today, though . . . thanks to a sudden jolt of energy brought to you by Mars and Uranus, accidents can be a part of your day if you don't take a second to think before acting.

AFFIRMATION FOR THE DAY:
Every day is mine to choose, and
today I choose peace and harmony.

BIG SPINS OF THE DAY:
Mars sextiles Uranus: 2:41 A.M. PST / 5:41 A.M. EST
Moon Void of Course: 2:55 A.M. PST / 5:55 A.M. EST until
Moon enters Virgo: 6:34 A.M. PST / 9:34 A.M. EST
Sun sextiles Jupiter: 7:48 A.M. PST / 10:48 A.M. EST

○◑◐●

SUNDAY

February 4

MOON IN VIRGO
SUCCESS RATING: ★★★

The second day of the Virgo Moon means that you've had time to acclimate to its energy and are feeling more comfortable. Since this is the weekend, it would be a good idea to start some sort of organizational attempt—get those papers filed, pay a few bills, and shoo the loafing golfers in your life out to the course.

You'll have plenty of energy available to you as the Moon takes a leisurely stroll through this constellation. Remember, Virgo is not a social sign, so you may not feel like being around a lot of people . . . don't be too critical of yourself if you feel compelled to take the phone off the hook. Also, your eyes will have no trouble finding areas around the house that need your attention.

Find some time later today to have an honest chat with someone in your life, because truth—and the ability to tell it—is available at your slightest request.

AFFIRMATION FOR THE DAY:
I am never alone.

BIG SPINS OF THE DAY:
None

○◑◐●

MONDAY

February 5

MOON IN VIRGO/LIBRA
SUCCESS RATING: ★★

More Virgo Moon energy is at hand: strong in the morning, and much weaker by the afternoon since the Moon is going Void of Course later today. This means that you should get the serious work done early (including meetings and contracts) while your mind's in good shape.

Your tolerance could strike a new low, so try to convert any thoughts of criticism into ones that are more compassionate. When regarding the people around you, remember that nobody *tries* to be incompetent (well, I can think of a couple of exceptions). Don't be too pushy today—there are those who will push back, and it just causes unnecessary friction.

You'll get almost everything done today within the time frame you set, and what you don't finish can be delayed until tomorrow with only minor distractions to contend with. This night is a perfect one to rest and prepare for tomorrow's social explosion.

AFFIRMATION FOR THE DAY:
I am perfect right now!

BIG SPINS OF THE DAY:
Moon Void of Course: 2:37 P.M. PST / 5:37 P.M. EST until
Moon enters Libra: 6:15 P.M. PST / 9:15 P.M. EST

FEBRUARY

○◑◐●

TUESDAY

February 6

MOON IN LIBRA
SUCCESS RATING: ★★

Left, right, left, right . . . that's how you walk with one foot in front of the other, and these directions may come in handy as you proceed through your day. It's not that you suddenly became stupid, but there will be times when you'll just be out of sync with the rest of the world. The truth is that everyone's likely to be a bit off today. It's like being in a place that's not so bad, yet still wishing that you were somewhere else.

Luckily, the Libra Moon is about charm and grace, so all you have to do is keep a smile and a comb handy. When all else feels out of whack, at least you'll look good. And it's not as if the day were a total bust: You can still have your meetings and get the job done as long as you realize that everything you do today is just an attempt to make the clock tick faster . . . nonproductiveness isn't really a big deal in the scheme of things.

AFFIRMATION FOR THE DAY:
I am a musical note in the Divine symphony.

BIG SPINS OF THE DAY:
None

○◑◐●

W E D N E S D A Y

February 7

MOON IN LIBRA
SUCCESS RATING: ★★★

The charming Libra Moon is back on track and will have you saying the right thing at the right time, although you may not even have a clue that it's happening—that's the kind of support surrounding you today. You'll likely feel a bit rebellious, but you'll look fantastic in the eyes of those who matter, so go forth with confidence. The culprits behind this little piece of magic are Venus and Uranus, which are making a wonderful aspect to each other, and the results will surprise you . . . literally.

Throw away convention and embrace the creative, "outside-the-box" guy or gal you really are. However, there could be just one individual who insists on acting as an authoritative curmudgeon in your life. He or she delights in reminding you where you're missing the mark, but please don't take the person seriously. It's a fleeting moment of jealousy—after all, if you weren't being all that charming, there would be nothing for him or her to attack. . . . This is your chance to rise above such petty power issues.

AFFIRMATION FOR THE DAY:
I'm in tune with the magic that perpetually flows through my life.

BIG SPINS OF THE DAY:
Venus conjuncts Uranus: 10:58 A.M. PST / 1:58 P.M. EST

○◑◐●

THURSDAY

February 8

MOON IN LIBRA/SCORPIO
SUCCESS RATING: ★★★★

Although you may need a bit of time in the morning to adjust to the changing Moon sign, most of the day presents you with fabulous opportunities, particularly in the areas of creativity, spirituality, art, music, and romance. I know those are just buzzwords but hopefully they'll remind you to pull out your metaphorical paintbrush and add strokes of color to your life.

The Scorpio Moon asks you to look below the form of everything and touch base with its essence. It's a classic lesson in not judging a book by its cover, but rather by its content. Today, listen to what's *not* being said, and let yourself be guided accordingly. Luck is in the air . . . tune in to and follow it—there's nothing in the way of feeling the magic!

AFFIRMATION FOR THE DAY:
I am radiant and have plenty of light to share.

BIG SPINS OF THE DAY:
Moon Void of Course: 3:39 A.M. PST / 6:39 A.M. EST until
Moon enters Scorpio: 7:10 A.M. PST / 10:10 A.M. EST
Sun conjuncts Neptune: 7:53 A.M. PST / 10:53 A.M. EST

○ ◑ ◐ ●

FRIDAY

February 9

MOON IN SCORPIO
SUCCESS RATING: ★★★

I'm not the type to espouse the idea that too much of a good thing is bad, but today is *so* smooth that you might just be tempted to go further than what's necessary to accomplish something. Now, this "something" could be anything from a shopping spree to a dogged chase for a much-needed signature. Whatever it is you want to pursue, understand that in a Scorpio Moon cycle, *nothing* will stop you from getting it . . . and that could be a problem.

Today's obsessive tendencies are partially due to the sign's relentless drive to get what it wants, but the Scorpio Moon isn't to be blamed entirely. There's also a little clash between Venus and Jupiter, the kind that makes it hard to feel as though you have enough, even when you may in fact have *more* than enough.

Today there's no such thing as "too much," but tomorrow, when you've had time to settle down, you may feel differently. Overall, there's nothing to caution you against moving forward—I'm just suggesting that you take a break here and there to check in!

AFFIRMATION FOR THE DAY:
I have all the support I need—right now.

BIG SPINS OF THE DAY:
Venus squares Jupiter: 3:32 A.M. PST / 6:32 A.M. EST

○◑◐●

SATURDAY

February 10

FEBRUARY

LAST QUARTER MOON IN SCORPIO
MOON IN SCORPIO/SAGITTARIUS
SUCCESS RATING: ★

A long (*very* long) Void of Course Moon, combined with a messy mix of Saturn, is making it a good day to rest and recoup. At least, that works for me—*you* may want to hit the stores in the hopes that shopping will distract you from potential depression. It doesn't matter what you do . . . the important thing to remember is that sometimes the roller coaster of life seems to hit a dip or two before swinging you up to the exciting high points.

A clash between the Sun and Saturn may present you with issues of authority that you must confront. These are completely resolvable, although it may take a willing compromise on the part of both parties concerned.

Certainly some of you will feel completely at home in today's seemingly undirected energy, and more power to you. The rest of us might come to your house tonight for some pizza and TV watching, since you shouldn't have to feel so good all by yourself!

The ringed planet, Saturn, will be closest in its approach to Earth—directly opposite the Sun—making it the best time to view and photograph the planet and its moons.

AFFIRMATION FOR THE DAY:
I am not what I feel!

BIG SPINS OF THE DAY:
Last Quarter Moon at 21° Scorpio: 1:52 A.M. PST / 4:52 A.M. EST
Sun opposes Saturn: 10:42 A.M. PST / 1:42 P.M. EST
Moon Void of Course: 2:40 A.M. PST / 5:40 A.M. EST until
Moon enters Sagittarius: 7:02 P.M. PST / 10:02 P.M. EST

○ ◑ ◐ ●

SUNDAY

February 11

MOON IN SAGITTARIUS
SUCCESS RATING: ★★

Although you may still be feeling some of the leftover effects of the Sun-Saturn clash, the fiery and inspired Sagittarius Moon encourages you to reach for the stars when you aim your sights. This is a great day to congregate with your spiritual community, or to just have coffee with a good friend to discuss the magic and mystery of life. It's important to fuel the part of you that wants to be inspired—otherwise you may seek what you desire in inappropriate ways.

Today's placements are hinting that if you must talk about the people in your life, you should do so as if they were in the room with you. Days that are filled with the Sagittarius Moon's energies aren't the best ones to divulge your secrets, and they're even worse times for engaging in potentially hurtful gossip.

Confucius once said that a wagging tongue today could end up biting your bottom tomorrow. Okay, maybe he didn't say those exact words, but you get the point. Be conscious of your words today, for they hold power.

AFFIRMATION FOR THE DAY:
I am a cherished natural resource.

BIG SPINS OF THE DAY:
None

FEBRUARY

○◑◐●

MONDAY

February 12

MOON IN SAGITTARIUS
SUCCESS RATING: ★★

It's another all-day Sagittarius Moon, and although you may feel more in the flow of its optimistic aims, there's another event happening that may impede any feeling of progress. Mercury, the planet that rules your focus, is about to begin moving backward. (Please read up on the Mercury Retrograde in Part I so that you can be prepared.)

Concentration may take extra effort . . . perhaps there are too many distractions coming your way, or maybe some unfinished work is starting to rear its head. Your focus of attention could be a bit tentative, and scheduled plans may begin to change. If you notice some of these effects, it could be that you're experiencing Mercury slowing down almost to a halt (it does this just prior to moving backward).

Most of the day is filled with supportive alignments, but you're cautioned to resist falling into the Sagittarius trap of feeling burdened and unappreciated. If you can avoid that setup, you'll be able to use your mind to envision great events coming to you—the clearer you make that mental picture, the more solid the results will be.

AFFIRMATION FOR THE DAY:
I accept everything that is in my life today.

BIG SPINS OF THE DAY:
Mercury Retrograde: See the "Understanding the Meaning of Retrograde" section in Part I.

○◑◐●

TUESDAY

February 13

MERCURY RETROGRADES
MOON IN SAGITTARIUS/CAPRICORN
SUCCESS RATING: ★

In the wee hours of the morning, the Moon leaves the inspired sign of Sagittarius and enters the productive sign of Capricorn. Perhaps you noticed that your dreams were intense last night, a way to assist you in clearing any subconscious cobwebs.

The big news of the day is that the Mercury Retrograde officially begins. Most astrologers would have you feeling fearful of signing any contracts—but if that were valid, many highly successful corporations wouldn't be in business. It's been reported that more than 50 percent of Fortune 500 companies were incorporated under a Mercury Retrograde. So the only things to fear during this period are rogue astrologers or uninformed laypeople who use the event as their excuse!

All that Mercury is symbolically asking us to do is go inward before going outward. Your psychic radar (a fancy name for intuition) is now on, and you may recognize just how much power your thoughts hold. So if you find yourself besieged by mechanical problems, you can be sure that you're being asked to listen more closely to your gut. There's also a good chance that for the next three weeks people whom you think about will appear in some form or another—perhaps by phone or even in person for a visit.

The low Success Rating of the day is due to an impending clash among Mars, Venus, and Saturn. It may be best to wait a couple of days to let yourself get acclimated to these new energies before stirring up new projects.

AFFIRMATION FOR THE DAY:
I direct the energies of my day so that they serve me in my highest good.

BIG SPINS OF THE DAY:

Moon Void of Course: 12:46 A.M. PST / 3:46 A.M. EST until
Moon enters Capricorn: 3:43 A.M. PST / 6:43 A.M. EST
Venus sextiles Mars: 2:37 P.M. PST / 5:37 P.M. EST
Mercury Retrogrades at 10° Pisces: 8:38 P.M. PST / 11:38 P.M. EST

○◑◐●

WEDNESDAY

February 14

FEBRUARY

MOON IN CAPRICORN
SUCCESS RATING: ★

I honestly think that there's a conspiracy to position Valentine's Day at a time of year when it's the most difficult to express warm feelings to our partners . . . but maybe we need to be reminded of love on those days when it's least likely to occur.

Don't take it seriously if you're unable to show your partner the kind of affection that this holiday seems to demand. The "planets of love" (Venus and Mars) are squabbling, and the Moon remains in the stoic sign of Capricorn, a combination that makes those warm feelings seem like they're a million miles away. If that sounds like a recipe for sharing a passionate evening, then you probably have one of those wonderful long-distance relationships that can afford the luxury of bypassing the petty details and jumping right into bed—er . . . I mean, *conversation.*

For most of you, this day will be perfect for getting some work done, with enough time left over to buy your partner a meaningful gift. If you're not in a relationship, this probably isn't the best day to meet someone (unless you like the idea of mutual commiseration), but you could certainly use today to trade phone numbers and then plan a real date for the weekend.

AFFIRMATION FOR THE DAY:
In others, I am able to see a
part of me that wants to be loved.

BIG SPINS OF THE DAY:
Moon Void of Course: 7:26 P.M. PST / 10:26 P.M. EST until tomorrow

○◑◐●

THURSDAY

February 15

MOON IN CAPRICORN/AQUARIUS
SUCCESS RATING: ★★★

The Moon slips into Aquarius this morning after a long Void of Course Moon that started last night. Hopefully you had a wonderful evening and are taking some time this morning to regroup . . . but there's no rush. The Moon in Aquarius won't be activating any planets, so you pretty much have a free day to make plans and carve a nice piece of productivity into your day.

Since this is a rebellious Moon, you may have to break a rule or two. Why not get a group together for lunch and compare notes on your Valentine's Day evening? It might be good for a couple of laughs! Today there's really nothing in the way of your making any advancement.

AFFIRMATION FOR THE DAY:
My mind patiently understands
that my feelings may need more time.

BIG SPINS OF THE DAY:
Moon Void of Course: until 8:36 A.M. PST / 11:36 A.M. EST
Moon enters Aquarius: 8:36 A.M. PST / 11:36 A.M. EST

○◑◐●

FRIDAY

February 16

MOON IN AQUARIUS
SUCCESS RATING: ★★★

An all-day Aquarius Moon means that you should be back on track and more clear than you've felt in a while, so take advantage of your ability to see the glass as half full and spread your optimism around. However, historically Aquarius is the sign that's known for loving humanity and hating humans, so let me explain. . . .

Imagine that you're on the committee for tenants' rights. You fight hard to see that each renter in your apartment building has freedom of expression. One evening, though, you go home to find that your neighbor has placed a political sticker (which you oppose) on his door, and you call to have him evicted. Love humanity, hate humans . . . get it?

Tomorrow brings a New Moon, known as a Dark Moon, and metaphorically speaking, you or a few people around you may feel a little depressed as a result. This is a natural response to the Dark Moon, and it's a way to release emotions that have accumulated over the last few weeks. Tonight would be a great time to light a candle and set an intention in motion for something that you'd like to receive over the next two weeks. Also, dreams will be meaningful tonight, so try to get to bed early.

AFFIRMATION FOR THE DAY:
I accept what is presented to
me each day with gratitude.

BIG SPINS OF THE DAY:
None

○◑◐●

SATURDAY

February 17

NEW MOON IN AQUARIUS
MOON IN AQUARIUS/PISCES
SUCCESS RATING: ★★★★

Happy New Moon! New Moons are rejuvenating times, although technically the Moon moves in front of the Sun showing us only its dark side. In the "old days" it was the period of receiving, since from this moment on, the Moon would be *receiving* light (a phenomenon called "waxing").

Today should bring a sense of renewal, a blank slate onto which you can write your story. Aquarius New Moons are usually filled with altruistic urges (for me, that may mean actually speaking to the neighbors!). Watch how your mind reacts to this wave of Aquarian energy, since it's a great way to learn about the different signs.

Don't expect to feel immediate zest: We have a morning Void of Course Moon, then the Moon enters Pisces, which isn't a sign that's known for its spirited high speeds. This just might be the perfect Saturday—that is, if you're willing to move slowly and let your intuition be your guide. The afternoon may bring people from your past into play, so keep your home tidy and be mentally ready for a visit.

AFFIRMATION FOR THE DAY:
In one instant I heal my family grievances and release them to a higher wisdom; that instant is now.

BIG SPINS OF THE DAY:
Sun sextiles Pluto: 5:04 A.M. PST / 8:04 A.M. EST
New Moon at 29° Aquarius: 8:15 A.M. PST / 11:15 A.M. EST
Moon Void of Course: 8:15 A.M. PST / 11:15 A.M. EST until
Moon enters Pisces: 10:31 A.M. PST / 1:31 P.M. EST

Happy Birthday, Pisces!

February 18–March 20

Feelings . . . for a Pisces, they're as automatic as breathing. In fact, feelings are *such* an integral part of this sign's reality that it may seem as if most Pisceans wouldn't even notice having more of them than the rest of us—but that's not really true. For instance, a Pisces could hop aboard a bus in a perfectly fine mood, sit for a while with other riders, and then get off that bus sporting a headache and low-level anxiety—not even realizing that, much like a sponge, he or she has just absorbed the feelings of the people who sat nearby.

When you meet a Pisces, *whom* you encounter depends on several factors with no common denominator. Influencing circumstances could include whom the person's living with, what the Piscean's thoughts were upon awakening, what television show he or she watched the night before . . . ad infinitum. It's the "sponge effect," and it's what makes it difficult to place this complex Water sign into any specific personality box, although there are key words and phrases that all people with this sign share: *compassion, magical thinking, healing abilities, addiction,* and *martyrdom.* If you're born under the sign of Pisces, honor yourself with a few minutes alone each day to release any accumulations that you picked up from the energy fields of those around you, which is a sure way to find *your* tender center.

Affirmations for Pisces:

The only true connection I need is the one with myself.

I can release the accumulation of others' energies just by my intention to do so.

I am not responsible for the pain of others.

○ ◑ ◐ ●

SUNDAY

February 18

SUN IN PISCES
MOON IN PISCES
SUCCESS RATING: ★★★

Say good-bye to objective reality as you know it and hello to a more personal reality that you can immerse yourself in: It's the world of Pisces, and you'll be swimming in it for the next 30 days as the Sun moves into this compassionate and chameleonlike sign.

You'll most likely notice that the world has a dreamlike quality to it, almost as if you could think of something and it would appear. That's how most Pisceans live their entire lives, but everyone gets this 30-day window of opportunity to play in it. If you're an intuitive person, you'll find this change very comfortable. However, if you're a left-brain, logical type, you may have a harder time adjusting—but don't fret . . . in just a few days you'll be an old pro at living your life as a mystic.

Today is good for letting yourself adjust to these changes. There may seem to be a lot of chaos around you in the first part of the day, but things will settle down. Rest and enjoy, as tomorrow promises some challenges.

AFFIRMATION FOR THE DAY:
Everything that I see in front of me
is a reflection of something within.

BIG SPINS OF THE DAY:
Sun enters Pisces: 5:09 P.M. PST / 8:09 P.M. EST

○◑◐●

MONDAY

February 19

MOON IN PISCES/ARIES
SUCCESS RATING: ★★

Move slowly this morning and allow the Moon to navigate you through the renewing sign of Aries. As you enter the world of the Ram, you may notice an increase in irritability, impatience, and absentmindedness. Even though this might seem a like problem, these emotions are actually tools to help you shake off the lingering effects of the Pisces Moon. Although things will clear up as the day progresses, there are some precautions you should take to ensure that you don't stir up unnecessary conflicts along the way:

1. Avoid power struggles. These are events that pit you against someone else in an attempt to establish who's the authority. You have nothing to prove, and if you're victorious, you win nothing except the ire of someone who might have been potentially helpful in the future.

2. Don't bark. Bite your tongue and find your center before speaking or acting. You're likely to appear rude even if you think that you sound like a songbird. Remember that the receivers of your words can twist things, too.

3. Be patient. Not everyone is going to be on the same treadmill that you are: Some are slower and some are faster. Eventually the pace evens out, so take a breath and let the natural timing take over.

I wouldn't commit to anything today . . . let the dust settle and take another look tomorrow.

AFFIRMATION FOR THE DAY:
I am the only one who can truly know what is best for me, and I listen closely to my inner guidance.

BIG SPINS OF THE DAY:
Moon Void of Course: 8:44 A.M. PST / 11:44 A.M. EST until
Moon enters Aries: 11:07 A.M. PST / 2:07 P.M. EST
Venus squares Pluto: 7:54 P.M. PST / 10:54 P.M. EST

○◑◐●

TUESDAY

February 20

MOON IN ARIES
SUCCESS RATING: ★

Okay . . . you're back in the flow. The fiery Aries Moon is teaching you all about getting what you want by providing you with the energy you need. You won't tolerate any whining today—in fact, you'll probably seem a little pushy to people you come into contact with. But don't be fooled, since they're under the same aggressive energy and will probably *call* you pushy just to start a fight.

Relationships are under a minor strain today as Venus prepares to leave Pisces and enter Aries. That means that you may be less inclined to yield to the demands of others and more likely to follow your own heart (and people just don't like that).

Don't read between the lines today, as most things are being presented at face value—the Aries Moon has no time for hidden agendas. Remember that you're still clearing up the past while Mercury is in retrograde, so keep your energy in balance. If you need to work off some excess steam, do so at the gym, not with your co-workers.

AFFIRMATION FOR THE DAY:
I see how things are connected to a bigger picture and take nothing personally.

BIG SPINS OF THE DAY:
None

○◑◐●

WEDNESDAY

February 21

FEBRUARY

MOON IN ARIES/TAURUS
SUCCESS RATING: ★

Venus is to Aries as the telephone booth is to Clark Kent: You're about to find your inner superhero! Are you ready to create real challenges and bully your way to the top? Competition, sports, and races to the finish line are now all part of your new reality. Gone are the compassionate days of the past month, along with the part of you that lets people jump ahead in the grocery-store checkout line just because they have fewer items. Also gone are the periods of sitting by the phone waiting for your special friend to call, as there's no time to waste on things that won't support you.

But did I mention that all of this feisty activity and aggressiveness has to wait until after the Void of Course Moon? In general (and in all seriousness), you should enjoy this day—but I'd refrain from new business ventures, just until tomorrow.

AFFIRMATION FOR THE DAY:
There is peace available to me every second of my life.

BIG SPINS OF THE DAY:
Venus enters Aries: 12:22 A.M. PST / 3:22 A.M. EST
Moon Void of Course: 9:42 A.M. PST / 12:42 P.M. EST until
Moon enters Taurus: 12:04 P.M. PST / 3:04 P.M. EST

○◑◐●

THURSDAY

February 22

MOON IN TAURUS
SUCCESS RATING: ★★

The Taurus Moon sends your attention to your body and to all things that bring you security. This is the kind of day that makes you want to blow off your diet and head for the nearest pastry shop! Part of the word *Taurus* is inside the word "res*tau*rant," and no Moon makes you appreciate food more than this one.

Beyond the desire to eat, this day has some interesting and helpful alignments. The Sun and Mercury are together today, indicating the end of the first phase of the Mercury Retrograde. You've finished clearing up the past and are ready to take on new projects for the future, and there's a good chance that you'll feel like a switch clicked on in your brain, bringing unusual clarity and awareness.

Today's rays help usher in excitement, giving you the boost needed to carve out a new path. No real impediments to your progress exist, but there aren't a great number of enhancements either—hence, the low Success Rating.

AFFIRMATION FOR THE DAY:
It is all good!

BIG SPINS OF THE DAY:
Sun conjuncts Mercury: 8:46 P.M. PST / 11:46 P.M. EST

FEBRUARY

○◑◐●

FRIDAY

February 23

FIRST QUARTER MOON IN GEMINI
MOON IN TAURUS/GEMINI
SUCCESS RATING: ★★

Due to an afternoon Void of Course Moon, you should use the morning to accomplish most of your work. Your temper may have a sensitive trigger that could surprise you, so try to stay aware of your moods as the day progresses.

As the Moon prepares to leave Taurus this afternoon, you might have to accommodate the shift by relaxing your expectations just a bit. Today, like yesterday, could be filled with every possible distraction you can think of . . . and then some. But if you expect such interferences, you'll most likely manage your way through them just fine.

After two days of basking in those earthy Taurus Moon energies, you could use some excitement, and today won't let you down. It's time to tackle any obstacles head-on so that old business will remain behind you as you prepare for the cycle that the New Moon initiates. The next New Moon is an Eclipse, which makes your discoveries today particularly powerful.

AFFIRMATION FOR THE DAY:
My life is full of possibilities
that I effortlessly manifest.

BIG SPINS OF THE DAY:

Moon Void of Course: 11:47 A.M. PST / 2:47 P.M. EST until
Moon enters Gemini: 2:42 P.M. PST / 5:42 P.M. EST
First Quarter Moon at 5° Gemini: 11:56 pm PST / 2:56 A.M. EST (Saturday)

○ ◑ ◐ ●

SATURDAY

February 24

MOON IN GEMINI
SUCCESS RATING: ★★

If you find that your mind is a whirlwind of random (and sometimes obsessive) thoughts, you aren't alone in that experience. For many, today will bring a plethora of mental activities, thanks to an already "thought-full" Gemini Moon connecting with an overexcited mental patient called Mercury. Since you're mostly conditioned to hang out in your mind, this won't seem like a problem for everyone—it may just look like an ordinary day with an extraordinary set of distractions (albeit most of them harmless).

Don't fret if you're in the group that finds this day to contain nothing more than a list of irritations seemingly designed to keep you preoccupied and away from your personal goals. "Irritations" are labeled as such only when things occur that you don't want . . . otherwise you'd call them "opportunities."

This is Mars's last day in Capricorn, and the push for productivity will come to an end, so give any task your last-ditch effort! It's also a great evening for a gathering with close friends.

AFFIRMATION FOR THE DAY:
What I really want, I have.

BIG SPINS OF THE DAY:
None

FEBRUARY

○◑◐●

SUNDAY

February 25

MOON IN GEMINI/CANCER
SUCCESS RATING: ★

There's a bevy of celestial activity today that could make you feel more comfortable at home than anywhere else. Mars is changing signs, an event that often carries its own set of speed bumps designed to slow you down while you adjust to the different focus.

For more than a month, Mars (the planet of action) has pushed you through the stoic sign of Capricorn at a relentless pace, creating the urge for "doing and building." Today your awareness is shifting into the less physically active sign of Aquarius, where you'll be given a chance to get an eagle-like perspective on your life. Your attention will move toward humanitarian causes—such as the environment, world politics, hunger, or whatever the "Aquarian activist" in you is called to do—and planetary changes like this usually require a day or two for you to adjust.

Later today the Moon will shift into the homebound sign of Cancer, aiming your focus on family and security. Watch how your moods change, and don't take them too seriously . . . it's a perfect day to let things settle.

AFFIRMATION FOR THE DAY:
There is nothing that I *must* do.

BIG SPINS OF THE DAY:
Mars enters Aquarius: 5:33 P.M. PST / 8:33 P.M. EST
Moon Void of Course: 5:21 P.M. PST / 8:21 P.M. EST until
Moon enters Cancer: 7:48 P.M. PST / 10:48 P.M. EST

○◑◐●

MONDAY

February 26

MOON IN CANCER
SUCCESS RATING: ★★

The all-day Cancer Moon may have you worrying more than usual about . . . well, just about anything. The Moon is at home in the sign of Cancer, which tends to accentuate your sensitivities, and on some level, you're feeling every nuance of change and responding like a barometer fluctuating with every minute change in pressure. This effect has a lot to do with Cancers' love of being at home, where they aren't as inundated with constant external input.

Tonight rolls in a very, very long Void of Course Moon, and although much can get done, it's often a random "luck of the draw" as to whether or not you can stay focused. Mercury's change in sign tonight isn't helping matters, and if you've been following this book, you now realize that a shift in signs requires an adjustment period . . . so get focused.

You can sign whatever you need to today with regard to business deals, but then get ready to perform random acts of kindness (or any other acts you choose). Family members may need your attention tonight, and you'll have plenty of it to give.

AFFIRMATION FOR THE DAY:
I am in the zone.

BIG SPINS OF THE DAY:
Mercury enters Aquarius: 7:01 P.M. PST / 10:01 P.M. EST
Moon Void of Course: 10:04 P.M. PST / 1:04 A.M. EST (Tuesday) until Wednesday

○◑◐●

TUESDAY

February 27

MOON IN CANCER
SUCCESS RATING: ★

An all-day Void of Course Moon may make it difficult to pay attention for too long to any one thing. (This would be a good day to read the Moon Void of Course section in Part I.) Although many people enjoy the freedom that this Moon offers, due to the resulting lack of focus, problems can arise from decisions that aren't thought all the way through. This is why you're advised to observe rather than act today—however, it's certainly *not* a law carved in stone.

For those of you who have already been working on certain ideas or projects for a while that don't require much more thought to complete, this can be a fine time to act. But if there's any doubt or confusion regarding some issue, it's best to wait just a day for more clarity. Misunderstandings are more prevalent today, so look for resolutions later.

AFFIRMATION FOR THE DAY:
My life is flowing in perfect
harmony with the Universe.

BIG SPINS OF THE DAY:
Moon Void of Course: All day and night

○◑◐●

WEDNESDAY

February 28

MOON IN CANCER/LEO
SUCCESS RATING: ★

February is certainly leaving in a forgettable way. Today's Leo Moon will help bring some optimism to the forefront, but a Saturn-Neptune connection isn't helping your spirits, since these two big players have a history of causing confusion in the world. This is the second of three rounds of this alignment—the first one occurred in August of 2006, and the last one will be in June of this year. Look back to the earlier one, see if you can "name the tune" that was being sung, and then see how it relates to the current time period.

Strains in world relationships may dominate, as Saturn in Leo represents control through pride, and Neptune in Aquarius stands for humanitarian ideals. It's likely that this is a conflict as to who has the "right" beliefs, and the result could be that all involved draw immovable battle lines.

If you bring that idea closer to home, you may find that you're battling a similar issue with something in your personal life. Take a look to see where you've drawn a line and become unwilling to budge—it could be a belief or conviction that you're holding about a particular situation. It might help if you try to release your stance and stay open to all opinions, but ultimately realize that none of us knows much. If you can't lighten up today, don't fret . . . March is bringing in some wonderful relief.

Take a moment today and make a list of things you're grateful for, particularly the ones that February brought you. Keep your mind on what's working, and avoid the pitfall of thinking that your happiness lies anywhere else but with you!

AFFIRMATION FOR THE DAY:
I am always in a state of gratitude, knowing that I have not been abandoned here.

BIG SPINS OF THE DAY

Saturn opposes Neptune: 4:02 A.M. PST / 7:02 A.M. EST
Mercury sextiles Pluto: 6:13 A.M. PST / 9:13 A.M. EST
Moon Void of Course: until 3:30 A.M. PST / 6:30 A.M. EST
Moon enters Leo: 3:30 A.M. PST / 6:30 A.M. EST

Thought for the Month

Managing Fear

In honor of the Mercury Retrograde, I'm going to be direct with you: Your fears about the Retrograde can cause a lot of problems—particularly when you have to decide to do something. Use this guide to help you figure out if a decision is fear based or not.

You can tell when a decision is being made *out of fear* when:

- You have an intense sense of urgency—a feeling that if you don't act soon, you'll lose something (another chance, opportunity, or what have you).
- There's a strong sense that what you need exists outside of you and you *must* do something to get it.
- You find yourself feeling abandoned or completely on your own.
- There seems to be a nonstop recycling of chatter in your mind.
- You repeatedly ask your friends for solutions to the same problem all under the guise of seeking advice, yet you don't seem to gain any insight.
- Your thinking is focused on the worst-case scenario and very few other possibilities.

You can tell when your decision is being made *without fear* when:

- You recognize that it's okay to act on something, because you really can accept any outcome.

- You can acknowledge that although you may not like your immediate situation, it *doesn't* define you or your future.

- You perceive that there's a part of you that will guide you perfectly, and you place your focus there.

- You recall that you have everything right now that you need to be joyful.

- You recognize that anxiety arises when you put your trust in your brain and not your Higher Mind.

- You remember that ultimately you don't have to make a decision now, especially if it disrupts your peace.

○◑◐●

MARCH 2007
SUMMARY

MARCH

When looking through the doorway into March, it's easy to see that important changes are coming. March is typically embraced as a pivotal month . . . after all, it does bring us spring (fall for our friends Down Under) and the inspiring—though hardly subtle—attributes of Aries, which alone are reasons to celebrate. But March 2007 has a few extra surprises: It harbors two Eclipses, hosts the end of the Mercury Retrograde, and presents the first of three important Jupiter-Saturn connections.

The Eclipses in this month are certainly dynamic. The one on March 3 is a Total Eclipse in Virgo, the same one that happened in March of 1988, setting off a chain of messy political events (do an Internet search for that year) . . . but things needed to be cleaned up at that time. How 1988 affected you personally is a matter of remembering not just March, but the entire year—so try to capture a theme and apply it to your life.

The first Jupiter-Saturn Trine occurs on March 16, taking place as part of a 21-year cycle, and it will happen two more times: in May 2007 and January 2008. In simple terms, this event is suggesting a time of harmony, when life will seem stable and solid (Saturn), while expansion will also seem possible (Jupiter)—which bodes well for the economy and any endeavors that you may undertake.

Here are some of the March highlights:

March 3:	Full Moon Eclipse at 13° Virgo
March 7:	Mercury Retrograde ends
March 16:	Jupiter trines Saturn
March 17:	Venus enters Taurus
March 18:	New Moon Eclipse 28° Pisces; Mercury enters Pisces
March 20:	Vernal (Spring) Equinox; Sun enters Aries
March 31:	Pluto Retrograde begins

○◑◐●

THURSDAY

March 1

MOON IN LEO
SUCCESS RATING: ★

It's an all-day Leo Moon, shining its optimistic rays on this first day of March. Keep in mind that if you feel an undertone of depression, it's the result of last month's Saturn-Neptune connection, which will lighten up as the days proceed. The less-than-chipper vibe is the reason why it's important to focus only on what's in front of you for a while.

Most of today's productive hours will start by noon (regardless of where you live) and continue throughout the day. Tonight holds a bit of romance for those of you who have a desire to pursue it, and the rest of you can simply enjoy the warm tone of the evening.

We're heading toward a Full Moon Eclipse, so there should be some excitement building. (Read about Eclipses on my Website, **www.12house.com**, and at the beginning of this book.) Start working out the details of your intentions now and you'll feel supported under this cycle. It's okay to feel emotionally wobbly as the Full Moon approaches, however, since it tends to have that effect.

Don't get involved in big signings, launchings, or purchases today. (Get used to that warning for a while.)

AFFIRMATION FOR THE DAY:
I say *yes* to receiving all the gifts that I desire!

BIG SPINS OF THE DAY:
None

○◐◑●

FRIDAY

March 2

MOON IN LEO/VIRGO
SUCCESS RATING: ★★★

For most of the morning, you'll be guided by the Leo Moon, which is hanging around long enough to see that you get all the accolades you could ever want before changing into Virgo later in the day. Morning miscommunications could set off a couple of minor irritations, so say nice things even if you aren't feeling them . . . it's best to give each situation the benefit of the doubt.

Later in the afternoon, you'll get an opportunity to tell the truth in a way that empowers you, thanks to a Pluto-Moon connection. The clarity will be remarkable, so make good use of it.

The scrutinizing eyes of the Virgo Moon will find any flaw that's waiting to be put right, but save your editing skills for the afternoon and your scathing criticisms for emergencies. Dinner plans should be minimal, as Virgo Moons don't encourage much socialization or rich foods.

AFFIRMATION FOR THE DAY:
I am perfect and complete just as I am.

BIG SPINS OF THE DAY:
Moon Void of Course: 11:03 A.M. PST / 2:03 P.M. EST until
Moon enters Virgo: 1:32 P.M. PST / 4:32 P.M. EST

○◑◐●

SATURDAY

March 3

FULL MOON ECLIPSE IN VIRGO
SUCCESS RATING: ★★★★

Lunar Eclipses are very powerful Full Moons that are part of big cycles that occur every 19 years. This Total Eclipse happened on the exact same day in 1988, and it's going to be visible around the world. Since the Full Moon is in Virgo, its energy is directed at awakening our discriminating palate. Under it, many flaws—from the global to the personal—will be exposed in order to be cleaned and purged. Watch the news (if you can bear it), and notice what your inner critic starts to pick on.

The Virgo Eclipse will also bring the qualities of service, solitude, and humor into your experience. Changes will also get set in motion: You may be fired, hired, or meet the most influential person in your life . . . it depends in part on where Virgo lies in your birth chart and is otherwise based on what your intentions are.

The Eclipse effect lasts two weeks and officially begins tonight (although you may have started to feel it weeks ago). Light a candle and jot down a list of your desires . . . the only reason to do so is to help keep you focused, since it will have no bearing on whether you receive what you wish for or not—that's between you and your heart. Venus is also part of this Eclipse, so what you love will definitely matter!

AFFIRMATION FOR THE DAY:
Among my greatest wishes,
experiencing gratitude is at the top.

BIG SPINS OF THE DAY:
The Full Moon Eclipse at 13° Virgo: 3:18 P.M. PST / 6:18 P.M. EST

○ ◑ ◐ ●

SUNDAY

March 4

MOON IN VIRGO
SUCCESS RATING: ★★★

It will be tough to beat yesterday's planetary show, but today will allow you to put the Eclipse to use. It's still an all-day Virgo Moon, so you may find satisfaction in going through your old clothes and donating them to charity—these Moons love helping you clear your clutter. Virgo is also very concerned with dietary needs and supplements, so a trip to your local health-food store may prove valuable and supportive.

Your pets could require a little TLC today, so be sure to give them some special attention. However, this is your day to do as you please with little interference, so save social events for another night of the week, and let yourself hole up to enjoy your own company. Once evening arrives, you can savor your quiet time by soaking in a long, relaxing bath; reading an engaging novel; or simply staying still and letting your mind come to a stop. Next week the pace picks up, so get some long-overdue rest.

AFFIRMATION FOR THE DAY:
Finding my inner stillness is effortless.

BIG SPINS OF THE DAY:
Moon Void of Course: 10:57 P.M. PDT /1:57 A.M. EDT (Monday) until tomorrow

○◑◐●

MONDAY

March 5

MOON IN VIRGO/LIBRA
SUCCESS RATING: ★★★

It's time for the annual Sun-Uranus connection, so expect the unexpected. When these two planets come together, there's an increase in the use of electronic equipment (computers, televisions, and so forth) and often a sudden desire to study offbeat sciences such as astrology. (Did I just call it "offbeat"? How rude!)

The fun part about today is that you're being guided by a social Libra Moon, so many of your escapades just might include your friends—the ones everyone else thinks are quirky! Sun-Uranus also excites the urge to break the rules, think outside the box, and seriously question authority. Pay attention to world events to see if you can find this energy acting out somewhere.

A word of caution, though: Try to stay grounded today, particularly if you want to purchase something new. This planetary connection is great for starting businesses that have an electronic or unconventional nature, and friendships and alliances you make under this aspect are likely to be unusual and instantaneous.

AFFIRMATION FOR THE DAY:
I feel electric!

BIG SPINS OF THE DAY:
Moon Void of Course: until 1:26 A.M. PST / 4:26 A.M. EST
Moon enters Libra: 1:26 A.M. PST / 4:26 A.M. EST
Sun conjuncts Uranus: 7:40 A.M. PST / 10:40 A.M. EST

○◑◐●

TUESDAY

March 6

MOON IN LIBRA
SUCCESS RATING: ★★

MARCH

Go to the theater, run to the museum, throw a party . . . just do something where you get to dress up and feel good about the way you look. The Libra Moon sometimes simply waits for an excuse to have tea with friends so that you can share a moment of sublime superficiality. It's your right under this Moon to seek out social ties and cast aside thoughts of being alone.

The Libra Moon likes people of all kinds, as long as nobody is immersed in heavy problems. It enjoys things light and easy and prefers that no one person dominate your attention.

Don't make important moves under today's Moon. Instead, wait for a period when the planets are more serious and less social—it's better to use the charm of the Libra Moon to win approval and make your more serious requests at a later time.

AFFIRMATION FOR THE DAY:
I deserve more.

BIG SPINS OF THE DAY:
None

○◑◐●

WEDNESDAY

March 7

MERCURY RETROGRADE ENDS
MOON IN LIBRA/SCORPIO
SUCCESS RATING: ★★

Late today, Mercury will cease moving backward, meaning that the Retrograde cycle is at an end. Many of you will celebrate; some of you will be sad, missing the psychic abilities that seemed to emanate during this cycle; and others won't care either way. Although you may want to rush out to sign your deals and make your purchases, it's just not a good idea . . . at least not yet.

Although Mercury is no longer appearing to move backward, it's also not going forward—that takes a day or two. Give the planet (and yourself!), time to settle down, and if you have unfinished work, get it done in the morning before the Moon goes Void of Course. Remember: Don't rush into *anything* for a couple of days.

The afternoon brings a serious Scorpio Moon that will begin the process of taking you inward. Follow the natural flow and start quieting down, since tonight promises to be calm and embracing.

AFFIRMATION FOR THE DAY:
I am never disconnected from my source.

BIG SPINS OF THE DAY:
Mercury Retrograde ends at 25° Aquarius: 8:38 P.M. PST / 11:38 P.M. EST
Moon Void of Course: 11:52 A.M. PST / 2:52 P.M. EST until
Moon enters Scorpio: 2:18 P.M. PST / 5:18 P.M. EST

○◑◐●

THURSDAY

March 8

MOON IN SCORPIO

SUCCESS RATING: ★★★★

MARCH

Friendships, art, romance, and music are just some of the things that may thrill you today, thanks to a wonderful link between Venus and Jupiter. Don't be surprised if you suddenly feel an inner confidence emerging, as well as a strong desire to act out a fantasy that you hold dear.

Of course, it doesn't hurt that the Moon is in sexy Scorpio, which fuels the fire of passion whenever it gets a chance. Those passions may include scary books or movies, or helping the characters on the TV show *CSI* solve their crimes . . . but whatever they are, you won't function very well today without them.

You should also begin feeling the forward motion of Mercury, and you may continue your progress with contracts and purchases with confidence.

AFFIRMATION FOR THE DAY:
My finances are abundantly overflowing.

BIG SPINS OF THE DAY:

Venus trines Jupiter: 3:16 A.M. PST / 6:16 A.M. EST

○◑◐●

FRIDAY

March 9

MOON IN SCORPIO
SUCCESS RATING: ★★★

There's an all-day Scorpio Moon and enough celestial activity to keep you hopping for most of the day. You may find yourself toting a serious mood around with you today, not because you're troubled, but because you most likely woke up with a long list of things that you "need" to do.

The morning is the optimal time to get your best work done, but you'll probably be up against a lot of distractions—ones that ultimately come from your deep desire *not* to do a lot of work. Blame Jupiter, since today the planet will tempt you with lighthearted possibilities that make playing hooky seem like a reasonable idea. If you're overwhelmed by the idea of cutting out on work today, consider doing it anyway. There's plenty of time next week to catch up, although there's also a good chance that you'll have more fun over the weekend if you know that you don't have a bunch of unfinished work waiting for you.

Tonight romantic vibes increase, as does your appetite—so solve both problems with a romantic dinner for two. If that's not a solution in your situation, then just do the luxuriant, deluxe-hot-bath thing . . . it will give you just what you need.

AFFIRMATION FOR THE DAY:
I am blessed in all areas of my life.

BIG SPINS OF THE DAY:
Venus trines Saturn: 12:41 A.M. PST / 3:41 A.M. EST
Sun squares Jupiter: 6:19 A.M. PST / 9:19 A.M. EST
Venus sextiles Neptune: 7:42 P.M. PST / 10:42 P.M. EST
Moon Void of Course: 5:53 P.M. PST / 8:53 P.M. EST until tomorrow

○◑◐●

SATURDAY

March 10

MOON IN SCORPIO/SAGITTARIUS
SUCCESS RATING: ★★

MARCH

The Sagittarius Moon plays a big part in setting the tone for your day by presenting you with a choice: magical or mundane. There's a part of Sagittarius that very much believes in magic, and people born under this sign tend to dedicate a big part of their lives to it. In that area of their world, they're the kings and queens—the sons and daughters of Jupiter, the biggest planet of the solar system. The other part of Sagittarius is mortal, however, and must deal with mundane realities, such as taking out the trash and going to work.

Today you'll be given a choice to follow the part of you that believes there's much more around you than what you see, or the part of you that thinks that what you see is what you get. It's really *your* choice today, because nothing else is influencing you.

I can't tell you which thought to embrace *(embrace the magic),* because *(embrace the magic)* that would *(embrace the magic)* be misleading *(embrace the magic)* you. So choose whatever supports you *(by the way, choose the magic).*

AFFIRMATION FOR THE DAY:
I embrace the magical part of myself completely.

BIG SPINS OF THE DAY:
Moon Void of Course: until 2:38 A.M. PST / 5:38 A.M. EST
Moon enters Sagittarius: 2:38 A.M. PST / 5:38 A.M. EST

○◑◐●

SUNDAY

March 11

LAST QUARTER MOON IN SAGITTARIUS
SUCCESS RATING: ★★

This is called the Last Quarter Moon because the Sun and Moon are at an angle that makes the Moon look sliced in two, symbolizing that you're halfway to the New Moon. It's designed to get you back on track and allow you to question your goals up to this point. So if you notice that you're annoyed today, you may be working at finding your center and illuminating all the extraneous intrusions along the way—the irritation just helps you to be ruthlessly honest.

Today will mostly focus on revealing the obstacles in your way that are preventing you from getting wherever it is that you're going. You may be exposed to a variety of different emotions, so just try to ride them out. Balance will be achieved shortly . . . avoid big decisions today.

AFFIRMATION FOR THE DAY:
I am so much more than my thoughts.

BIG SPINS OF THE DAY:
Last Quarter Moon at 21° Sagittarius: 8:55 P.M. PDT / 11:55 P.M. EDT

○◑◐●

MONDAY

March 12

MOON IN SAGITTARIUS/CAPRICORN
SUCCESS RATING: ★★

The Moon shifts from fiery Sagittarius to earthy Capricorn today, and that can require a bit of an adjustment (a big one for some of you). Sagittarius loves to keep the energy fresh and new, while Capricorn wants things steady and familiar. Bridge the gap between the two by working in the morning and playing in the later part of the day—that way, both Moons will be honored.

You'll know the precise moment when it's time to shift your focus: Capricorn will add a stoic quality to the air, and you may begin to feel down. Before you panic, remember that depression is part of the Capricorn Moon experience, and it's helping you evaluate your circumstances before it sends you into action.

You can pretty much do whatever you want today, but just be aware of the interval of the Void of Course Moon.

AFFIRMATION FOR THE DAY:
I am the pearl in this oyster called Earth.

BIG SPINS OF THE DAY:
Moon Void of Course: 11:27 A.M. PDT / 2:27 P.M. EDT until
Moon enters Capricorn: 1:35 P.M. PDT / 4:35 P.M. EDT

○◑◐●

TUESDAY

March 13

MOON IN CAPRICORN
SUCCESS RATING: ★★★

"Steady and ready" could be a fitting mantra for the Capricorn Moon today. This Moon has an ability to make the achievement of your aims seem like the most important task you have to do. If you aren't the goal-setting type, then focus your attention on unfinished projects or your friends . . . you might even want to take a sober look at your finances.

You may find that the effects of this Moon make your moods more serious and self-questioning. It will certainly be harder to sit around holding frivolous conversations under the Capricorn Moon's watch.

Use this day fully by doing something that allows you to feel productive—it could be as simple as finishing a book that you started or helping a friend complete a project. *Purpose* is your theme for today, so if you don't have one, make one up.

Do something tonight outside of your usual ritual, and be assured that you'll like the outcome.

MARCH

AFFIRMATION FOR THE DAY:
What I do does not define me.

BIG SPINS OF THE DAY:
None

○◑◐●

WEDNESDAY

March 14

MOON IN CAPRICORN/AQUARIUS
SUCCESS RATING: ★★

If you feel as though the task-oriented Capricorn Moon has imprisoned you, help is on the way. The stoic and purposeful Capricorn Moon gives way to the rebellious and energetic Aquarius one by midafternoon.

Tie up all those loose ends this morning, and then give things a rest until tomorrow. You're on a roll and everything's about to get pretty sweet, but show some restraint and let the change in energies find a balance.

You can certainly afford to get in some playtime tonight and even a little *rest* (yikes, I said the *R* word under a Capricorn Moon!). Don't overthink things today, because it's too easy to turn a single thought into a whirlwind of mental chatter that prevents you from feeling.

Apart from the Void of Course Moon, there's no reason why you shouldn't make permanent commitments today—just make sure there are reasons why you *should.*

AFFIRMATION FOR THE DAY:
I can change my mind freely
without negative consequences.

BIG SPINS OF THE DAY:
Moon Void of Course: 1:22 P.M. PDT / 4:22 P.M. EDT until
Moon enters Aquarius: 7:53 P.M. PDT / 10:53 P.M. EDT

○◑◐●

THURSDAY

March 15

MOON IN AQUARIUS
SUCCESS RATING: ★★★★★

Finally, you have a day where you can direct your attention to a project and not worry about big distractions taking you off course. Aquarius Moons can be idealistic, encouraging you to contemplate how you'd end world hunger or shelter the homeless. It's the sign's idealism that rejuvenates your hope for humanity and your sense of global family . . . but make sure it's not taking you away from your duties at hand.

Today offers a wonderful connection between Venus and Chiron (the rogue comet) and suggests that if you meet someone today or take your current relationship to another level, you're likely to have a bond that lasts forever. This also applies to businesses that you may launch or contracts that you enter into today . . . the fact that there's no Void of Course Moon assures you that the green light is lit—so go for it!

AFFIRMATION FOR THE DAY:
I am always ready to receive
all that is in my highest good.

BIG SPINS OF THE DAY:
None

○◑◐●

FRIDAY

March 16

MOON IN AQUARIUS/PISCES
SUCCESS RATING: ★★★★★

MARCH

Have you been attempting to give birth to a creative idea? Perhaps you've been trying to conceive a child? Today the planets are forming what's known as a *fertility aspect,* and they're supporting you in planting whatever seeds you might want to cultivate.

This is one of the more active days of the month, and it would serve you well to use it to launch whatever projects you've had in the works. It could be that you've wanted to get something off your chest, or perhaps your creativity well hasn't been flowing lately. . . . Well, this is the day that things will turn around.

You may have the feeling that there's a safety net below you, as if to reassure you that you can't fail and you'll be secure in your new goal. It's very likely that discussing something personal with a colleague or friend could assist you in achieving the clarity you seek—perhaps you'll gain insights that you would have overlooked otherwise.

The planets are on your side today, so make use of them, and write your thoughts in a journal for even more revealing insights. This is a green-light day: Anything you start has a great chance at a happy ending.

AFFIRMATION FOR THE DAY:
I love my smile and its effect on those around me.

BIG SPINS OF THE DAY:
Jupiter trines Saturn: 3:48 P.M. PDT / 6:48 P.M. EDT
Mercury sextiles Pluto: 4:30 P.M. PDT / 7:30 P.M. EDT
Venus trines Pluto: 5:15 P.M. PDT / 8:15 P.M. EDT
Mercury sextiles Venus: 6:23 P.M. PDT / 9:23 P.M. EDT
Moon Void of Course: 9:02 P.M. PDT / 12:02 A.M. EDT (Saturday) until
Moon enters Pisces: 10:31 P.M. PDT / 1:31 A.M. EDT (Saturday)

○◑◐●

SATURDAY

March 17

MOON IN PISCES
SUCCESS RATING: ★★★

It may very well seem that the luck of the Irish is with you under this dreamy Pisces Moon. The powerful effects of yesterday's planets will feel even stronger today because you've adjusted to them.

Today is auspicious as Venus moves into its home sign of Taurus. If you're a Taurus or Libra by birth, you'll very likely enjoy a particular ease—but everyone else will also benefit from the comfort that this placement brings. Hot baths, massages, and other bodily treats beckon you under this aspect, and the Pisces Moon will simply enhance these sensations.

Don't fret about not having the energy level that you're used to . . . you aren't supposed to be exerting yourself much today. Kick back, and let yourself *feel* what's going on around you, since today your intuition is particularly fine-tuned.

There's a New Moon Eclipse tomorrow evening, so you may find it useful to prepare your goals. This Eclipse wants you to plant seeds of intentions in order for you to see them become manifested over the next few weeks. Write down your desires and save them, but you don't have to worry about detailing your requests perfectly, as the Universe isn't trying to hurt you.

AFFIRMATION FOR THE DAY:
I am worthy of real love.

BIG SPINS OF THE DAY:
Venus enters Taurus: 3:01 P.M. PDT / 6:01 P.M. EDT

○◑◐●

SUNDAY

March 18

SOLAR ECLIPSE IN PISCES
MOON IN PISCES/ARIES
SUCCESS RATING: ★★★

MARCH

The Moon will be in front of the Sun tonight, forming a Partial Eclipse that won't be visible in the U.S. (except for in Alaska), but it will be observable in parts of Asia. However, whether you can see it or not, you'll definitely *feel* the power of this Eclipse.

Eclipses tend to set cycles into motion that are 19 years in duration. In other words, this very Eclipse occurred exactly 19 years ago (1988), in the identical sign, and at the same degree. If you can't remember that time period, it doesn't matter . . . what's important is that you're beginning a new cycle, one where the themes are *compassion, spirituality,* and *connection*—all the key words for Pisces. Take notice of what's happening in the world, as these Eclipses tend to have a global impact, but also pay attention to how your focus changes in your daily life.

This is a day to dream and to dream big. Pisces Moons normally bring you nostalgic feelings, the kind that makes the past seem like it's the present, and the opportunity is finally there to purge the residual old hurts. Be on the lookout for people you haven't heard from in years, since they have a way of showing up during this type of clearing process.

Don't worry if you feel a decrease in your energy today—that's part of the effect of the clearing. Within a couple of days, you'll be the embodiment of spring!

AFFIRMATION FOR THE DAY:
I embrace and then completely release my past.

BIG SPINS OF THE DAY:

Mercury enters Pisces: 2:35 A.M. PDT / 5:35 A.M. EDT
Partial Solar Eclipse at 28° Pisces: 7:43 P.M. PDT / 10:43 P.M. EDT / 3:43 UT
Moon Void of Course: 8:59 P.M. PDT / 11:59 P.M. EDT until
Moon enters Aries: 10:42 P.M. PDT / 1:42 A.M. EDT (Monday)

○◑◐●

MONDAY

March 19

MOON IN ARIES
SUCCESS RATING: ★★

Shake off the powerful blanket of feelings brought on by the Eclipse, and get your motors revved for the day. The Aries Moon is full of fire and has the energy to get you motivated. If you start to feel antagonistic toward someone or something, then you're trying to use anger to help you snap out of yesterday's emotional immersion. However, if you understand this process, you'll be less likely to make the mistake of acting or speaking inappropriately—saving you from the uncomfortable process of having to suck up tomorrow.

You could very well notice the emergence of a power struggle between you and an authority figure. Since the Moon is in Aries and the Sun will be there tomorrow, please refrain from lashing out, and instead, review the conflict internally. Imagine that the person you see as the problem is only reflecting an inner struggle back to you, one that you need to work out with yourself. Anger directed toward anyone today isn't worth it.

On a final note, say good-bye to the Sun in Pisces today by taking a moment to reflect on the last 30 days . . . and then get ready to celebrate spring!

MARCH

AFFIRMATION FOR THE DAY:
I experience my feelings without judgment or fear.

BIG SPINS OF THE DAY:
Sun squares Pluto: 3:11 P.M. PDT / 6:11 P.M. EDT

Happy Birthday, Aries!

MARCH 20–APRIL 20

The symbol for independent Aries is the Ram—head down, horns out, and charging forward! It's easy to confuse the sign's determined thrust with rudeness, but people born under Aries are really just doing what comes most naturally: moving right along and letting no obstacles hinder them. Born with the force of spring, Aries natives carry the fire of inspiration deep within . . . so you can hardly blame them for not sitting still.

Possessing the spirit of the warrior, these individuals despise the appearance of weakness and revel in strength. Challenged at an early age to be tough and independent, people with this sign are unconsciously prepared at all times to champion a cause—and where none exists, they will have no trouble creating one. It's the Aries nature to go where angels fear to tread, and they share their courage with you when you can't find your own. They typically hate the thought of a traditional domestic life, but many do fully accept the *challenge* (a big Aries key word) and become truly amazing parents.

It's the innate desire of those born under this sign to experience their spiritual nature, and when they become impassioned, it will be likened to a religious experience . . . they fuel their fire by motivating and inspiring others. Listen closely when the Aries speaks: Profound words are often imparted, and although he or she might not always listen to his or her own brilliance (there's just no time!), *you'll* be amazed if your ears are attuned to it.

AFFIRMATIONS FOR ARIES:

My passions serve me, and I can trust them fully.

I have the courage I need to face any life situation with compassion.

I am strong enough to let my guard down.

○◑◐●

TUESDAY

March 20

VERNAL EQUINOX
SUN IN ARIES
MOON IN ARIES/TAURUS
SUCCESS RATING: ★★

Vernal is Latin for "belonging to spring," and *Equinox* means "equal night." This means that day- and nighttime are of equal length today—a perfect symbol for regaining our inner balance as we begin our journey into spring.

You may not be aware that the official time of spring and that of Aries are the same, but they are. So, since today is very much like an astrological New Year cycle, take a moment to make peace with your past and embrace what's in your present. You'll most likely enjoy a vast amount of energy, particularly in the morning, and there are two astrological changes taking place: (1) The Sun is entering Aries; and (2) the Moon is going into Taurus. You may need the entire day to adjust to this new cycle (thus the reduced Success Rating).

Don't fret about having a lower level of motivation . . . you'll rebound quite quickly this week. Pass on the signing of important papers today, unless you're absolutely compelled to do so.

AFFIRMATION FOR THE DAY:
I am always home and there is no place like it.

BIG SPINS OF THE DAY:

Sun enters Aries (Vernal Equinox): 5:08 P.M. PDT / 8:08 P.M. EDT
Moon Void of Course: 8:34 P.M. PDT / 11:34 P.M. EDT until
Moon enters Taurus: 10:16 P.M. PDT / 1:16 A.M. EDT (Wednesday)

○◑◐●

WEDNESDAY

March 21

MOON IN TAURUS
SUCCESS RATING: ★★★

MARCH

You may have a hard time getting out of bed this morning due to the sensual Taurus Moon, which tends to make you want to move slowly while it increases your personal desires. Today's theme centers on learning how to tame the Bull of passion—something you're bound to have plenty of.

There's great sexual energy in the air, and you can direct this seductive aspect to your benefit in your work. However, you should take some precautions: Don't confuse this energy with love—it's raw and powerful passion, and it can leave as quickly as it came. Perhaps you could better harness it during a job interview in order to appear enthusiastic about the prospective position . . . in other words, use this excitable energy where it will ensure that everyone feels positive all around.

You'll get some support in restraining your aggressions, which is a good thing, since placing boundaries around your passions could prevent hurt feelings later. Overall, it's a powerful day—one that, if used consciously, could help you advance your goals.

AFFIRMATION FOR THE DAY:
My desires are lovely and supportive.

BIG SPINS OF THE DAY:
None

○◑◐●

THURSDAY

March 22

MOON IN TAURUS/GEMINI
SUCCESS RATING: ★

An all-day Void of Course Moon makes this a day that could go any way you choose. The planets are taking a tough position, as if to keep us alert and aware. It's likely that you'll experience a multitude of distractions, making it difficult to perform your normal duties. It may seem unfair that on the day you need it the most, the safety of your routine is replaced by other matters that need your attention.

The hallmark of today is a yearly opposition between Mars and Saturn. At stake is your ability to do what you'd like without restraint—but at the same time, Saturn is reminding you that duty and responsibility take precedence. If you push too hard, you may feel as though you're driving with one foot on the gas pedal and the other on the brake: It's not good for the "car" (you), and it can create more problems later. Use today to be a conscious observer . . . keep a notebook with you, write down which issues emerge that you'd like to address, and tackle them tomorrow.

AFFIRMATION FOR THE DAY:
I have all the validation that I need.

BIG SPINS OF THE DAY:
Mars opposes Saturn: 12:35 A.M. PDT / 3:35 A.M. EDT
Moon Void of Course: 8:12 A.M. PDT / 11:12 A.M. EDT until
Moon enters Gemini: 11:07 P.M. PDT / 2:07 A.M. EDT (Friday)

○◑◐●

FRIDAY

March 23

MOON IN GEMINI
SUCCESS RATING: ★★★

Well, if you've been looking for your missing energy, you may be in for a pleasant surprise, thanks to a superactive Mars and a little help from Jupiter. It seems that ever since the first day of the spring, we've been asked by the planets to learn some patience. This is an ironic message, because the start of spring isn't symbolized by anything that looks remotely like patience—it is, after all, a season ruled by Mars, *the* planet of action. But if you look around, you might just find the reason for this unusual request. Ask yourself if there's a gift that recently came into your life that you might have passed by if you'd been in high gear.

Today you shift into the gentle wind of a Gemini Moon, and it urges you to get connected. Perhaps it's time to finish that book or call your old friend, tasks that you've had on your eternal list of things to do. And speaking of Gemini communication, keep your eyes on the national news (if you can stand it) . . . there may be something important going on.

AFFIRMATION FOR THE DAY:
Endless showers of peace lovingly
and ceaselessly flow over me.

BIG SPINS OF THE DAY:
Mars sextiles Jupiter: 9:02 A.M. PDT / 12:02 P.M. EDT

○◑◐●

SATURDAY

March 24

MOON IN GEMINI
SUCCESS RATING: ★

Although it's very possible that this day could bring you great pleasure, you may feel an undertone of malaise—or to put it more "scientifically," just plain *yucky*. Today two major planets are making a very short but unusually uncomfortable aspect. Simply being aware of this can help you maneuver through it unscathed.

It's possible that you'll uncover some worry or fear that's been locked inside of you. Maybe you'll hear something on the news, or it could be something less definable. However, finding the source of it doesn't matter—how you respond to it does.

Once you recognize that fear arises when you choose not to trust your Divine connection, you have a better chance of surrendering it in favor of a different idea. You're getting the assistance of Venus today, suggesting that you'll find great comfort in doing something you love. Perhaps musical or artistic experiences, or just spending time with a loved one watching a romantic comedy (comedies are a good idea), could help channel any heavier emotions that may emerge.

Relax and connect today with people you care about, and avoid trying to make progress in any arena. Clarity is just a hot bath away!

AFFIRMATION FOR THE DAY:
All that I need, I have.

BIG SPINS OF THE DAY:
None

○◑◐●

SUNDAY

March 25

FIRST QUARTER MOON IN CANCER
SUCCESS RATING: ★

MARCH

The Moon slips into Cancer in the wee morning hours and starts bringing your feelings to the forefront. Cancer Moons tend to keep your focus on the home and family, making this the perfect day to decompress (love that word!).

Look around and notice if your home needs a little sprucing up, and then direct your energy toward beautifying it. Your natural tendency will be to get creative, thanks to a Mars-Neptune connection. This aspect can also move you to connect with your spirituality, whether through a book or by actually visiting a place where similarly minded people are gathered.

The Sun and Moon are in their First Quarter, reminding you to take a peek and see where you may have left your own personal goals behind in favor of someone else's. You'll be supported in recovering them, and—in the process—in finding your own inner voice.

AFFIRMATION FOR THE DAY:
Nothing I do can disrupt my Divine connection.

BIG SPINS OF THE DAY:

Moon Void of Course: 12:57 A.M. PDT / 3:57 A.M. EDT until
Moon enters Cancer: 2:49 A.M. PDT / 5:49 A.M. EDT
Mars conjuncts Neptune: 10:39 A.M. PDT / 1:39 P.M. EDT
First Quarter Moon 5° Cancer: 11:17 A.M. PDT / 2:17 P.M. EDT

○◑◐●

MONDAY

March 26

Moon in Cancer
Success Rating: ★

Today brings a very long Void of Course Moon that begins in the morning and lasts until tomorrow. In a way, this day can help you unhook yourself from the heavier emotions that you may be carrying.

Most astrological consultants would advise you not to make large purchases or sign important documents today, simply because your focus may not be fully engaged, and I have to agree with my colleagues up to a point. However, if you feel strongly moved to engage in business as usual and feel connected to both your mind and intuition, then go for it! Only *you* know what you're feeling today—all I can do is tell you about the trends. However, if you're reading this, you're already a trendsetter!

Finally, don't worry about the lethargy that may be in the air, as the tide will soon be turning.

Affirmation for the Day:
Failure is an illusion that occurs when
I have chosen to feel separate from my source.

BIG SPINS OF THE DAY:
Moon Void of Course: 7:36 A.M. PDT / 10:36 A.M. EDT until tomorrow

○◑◐●

TUESDAY

March 27

MOON IN CANCER/LEO
SUCCESS RATING: ★★

If you find yourself thinking, *For every two steps forward, I seem to go one step back,* then take comfort in the fact that you aren't alone. Of course, your state of mind isn't pointing to a true phenomenon . . . you can't go backward, although it certainly *feels* as if you can.

The Moon is switching signs today and asks you to make the transition from worried and concerned to perky and optimistic (it's not as easy as it sounds). There's a good chance that you've recently introduced yourself to a new passion and now have to adjust to the responsibilities that come with it. For many odd reasons, this could take a toll on a close relationship, but the effect is short-lived as long you don't make it too real by reacting to it. Let things find their balance in their own time.

If you remember nothing else today, keep in mind that you don't have to control everyone's feelings. This will prevent you from adding one more responsibility to your already full list of things to do.

MARCH

AFFIRMATION FOR THE DAY:
I release the outside world as
my primary source of self-worth.

BIG SPINS OF THE DAY:
Moon Void of Course: until 10:05 A.M. PDT / 1:05 P.M. EDT
Moon enters Leo: 10:05 A.M. PDT / 1:05 P.M. EDT

○◑◐●

WEDNESDAY

March 28

MOON IN LEO

SUCCESS RATING: ★★

A radiant Moon in Leo can turn the most dismal day into a sparkling playground if you allow it to. There's no doubt that something in your life is requiring much of your time. Although it may be enough of a reward for you to know that you're making a difference, you have to make sure that it doesn't consume you.

The Leo Moon is about recognizing your individual self and embracing it, regardless of the opinion of those around you. This is a day to take note of what you're doing and to allow yourself a sense of personal pride. You've accomplished some amazing things up to this point, and you deserve a moment to celebrate.

Now that you know how good it feels to get such acknowledgment, turn around and give it to others. Find someone in your life who's your unsung hero and thank him or her for the support. *You'll* be a hero, and you could very well turn this potential "pumpkin" of a day into your gilded carriage instead!

AFFIRMATION FOR THE DAY:
I deserve time to celebrate myself.

BIG SPINS OF THE DAY:
None

○◑◐●

THURSDAY

March 29

MOON IN LEO/VIRGO
SUCCESS RATING: ★★

I'm really not trying to be stingy on the Success Ratings—but this *is* a time of adjustment, and we have to be careful not to move too quickly, lest we fall and scrape our knees. The potential for arguments is too high today to encourage running out and launching our own business or taking a personal risk of any kind.

MARCH

Try to focus on your broader goals, even if matters that are more personal seem to be lingering. Your relationships are going through real changes as another part of you emerges. Think of it as shedding an outer shell so that a "new you" can come forth. It's a process that can create resistance from those close to you, who may not really understand it.

You're ready for change . . . you just may not be ready to admit it. Avoid any direct confrontations today—bite your tongue if you have to. There's a much better place for your energy today: It's needed right where you are.

AFFIRMATION FOR THE DAY:
I extend a loving thought to everyone I meet and simultaneously extend that thought to me.

BIG SPINS OF THE DAY:
Moon Void of Course: 6:25 P.M. PDT / 9:25 P.M. EDT until
Moon enters Virgo: 8:28 P.M. PDT / 11:28 P.M. EDT

○◑◐●

FRIDAY

March 30

MOON IN VIRGO
SUCCESS RATING: ★★

An all-day Virgo Moon calls forth your inner loner. Sometimes you need to release the accumulation of energy that you've been storing throughout the week, but the timing and setting have to be right. Be sure to add "Take a hot bath" to your list of things to do—then really do it. This way, you can focus, knowing that you've slotted in time for yourself, since it may seem that others are tugging at you for help throughout the day . . . and under a Virgo Moon, you're often compelled to give it to them.

Thankfully, the Moon also supports you in achieving organization, so this would be a perfect day to get focused on details that you've been ignoring. Straighten up your desk, file your papers, and find ways to make your work and home spaces more efficient. This is a great way to pass the day, and you'll have full planetary support.

Be cautious about using criticism as your way to give feedback, since the Virgo Moon tends to give you a razor-sharp mind—and a tongue to match. This behavior is an unconscious way to set boundaries and protect yourself from overgiving, so be discriminating about when you say "yes" in the first place. That way, you won't have to hurt someone's feelings later.

Finally, don't forget to make the last item on your to-do list a reality!

AFFIRMATION FOR THE DAY:
"Perfect" is the only way to describe my life.

BIG SPINS OF THE DAY:
None

○◑◐●

SATURDAY

March 31

MOON IN VIRGO
SUCCESS RATING: ★★

Did you have trouble sleeping last night? If so, you were just feeling the effects of the Virgo Moon. This Moon focuses your mind in a way that allows you to see the flaws in everything in order to help you pinpoint which areas most need help.

Today brings you a bevy of activity, along with a few surprises that have been long overdue. It's almost as if March wants you to have fond memories of your journey over the last 30 days. Pluto will move backward today, and it's ready to begin its retrograde journey, which lasts until September. Scorpios will feel this impact most strongly, since Pluto is the ruling planet of that sign, but everyone will notice a sense of withdrawal.

Review the areas of your life that empowered you over the past month, and make note of the areas that didn't. Remember to experience gratitude for all the gifts that appeared, while you release and forgive the experiences that didn't feel supportive.

Get to bed early tonight, and give your mind some time to unwind. And don't do a lot of analysis, as this is unproductive.

AFFIRMATION FOR THE DAY:
I am an astounding example of living life in gratitude.

BIG SPINS OF THE DAY:
Venus sextiles Uranus: 1:22 A.M. PDT / 4:22 A.M. EDT
Pluto goes Retrograde: 1:02 P.M. PDT / 4:02 P.M. EDT

Thought for the Month

WHERE ARE THE "GRAND" GRANDMOTHERS?

MARCH

Not long ago, three generations of women walked into my store—a grandmother, her daughter, and her daughter's daughter—all beautiful, all fashionable. I was surprised when they told me about the nature of their relationship, because the two mothers looked like sisters. They seemed to expect this shock and gratuitous flattery, and I generously (and genuinely) supplied both.

The encounter made me fondly remember my own grandmother, with her housedress, flip-flop slippers, swollen ankles, and slightly tilted head. To me, she was the most spiritual woman in the world, and even her cooking was a special experience. Most important, though, I always felt her love.

One day when I was mowing her lawn, a couple of strangers walked up to her home and rang the doorbell. They were lost and trying to find someone else's house, so she took them in and fed them! When I joined them later, they were in the kitchen (where else?), laughing. My grandmother's motto was: "The pot is never empty if your faith is full." These strangers left her home different people, and I knew it was because my grandmother—this angel—had touched their lives.

My grandmother was also a storyteller. Each tale was part of her kindness, and she would share those that related to whatever I was too shy to talk about directly. Now whenever I see an unbelievable act of compassion, I think of her, and when I'm in a situation where I'm not sure what to do, I try to respond as she would, because she always acted from her own heart.

This Thought for the Month isn't about having grandmothers who are like mine . . . it's about the spirit of *all* grandmothers. Every time we listen closely to a person in pain, offer help without resenting it, cook a special meal, or mend someone's wound, we're bringing in that "grand" spirit.

○◑◐●

APRIL 2007
SUMMARY

Sometimes when I'm interpreting the energies of a month, I feel as if I'm a psychiatrist evaluating the stability of a client. If I were indeed a psychiatrist (which I'm not), and April were a client (which it's not), I'd probably diagnose it as having a passive-aggressive personality, just based on my first impression. Technically, *passive-aggressive* refers to someone who gives the appearance of being cooperative, yet holds an underlying hostility, and I hastily pasted that classification onto April. This was due to the fact that I saw the wonderful Full Moon in Libra occurring on just the second day and was thrilled by this early gift, but as I studied the month further, I found several planets squabbling so intensely that I felt my "client" was clearly harboring antagonistic feelings while pretending to be appealing.

Later, having looked deeper into April's "mind," it was clear that I had to change my diagnosis. The month wasn't harboring any hostilities—it just wasn't coughing up any of the good stuff. There are no days with Success Ratings over three stars, no super-romantic days, no spectacular days in which to start a business, and no *This-is-the-best-day-of-your-life* kind of days. April is clearly being stingy and, therefore, has been given the diagnosis of anal-retentive.

So there we have it: April is simply holding out on us. However, your personal birth chart may combine with the planets of a particular day to make absolute magic. So, if you experience something that doesn't fit with what you read, go with your gut.

Here are some of the April highlights:

April 2: Full Moon in Libra
April 5: Jupiter Retrogrades
April 6: Mars enters Pisces

April 10: Mercury enters Aries
April 11: Venus enters Gemini
April 17: New Moon in Aries
April 19: Saturn goes Direct
April 20: First day of Taurus
April 27: Mercury enters Taurus

○◑◐●

SUNDAY

April 1

MOON IN VIRGO/LIBRA
SUCCESS RATING: ★

I would have loved to play an April Fool's joke on you and tell you about the crashing of two planets that would end the world as we know it, but I have the legitimate worry that many of you might take it seriously. I wouldn't blame you, though, since there's so much gloom-and-doom astrology out there that it would be only natural for you to take the bait.

Today's planetary rays are activating your mind, and you may notice an increased alertness that actually makes it *difficult* to focus. Mercury, the planet of thinking, has connected to Uranus, the planet of sudden jolts—so lay off the coffee today, and try to avoid the countless distractions that are waiting to annoy you. You may feel exhilarated by the new charge of power, but it can also be overwhelming. It's best to lay low during times of such high energy and leave large-ticket items off your list of things to buy until the dust settles.

As the moon moves into Libra, you may also find it important to make a connection with someone you're close to. . . .

AFFIRMATION FOR THE DAY:
I observe my mind and realize that
it is only a small part of my complete self.

BIG SPINS OF THE DAY:
Moon Void of Course: 6:39 A.M. PDT / 9:39 A.M. EDT until
Moon enters Libra: 8:45 A.M. PDT / 11:45 A.M. EDT
Mercury conjuncts Uranus: 11:30 A.M. PDT / 2:30 P.M. EDT

○◑◐●

MONDAY

April 2

FULL MOON IN LIBRA
SUCCESS RATING: ★

Welcome to the first Full Moon of spring, called the Full Pink Moon because the herb *moss pink* is one of the most prevalent flowers early in the season. Pink is also one of the colors representing the heart. Of course the heart is a symbol of relationships; and relationships, in turn, are symbols of Libra—the sign in which the Full Moon falls.

This Libra Full Moon activates the desire in all of us for personal connections. Think of your kinship to everything—pets, friends, colleagues, and even nature—because that's where this Full Moon will direct your attention.

You may find that you have many questions emerging about your relationships. Perhaps you're feeling less understood than usual, or maybe someone wants something from you that you can't give. Examining what *you* want is all part of this cycle, but don't try to figure everything out today, since clarity will find you soon enough.

Libra Moons are always great times to participate in group functions . . . perhaps dinner with friends, or an evening out on the town (although make it an early one because this is the workweek). It's not a great time to land on any one conclusion, since too much is still being worked out, but it *is* a great day to distract yourself by doing something that brings beauty into your life. Buy something nice for your home or office—or, better yet, for yourself!

AFFIRMATION FOR THE DAY:
I breathe in the remembrance of my true loving connection: my connection to the Divine.

BIG SPINS OF THE DAY:
Venus squares Saturn: 12:01 A.M. PDT / 3:01 A.M. EDT
Full Moon at 13° of Libra: 10:16 A.M. PDT / 1:16 P.M. EDT

○◑◐●

TUESDAY

April 3

MOON IN LIBRA/SCORPIO
SUCCESS RATING: ★

There are some hangover effects lingering from yesterday's Full Moon, and although you'll probably be feeling better, you still have some sorting out to do. You may find that you're a little more depressed than usual—that's because the ruler of your mind, Mercury, is taking a serious turn that's designed to help you look objectively at your life.

Not much may move you today, or you could find yourself completely dedicated to distracting yourself through idle chatter, shopping, or nose-diving into work. This is one of those days that gets progressively better as time moves on, and by midday, you'll most likely feel back in control.

There's a Void of Course Moon later in the evening, a great time to release and relax as the Scorpio Moon takes hold.

AFFIRMATION FOR THE DAY:
My happiness is easily found within me.

BIG SPINS OF THE DAY:
Moon Void of Course: 7:31 P.M. PDT / 10:31 P.M. EDT until
Moon enters Scorpio: 9:37 P.M. PDT / 12:37 A.M. EDT (Wednesday)

○ ◑ ◐ ●

WEDNESDAY

April 4

MOON IN SCORPIO
SUCCESS RATING: ★★

Help! I've fallen in love and I can't get up! If that's not you, then you'll likely be hearing about it from someone in your extended family. Venus and Neptune—the planets that have to do with romantic love—are fighting, and usually their battle brings someone to his or her knees. The good part of this experience is that once the clash of these planets begins, it's essentially already over.

If love hasn't run you down, then you may find your head wrestling with an issue that wants resolution. But hear this: The best action is *in*action.

Become the observer of your life, and watch as your mind searches, seeking answers . . . all the while remembering that you don't need them. With the Scorpio Moon at your disposal, all you have to do is fearlessly stay present with your feelings. Truth emerges when you remain steady, not when you're bouncing around trying to control circumstances. If you can manage to stay in a fixed position, you'll very likely spot all the craziness jumping around you. Sometimes it's more fun to just watch the roller coaster, instead of ride it.

This evening, Mars and Pluto will bring a form of courage and focus—and not only is it needed, it's welcomed. Avoid signing anything of importance, though, since there's just not enough clarity.

AFFIRMATION FOR THE DAY:
Why not?

BIG SPINS OF THE DAY:
Mercury squares Jupiter: 12:18 A.M. PDT / 3:18 A.M. EDT
Venus squares Neptune: 11:16 A.M. PDT / 2:16 P.M. EDT
Mars sextiles Pluto: 5:17 P.M. PDT / 8:17 P.M. EDT

○◑◐●

THURSDAY

April 5

MOON IN SCORPIO
SUCCESS RATING: ★★

By now, you're well adjusted to the internal focus brought by the Scorpio Moon, which attempts to drive out any lurking fears. You may have noticed an increase in your desire to solve mysteries—be they real or ones that you've encountered through a book or movie.

Chances are you've found something to obsess about and have spent hours researching all the answers. Well, good for you, because it means that you're in the flow of the celestial energies (which, by the way, are about to change yet again).

Today, Jupiter, the biggest planet in the solar system, stops moving forward and begins a backward journey lasting until fall. You Sagittarians will notice the strongest shift in your focus because Jupiter is your planetary ruler; the rest of you will sense a more subtle change in direction as the planet's backward motion encourages you to investigate exactly what it's going to take to make your dreams come true.

AFFIRMATION FOR THE DAY:
I safely look within and release all fear.

BIG SPINS OF THE DAY:

Jupiter goes Retrograde: 4:54 P.M. PDT / 7:54 P.M. EDT
Moon Void of Course: 7:55 P.M. PDT / 10:55 P.M. EDT until tomorrow

○◑◐●

FRIDAY

April 6

MOON IN SCORPIO/SAGITTARIUS
SUCCESS RATING: ★★

In the wee hours of the morning, Mars left the sign of Aquarius and entered Pisces. The planet of passion and aggression, Mars will direct your interests from the world of ideals into the realm of feelings.

While in Pisces, Mars may slow you down so that you use your intuition as guidance rather than your mind. For the more intellectually driven among you, this shift can create a feeling of disorientation, but it won't take long to acclimate to the change. Before long, you'll notice how easy it is to choose something simply because it feels right, regardless of all the research you've compiled on it.

Mars in Pisces can often mean that the past comes to life in some form. Maybe an old friend or family member reemerges, or perhaps it's an old project that renews your interest. Whatever it is, you'll find it familiar, and you'll be willing and able to deal with it. But don't be surprised if you start misplacing things over the next month . . . this isn't the most organized placement for Mars, so stay one step ahead of yourself.

The Moon enters Sagittarius by midmorning and may overstimulate some of you, so ride the wave for a bit prior to making any big decisions today.

APRIL

AFFIRMATION FOR THE DAY:
I can do it!

BIG SPINS OF THE DAY:
Mars enters Pisces: 1:49 A.M. PDT / 4:49 A.M. EDT
Moon Void of Course: until 9:57 A.M. PDT / 12:57 P.M. EDT
Moon enters Sagittarius: 9:57 A.M. PDT / 12:57 P.M. EDT

○◑◐●

SATURDAY

April 7

MOON IN SAGITTARIUS
SUCCESS RATING: ★★

If you think April is being stingy in doling out the number of stars for the Success Ratings, you're absolutely correct. The planets are in a state of change that lasts for about two weeks, and although you may be directed to refrain from big projects and expenditures, your intuition is now fully activated, so you can trust your inner guidance. Just remember: When deciding what to do, the answer that has no fear attached to it is probably the best one.

The all-day Sagittarius Moon will keep you lighthearted for most of today, making it perfect for an adventure into the world. Mercury is warming up nicely to Venus, creating an urge to connect with others. It's an ideal time to add compliments and gratitude to your dialogue. Even when people think they're "all that," if *you* appreciate what they do, tell them—it will make a difference today.

AFFIRMATION FOR THE DAY:
The love that I extend is that which I am giving myself.

BIG SPINS OF THE DAY:
Mercury sextiles Venus: 9:10 A.M. PDT / 12:10 P.M. EDT

○◑◐●

SUNDAY

April 8

MOON IN SAGITTARIUS/CAPRICORN
SUCCESS RATING: ★★★

Japan is celebrating Buddha's birthday today, and the Sagittarius Moon dominates and brings to light the struggle between your spiritual and mortal selves. On the one hand, this Moon reminds you that you're a blessed child of the Divine and deserve to be treated as such . . . but on the other hand, there's trash that has to be taken out and jobs that require your attendance.

You have the opportunity to bridge those realities so that you can bring your magic into your humanness. Focus on what works today, and notice how easy and fulfilling it is to accomplish anything that you place your attention on.

An early-evening Void of Course Moon suggests that you leave work *at* work tonight and relax. A nice dinner with friends is completely on the menu!

AFFIRMATION FOR THE DAY:
I will always be more than
my thoughts can comprehend.

BIG SPINS OF THE DAY:
Sun trines Saturn: 4:56 A.M. PDT / 7:56 A.M. EDT
Moon Void of Course: 6:35 P.M. PDT / 9:35 P.M. EDT until
Moon enters Capricorn: 8:36 P.M. PDT / 11:36 P.M. EDT

○◑◐●

MONDAY

April 9

MOON IN CAPRICORN
SUCCESS RATING: ★★★

Dream big today! The Sun and Jupiter are holding hands, lifting you up to places as far as your imagination will take you. It won't feel all that dreamy, though, thanks to the sober Capricorn Moon, but that's a blessing, because now you can have that bridge—the one that links your inner magic with the physical world.

This connection of Jupiter and the Sun can give you a feeling of being bigger than life. This could encourage you to overindulge, so keep an eye on excesses. Although this is considered a lucky connection, you do have to put effort into anything that you want results from.

You could get some good news in financial matters, so look and see if there's anything that you need to do about your money (investment changes and so on). This is also a great time for travel.

Aim your desires at tangible things, and don't be pushy toward others. This planetary combination won't feel good to individuals who dislike overly expansive energies. Don't try to figure it all out . . . just follow your own flow.

AFFIRMATION FOR THE DAY:
I am part of a bottomless well of healing energy.

BIG SPINS OF THE DAY:
Sun trines Jupiter: 5:07 P.M. PDT / 8:07 P.M. EDT

○◑◐●

TUESDAY

April 10

LAST QUARTER MOON IN CAPRICORN
SUCCESS RATING: ★★

Thankfully, you're being guided by the responsible Capricorn Moon on a date when Mercury is changing signs and the Sun and Moon are doing their biweekly squabbling. The outcome is likely to be a very productive day with little time for standing around the metaphorical office watercooler.

The Last Quarter Moon (the astrological name for this bickering between the Sun and Moon) is a period for finding obstacles. No, that's not a typo—it's really the time when you must see what's in the way of having what you want. So, if you find yourself putting out a lot of fires, try to remember that what you're really doing is preventing problems from getting bigger later in the week.

As Mercury leaves the sign of Pisces and enters Aries, you may find that your tongue develops a mind of its own. Be watchful of your words tonight (and for the next 30 days) . . . you're almost over this bumpy ride!

AFFIRMATION FOR THE DAY:
I can release the steering wheel
and leave the driving to the Divine.

BIG SPINS OF THE DAY:

Mercury squares Pluto: 12:23 A.M. PDT / 3:23 A.M. EDT
Last Quarter Moon at 20° Capricorn: 11:04 A.M. PDT / 2:04 P.M. EDT
Mercury enters Aries: 4:07 P.M. PDT / 7:07 P.M. EDT

○◑◐●

WEDNESDAY

April 11

MOON IN CAPRICORN/AQUARIUS
SUCCESS RATING: ★★★

Out with the old and in with the new . . . that's the message the Aquarius Moon brings in today. After more than two days of towing the line, you should be ready to break some rules and allow some playtime into your life.

Today brings you some of the most success-driven aspects you've seen all month. Turn on your favorite music, and let the inspiration move you. This is the last day for Venus to hang out in the Taurus constellation, so why not let yourself have one more juicy, sensual, relaxing, body-dropping, feel-good moment with your masseuse or masseur? It's not that you can't get a massage later, but there's something about having Venus in Taurus that makes physical experiences more pleasurable.

Be sure to let someone know how much you appreciate him or her today. Perhaps this is the time to ask for that raise, or at least to give the boss something to remember you by. Also, tonight books and conversations will start having a stronger appeal.

APRIL

AFFIRMATION FOR THE DAY:
I can have what I want.

BIG SPINS OF THE DAY:
Moon Void of Course: 2:57 A.M. PDT / 5:57 A.M. EDT until
Moon enters Aquarius: 4:23 A.M. PDT / 7:23 A.M. EDT
Sun sextiles Neptune: 12:33 P.M. PDT / 3:33 P.M. EDT
Venus enters Gemini: 7:15 P.M. PDT / 10:15 P.M. EDT

○ ◑ ◐ ●

THURSDAY

April 12

MOON IN AQUARIUS
SUCCESS RATING: ★★

An all-day Aquarius Moon may leave you feeling a little detached today, which you'll be able to sense because *everyone else* is acting distant.

First let's define *detached:* It actually means "feeling more like an observer than a participant." Detachment isn't a bad thing—it's just something to be aware of, and it's often quite useful in dealing with difficult situations. For example, notice how easy it is to allow others to have their feelings today without the accompanying urge to "fix" them. This allows you the perspective you need to decide what you'd *like* to do, rather than what you think you *must* do.

Avoid explaining yourself today, and forgo signing any contracts until next week . . . clarity is on the way!

AFFIRMATION FOR THE DAY:
I am in touch with the part of me
that never wavers, the part that is eternal.

BIG SPINS OF THE DAY:
None

○◑◐●

FRIDAY

April 13

MOON IN AQUARIUS/PISCES
SUCCESS RATING: ★★

Yes, it's Friday the 13th! Do you still believe that our perfectly arbitrary system of numbering the days of the month has the power to cause bad luck? If so, you owe it to the fulfillment of your life to stop that kind of thinking, if only because of the fact that your thoughts do indeed create!

The Moon's entrance into Pisces heralds a time of remembering your wonderful connection to all life, and this is a perfect day for it. People from your past may appear just to remind you of your impact on their lives, and nostalgic memories could flood you with a multitude of feelings. For many of you, the transition into Pisces will feel a little depressing—but trust me, that's just how you're interpreting the natural process of adjustment, and it will soon pass.

Today will probably feel surreal and full of tiny little miracles, each one with a message just for you. Try to avoid getting too far into someone else's business: People do love to complain about their circumstances, and sometimes all they need is a kind ear, nothing more. And finally, be good to yourself today . . . after all, it's been a long week.

AFFIRMATION FOR THE DAY:
My past, my present, and my future are all part of my dream, and none of them are real.

BIG SPINS OF THE DAY:
Moon Void of Course: 6:50 A.M. PDT / 9:50 A.M. EDT until
Moon enters Pisces: 8:39 A.M. PDT / 11:39 A.M. EDT

○◑◐●

SATURDAY

April 14

MOON IN PISCES
SUCCESS RATING: ★★★

Wow, it's actually quiet on the celestial weather front today. A magical Pisces Moon floods you with random notes from a song long forgotten as your mind floats on a mystical path. This is hardly a day to do anything that requires your concentration—that includes driving, sawing, or working machinery of any kind (unless you feel utterly confident that you're not intoxicated with the Pisces flow).

Observe your associations today and see if they seem almost dreamlike. That's the magic of Pisces . . . it's as if a bubble has surrounded you. Relax and enjoy this perfect day for being a lounge lizard (or is it couch potato?). There's really nothing in the way of having the experience you'd like to enjoy today.

AFFIRMATION FOR THE DAY:
I am wrapped in a blanket of love—
always protected, always warm.

BIG SPINS OF THE DAY:
None

○◑◐●

SUNDAY

April 15

MOON IN PISCES/ARIES
SUCCESS RATING: ★★★

Enjoy the rest of the magical "Pisces floating session" in the morning, because a fiery, feisty Aries Moon makes a Ram's entrance midday. In contrast to yesterday, you may not have the temperament or desire to stay at home and "float," so make some plans for the things you'd like to accomplish.

Be careful today . . . sometimes it's easy to use anger as a way to help you get motivated, but you don't want to aim it at the people in your life. Remember that if you feel the urge to unleash your temper on someone, you're probably just using the person to get your adrenaline going, and there are better ways to do so.

Start by setting goals, and then stick with them today. Make your achievements important—not because they are, but because you'll most likely feel better having accomplished them. There's nothing to stop you from having a fabulous day (unless, of course, you punch someone!).

AFFIRMATION FOR THE DAY:
I am not what I do.

BIG SPINS OF THE DAY:
Moon Void of Course: 8:02 A.M. PDT / 11:02 A.M. EDT until
Moon enters Aries: 9:47 A.M. PDT / 12:47 P.M. EDT

○◑◐●

MONDAY

April 16

MOON IN ARIES
SUCCESS RATING: ★★★

The Aries Moon gets the full spotlight today, and you'll probably prosper from the exuberance that it's radiating. The only thing that could possibly dampen your spirits is the natural low-level anxiety that comes the day before a New Moon, so if you feel a little less than exhilarated today, don't worry—you're just in tune with this lunar lull.

The New Moon is dark because it moves directly in front of the Sun, leaving you unable to see it. On an emotional level, it seems as if the light is gone, but it's actually the beginning of your new cycle.

The New Moon occurs very early tomorrow morning, so be sure to grab your favorite candle and light it tonight. Write down a prayer or affirmation for what you'd like to see unfold, and remember to review all that you're grateful for.

AFFIRMATION FOR THE DAY:
I desire to embrace the gift of gratitude.

BIG SPINS OF THE DAY:
None

○◑◐●

TUESDAY

April 17

NEW MOON IN ARIES
MOON IN ARIES/TAURUS
SUCCESS RATING: ★★★

Happy New Moon! It may take you a few hours to get into the flow of this Moon, but it's the start of the new energies that will turn this month around (goodness knows, it needed a change). Under the guidance of the Ram, you'll learn how to forge ahead toward what you desire, initiate your goals, and confront your fears with remarkable courage. This Moon is letting you know that you have an adventure ahead, and over the next two weeks, you'll be challenged to keep on track and reach your goals.

The midmorning brings in the Taurus Moon, which will get you back in touch with your body and earthly surroundings. It's a great day to discard old items that are no longer of use—a way to clear your clutter and make room for new things to enter. This is a powerful cycle, so remember to stay the course.

AFFIRMATION FOR THE DAY:
I am a beloved child of the Divine . . . hear me roar!

BIG SPINS OF THE DAY:

New Moon at 27° Aries: 4:37 A.M. PDT / 7:37 A.M. EDT
Moon Void of Course: 7:27 A.M. PDT / 10:27 A.M. EDT until
Moon enters Taurus: 9:12 A.M. PDT / 12:12 P.M. EDT

○◑◐●

WEDNESDAY

April 18

MOON IN TAURUS
SUCCESS RATING: ★★★

The all-day Taurus Moon beckons you to break with your diet and indulge your food fantasies . . . this Moon is all about what makes your body scream in delight! (*Hint:* Try everything that's plush and pleasurable.)

The afternoon hours may bring a problem to the forefront where you could have to choose between short-term discomfort and long-term gain, or vice versa. When Taurus dominates the day, however, you tend to hold on to what's familiar and secure, rather than venturing into new territory.

Don't let today be a struggle. Instead, strike a deal with yourself: For everything that you have to sacrifice (for the sake of work or someone else), you get to buy yourself something decadent. Be sure to show your appreciation to those who deserve it, though, since it's always good to give what you want to receive.

AFFIRMATION FOR THE DAY:
Change is good.

BIG SPINS OF THE DAY:
Moon Void of Course: 7:30 P.M. PDT / 10:30 P.M. EDT until tomorrow

○◑◐●

THURSDAY

April 19

MOON IN TAURUS/GEMINI
SUCCESS RATING: ★★

The Moon will transition into Gemini midmorning, igniting the urge to communicate. Don't be surprised if you're inundated with messages and phone calls asking for your time. The Sun and Pluto are in wonderful harmony, and that gives you the air of being able to do anything that you put your mind to . . . it's a nice energy to have on a day such as this, which is the last one with the Sun in Aries.

Maybe now is a good time to tell you that Saturn is about to go direct. Since this planet rules duties and responsibilities, you may find that something you're in charge of suddenly needs more attention than you'd anticipated. It won't matter, though, because with the Sun-Pluto aspect in full bloom, you can face anything today!

AFFIRMATION FOR THE DAY:
I have everything I need to complete all that I desire.

BIG SPINS OF THE DAY:
Sun trines Pluto: 12:32 A.M. PDT / 3:32 A.M. EDT
Moon Void of Course: until 8:52 A.M. PDT / 11:52 A.M. EDT
Moon enters Gemini: 8:52 A.M. PDT / 11:52 A.M. EDT
Saturn goes Direct: 2:00 P.M. PDT / 5:00 PM EDT

Happy Birthday, Taurus!

APRIL 20–MAY 21

Taurus symbolizes the deep and stable roots of an oak tree, and this Earth sign focuses on all that's physical and tangible. Taureans touch, feel, and sense the world surrounding them, never losing their insatiable need to live adequately and securely. The symbol for Taurus is the Bull, and although this can refer to a stubborn streak, it also represents bullish desire. People born under this sign absolutely love *things*—perhaps to create a feeling of security—and most Taureans develop a refined taste for the best of everything in every category.

Speaking of taste, do you remember how I pointed out that the name of Taurus is partially embedded in the word "res*taur*ant"? Indeed, some of the finest cooks in the world happen to be of this sign—after all, who's better qualified to handle earthly delights? Taureans' sensuality in cooking also carries over to their bodies, and there isn't a single sign that comes close to having the responsiveness Taurus does when it comes to physical pleasure. Massages, hot baths, and trips to the spa are all examples of the way that those born under this sign love to pamper themselves. . . . And when you need your obstinate Bull to move a little faster, two things are astonishingly effective—flattery and gifts!

AFFIRMATIONS FOR TAURUS:

I have everything I need to feel safe and secure.
My body tells me all I need to know.
I can trust change, for I know how life works.

○◑◐●

FRIDAY

April 20

SUN IN TAURUS
MOON IN GEMINI
SUCCESS RATING: ★★★

For the next 30 days, the Sun will be in Taurus, bringing your attention to the Earth and all that goes with it. Notice how powerful showing appreciation is, and observe how much more meaningful gifts are in these upcoming weeks—those two tips alone will prove to be invaluable tools during Taurus's reign.

Your possessions can take on a whole new meaning during the Taurus season. Items that you didn't give away under the Aries cycle are unlikely to be going anywhere under this one . . . Taureans never give up their things, and neither will you while the Sun is visiting the sign of the Bull. You'd also be wise to use your body's wisdom to make decisions—if something feels good, it probably is.

The Gemini Moon helps you maintain a light and easy attitude, even though today may be filled with distractions, and you could feel overwhelmed. Regardless of your assessment of the week—or your performance during it—wait until after the weekend to rev back into work mode. Try to enjoy the world around you, since you've been through a lot in the past few days. Hot baths and big meals are calling you tonight.

AFFIRMATION FOR THE DAY:
I remember to breathe in feelings of support, and exhale judgments and hurts.

BIG SPINS OF THE DAY:
Sun enters Taurus: 4:07 A.M. PDT / 7:07 A.M. EDT

○◑◐●

SATURDAY

April 21

MOON IN GEMINI/CANCER
SUCCESS RATING: ★★

Move slowly today, and allow yourself time to adjust to the change in Moon signs. Your brain may need an extra cup of coffee to seem normal, while your stomach could require an antacid just to feel settled down.

Saturn is now retrograde, the Sun is in Taurus, and the Moon is getting ready to change signs . . . it's enough to make you feel as if you're on a roller-coaster ride. Use today to find your center, and the Cancer Moon will help you by creating the urge to spruce up the house and make things cozy. Nostalgia could rule the tone of today, inviting you to reach for a good classic movie.

Mercury is activating your vocal chords through its association with Jupiter, so you might feel compelled to grab the phone this afternoon. Show some restraint in your topics of conversation, however, as engaging in any form of malicious gossip could find its way back to haunt you. If you can't say something nice about someone today, don't broach the subject at all.

AFFIRMATION FOR THE DAY:
I deserve to be pampered, and I am open to volunteers.

BIG SPINS OF THE DAY:
Mercury trines Saturn: 12:10 A.M. PDT / 3:10 A.M. EDT
Moon Void of Course: 8:53 A.M. PDT / 11:53 A.M. EDT until
Moon enters Cancer: 10:51 A.M. PDT / 1:51 P.M. EDT
Mercury trines Jupiter: 3:40 P.M. PDT / 6:40 P.M. EDT

○◑◐●

SUNDAY

April 22

MOON IN CANCER
SUCCESS RATING: ★★

Thanks to the Moon's alignment with Mars, there's an early boost of energy for you this morning. (No, it doesn't come from your coffee cup.) The biggest problem today will be knowing when to slow down, since there's even more energy available to you because of the Moon's continued connection to all the action planets.

The only words of caution you need today are the ones that all parents around the world have said to their kids at some point: "Slow down!" There's nothing wrong with enjoying the velocity of the day, but too much speed can lead to carelessness.

This is a great time to get out and embrace family and friends . . . as long as your mood can hold up. That is, if you find yourself getting crabby, it's time to go. Tonight a little tension could occur in the relationship department—curb your tongue if you can't say something positive.

AFFIRMATION FOR THE DAY:
I am a magnificent individual
and am becoming more so each day.

BIG SPINS OF THE DAY:
Mercury sextiles Neptune: 9:12 P.M. PDT / 12:12 A.M. EDT (Monday)
Venus squares Mars: 10:30 P.M. PDT / 1:30 A.M. EDT (Monday)

○◑◐●

MONDAY

April 23

FIRST QUARTER MOON IN LEO
SUCCESS RATING: ★★

Racing around trying catch up with lost time isn't going to work for you today. The Void of Course Moon is abnormally long, and the celestial bickering is just too distracting for you to have any focus. This day is good for slow starts, such as cleaning up old, unfinished business and having horrendously pointless phone chats that are longer than they should be.

You must be wondering why you should even get out of bed today, and I'll tell you . . . because you matter! Days like this are needed to remind the less fortunate (or less awake) that everything in life isn't about productivity. Things that matter can be as simple as putting a smile on the face of someone who's had a worse week than you, or reminding another person that he or she makes a difference. Don't fall so deeply into your rut that you can't imagine your mood having any effect. The afternoon Leo Moon will help you find your own smile and keep it on *your* face!

AFFIRMATION FOR THE DAY:
I extend the love . . . effortlessly.

BIG SPINS OF THE DAY:
Moon Void of Course: 2:12 A.M. PDT / 5:12 A.M. EDT until
Moon enters Leo: 4:39 P.M. PDT / 7:39 P.M. EDT
First Quarter Moon at 4° Leo: 11:37 P.M. PDT / 2:37 A.M. EDT (Tuesday)

○◑◐●

TUESDAY

April 24

MOON IN LEO
SUCCESS RATING: ★★★

For most of the day, you'll feel larger than life (and I'm not talking about your weight!). The Leo Moon tends to guide you into a sense of childlike wonder and innocence. If possible, look to the arts for a way to express your creative side, and don't obsess about what isn't working in your life (leave that for the Virgo Moon).

Be careful of overindulgence, as there's a tendency to bite off more than you can chew. But heck, it's a Leo Moon . . . if you can't eat like royalty today, then there's no point in having this Moon at all!

Tonight you could encounter a frustrating situation that will be made worse if you create a drama out of it. Keep your cool in all matters today—know that the luck inherent in this Moon will prevail.

AFFIRMATION FOR THE DAY:
I invite and allow success in my life.

BIG SPINS OF THE DAY:
None

○◑◐●

WEDNESDAY

April 25

MOON IN LEO
SUCCESS RATING: ★★

Today you could wake up from a sound sleep full of dreams, only to face a dreamlike reality. The Moon is making many connections right now, but none of them helps your head feel as if it's completely out of the clouds: *Look! There's clarity . . . no, wait . . . it was there just a minute ago!* If anything is clear today, it's that you're *not* going to be all that clear. Many of you will enjoy the free-association feel of the day, and those of you who do manage to keep an unclouded mind may see that such a quality is sorely lacking in the people around you.

It's a Leo Moon, and without a *little* drama, there would be no excitement. However, don't make big purchases today unless you've thought them through. It's always fine to support your local merchants if you have the discretionary funds, but don't be too extravagant!

Venus is making a wonderful connection to Chiron, the rogue comet, which can indicate that an important person is due to enter your life.

AFFIRMATION FOR THE DAY:
I generously give and graciously receive.

BIG SPINS OF THE DAY:
Venus trines Chiron: 12:19 A.M. PDT / 3:19 A.M. EDT

○◑◐●

THURSDAY

April 26

MOON IN LEO/VIRGO
SUCCESS RATING: ★★★

The Moon enters Virgo in the early hours of the morning, giving you the eyes of an eagle and an even sharper mind. Today's the day that you're going to "slice and dice" through any mess. It's also the one that can save you from any slothful habits you've acquired over the last couple of days.

Your mind is clear and your intuition is finely tuned. Precision will matter today—it's perfect if you have editing to do, but you can also use the time to write, read, or perform the favorite Virgo activity . . . clean!

Be a little cautious in your interactions, as the aspects today could make you very critical of others, which isn't so bad if you keep it to yourself. The energy continues on throughout the evening, when you may be in for a surprise—the kind that gives you a situation where there's a difficult choice to be made. For example, you could be exhausted and looking forward to sleep, when a friend calls you with a relationship emergency. Do you go to bed, or do you go over there to be supportive? The correct answer is . . . unplug the phone when you first get home.

AFFIRMATION FOR THE DAY:
I see the perfection in everything around me.

BIG SPINS OF THE DAY:
Moon Void of Course: 12:03 A.M. PDT / 3:03 A.M. EDT until
Moon enters Virgo: 2:25 A.M. PDT / 5:25 A.M. EDT
Mercury trines Pluto: 10:05 A.M. PDT / 1:05 P.M. EDT
Venus squares Uranus: 8:21 P.M. PDT / 11:21 P.M. EDT

○◑◐●

FRIDAY

April 27

MOON IN VIRGO
SUCCESS RATING: ★★

Much of yesterday's Virgo influence is still in effect . . . with one major difference: Mercury (the planet that rules Virgo) entered Taurus in the early morning. This shift adds a softer component to the Virgo Moon and a stronger desire to have the environment in perfect shape. It's a great day to shop the health-food store and stock up on those vitamins and wholesome foods, and you may want to donate a carload of clothing to the thrift stores.

Virgo Moons make us love bargains, and with Mercury in Taurus, we'll have the stamina to find them. If you can get up the momentum, this is likely to be one of the most productive days of the month for you—sometimes it's just a matter of starting anywhere and letting one thing lead to the other. But if you can't devote a whole day to a project, then don't open your closet door!

AFFIRMATION FOR THE DAY:
There is an endless supply of resources available to me.

BIG SPINS OF THE DAY:
Mercury enters Taurus: 12:16 A.M. PDT / 3:16 A.M. EDT
Venus sextiles Saturn: 1:07 P.M. PDT / 4:07 P.M. EDT

○◑◐●

SATURDAY

April 28

MOON IN VIRGO/LIBRA
SUCCESS RATING: ★

You've had two full days of getting productive, but neither of them contained a Mars-Uranus connection. . . . This volatile combination of planets is like having a supercharged battery plugged into your head! The good news is that it does bring lots of energy; the bad news is that it's rarely controllable.

You have the strength to handle any circumstance, but be sure to avoid taking on more than you need to. History shows that the Mars-Uranus aspect can produce accidents resulting from carelessness—so take a breath before leaping, and get a second opinion before making spontaneous purchases.

AFFIRMATION FOR THE DAY:
I can handle all circumstances that come my way.

BIG SPINS OF THE DAY:
Venus opposes Jupiter: 5:44 A.M. PDT / 8:44 A.M. EDT
Moon Void of Course: 12:15 P.M. PDT / 3:15 P.M. EDT until
Moon enters Libra: 2:46 P.M. PDT / 5:46 P.M. EDT
Mars conjuncts Uranus: 9:37 P.M. PDT / 12:37 A.M. EDT (Sunday)

○◑◐●

SUNDAY

April 29

MOON IN LIBRA
SUCCESS RATING: ★★

If you happen to be in utter confusion about matters relating to your relationships, please know that you're not weird and you're not wrong—no one is. The cosmos is supporting you in healing your wounds associated with others, since the planetary cycles often do support you in resolving issues that are theme related. Since this is the relationship-oriented Libra Moon, and Venus is commingling with Jupiter and Saturn, it makes sense that you may be having a difficult time maneuvering in your relationships (including those with bosses, colleagues, and neighbors).

The main theme surrounding your social conundrum is *freedom.* If that theme emerges, don't panic—instead, take a look at what areas of your life you may have neglected in lieu of your relationship. Remember, I just said to "take a look"—I didn't say that you should act on anything. It's a day to be aware, since truth will emerge in its own time . . . and, needless to say, *no signing of de contracts!*

APRIL

AFFIRMATION FOR THE DAY:
Today I release all my fears and place them in my light, where they immediately disappear.

BIG SPINS OF THE DAY:
None

○◑◐●

MONDAY

April 30

MOON IN LIBRA
SUCCESS RATING: ★★

Dear April,

First, I'd like to say thank you for all the lessons that you pitched on me this month. You certainly did a fine job slinging the dirt . . . after all, you were host to the "earthy" sign of Taurus. I don't recall a single day where you gave five-star permission for anything, but I do remember a day with five clashing planets and two retrogrades! Let's see . . . you don't bring spring, you don't even bring in daylight savings time anymore, and you had some days with Void of Course Moons lasting for weeks (well, it felt like weeks). What I will say for you, April, is that you gave me something I needed more than anything: You gave me a greater faith in myself than I've ever had, and you made me dig pretty deep to find and remember my connection to the Divine. I guess that's a pretty big gift, so you're off the hook . . . but next year you'd better have some sugar in your lemonade, or I'm kicking your rear!

Until then. . . .

Love, Mark

Massive energy abounds today as we say good-bye to April. We should be able to make amends with anyone we've been on the outs with by sharing our hearts and being honest. The Libra Moon makes the truth palatable, although we often underestimate people's ability to handle it.

AFFIRMATION FOR THE DAY:
Nothing enters my life that cannot at some point be considered a gift.

BIG SPINS OF THE DAY:
Mars squares Jupiter: 3:22 P.M. PDT / 6:22 P.M. EDT
Venus trines Neptune: 6:34 P.M. PDT / 9:34 P.M. EDT

Thought for the Month

Remember You

Mountains look high when we're standing at their base. The peaks that once seemed so accessible, so close, now seem a million miles away, and the distance back to the home that we left behind seems even farther. So here we are: We can't turn back (we've already been there), and if we let our minds chatter too long, we'll stand here frozen as though we're deer in headlights. So on we go toward the peak like brave soldiers, with little encouragement—save for that of the people who count on us to survive—and a vague promise of something better. The end is unknown, but our courage is unquestionable.

That's *you* at the mountain. . . . Without question, every single individual reading this is making a choice to move forward, without knowing the outcome. Each of you has at least one person counting on you to make it, and every one of you is willing to try, regardless of how your mind assesses the situation.

Beyond any doubt, you're brave to be here and facing your fears. Each second, you're making choices for your survival with courage and conviction. No matter what your mind tells you—no matter what you think you believe about yourself—you deserve the kind of tribute that we save for heroes.

This month, you've mustered up the wisdom to appreciate who you are and what you're going through. Now let real compassion surround you . . . then, in your mind, extend that compassion to all the people you can, recognizing that they are being just as courageous.

MAY 2007

SUMMARY

This month manages a couple of good slaps, calling attention to some very powerful alignments. For starters, the entire Moon cycle (Full, Last Quarter, New, and First Quarter) will take place in the fixed signs (Scorpio, Aquarius, Taurus, and Leo), which are pretty close in nature to what the label implies: static, immovable, stubborn, and so on. When the Moon cycles through these signs, you can expect your choices to be limited and your learning to be specific. The fixed Moons of May are offering you an anchor to help you remain true to your center while the future evolves into history. In other words, this month has a lesson to teach you, and it will do so whether you feel ready or not. May is trying to give you a hint about flowing with the upcoming tide, which will be big at times and always interesting.

Take your mind back to the year 2000. . . . Remember all the fuss over Y2K? That was the year that Jupiter squared Uranus—and the two giants are at it again this month. Back then, they were in Taurus and Aquarius (fixed signs), but this year they'll be in Sagittarius and Pisces (mutable signs). In 2000, Jupiter wanted you to get back to your roots of security while you struggled against the technological push of Uranus in Aquarius, but balance was eventually found. In 2007, Jupiter will be seeking ways for you to maintain your spiritual diversity while battling Uranus's drive to bring humanity under one belief. . . . It's all starting under May's domain.

May highlights:

May 2: Full Moon 12° Scorpio
May 8: Venus enters Cancer
May 11: Mercury enters Gemini

May 15: Mars enters Aries
May 16: New Moon 26° Taurus
May 21: Sun enters Gemini
May 24: Neptune goes Retrograde
May 28: Mercury enters Cancer

◐

○◑◐●

TUESDAY

May 1

MOON IN LIBRA/SCORPIO
SUCCESS RATING: ★★★

Happy May Day! Do you know where your maypole is? Many countries around the world celebrate this date for various reasons, ranging from labor-movement victories to the coming of summer. Today you begin your journey into May with exuberance, curiosity, honesty, and fearlessness. Your intuition is high and your determination is unwavering . . . pay attention to where your thoughts take you.

Tomorrow's Full Moon occurs early in the morning and will illuminate your mind, thanks to a special Mercury alignment (see tomorrow's forecast for more information). It's not a bad idea to make a list of what you desire—or pull out your old list from the last New Moon—in anticipation of the Full Moon's harvest.

If you're comfortable with your intuitive side, you'll maneuver through this day with few, if any, obstacles. If you're a left-brain type, you may want to get a second opinion before moving ahead with any big decisions. And everyone should remember that Full Moons can accentuate emotional highs and lows.

AFFIRMATION FOR THE DAY:
I am connected deeply to all that I see.

BIG SPINS OF THE DAY:
Moon Void of Course: 1:07 A.M. PST / 4:07 A.M. EST until
Moon enters Scorpio: 3:42 A.M. PST / 6:42 A.M. EST

○◑◐●

WEDNESDAY

May 2

FULL MOON IN SCORPIO
SUCCESS RATING: ★★★★

The first Full Moon of May is celebrated as Buddha's birthday by millions. It's a spectacular time for celebrations of any kind, as Mercury and the Sun are making what's known as a *Superior Conjunction*. This means that Mercury is away from Earth, on the other side of the Sun, so it's benefiting from unobstructed solar rays. This means that your mind is illuminated with a type of clarity that you haven't felt in some time.

When your mind is activated, your ability to manifest your thoughts is enhanced, so if you've ever believed that your thoughts create your reality, believe it today. See the beauty in your life, and find gratitude in your thinking, for it will make a difference in the course of your week.

Soak up the Full Moon in Scorpio, and feel the deep journey that it takes you on. This is a great day to launch a business that has to do with communication, and it's also perfect for having an intimate chat with a loved one. If fears emerge, feel them, embrace them, and release them . . . they should be given no more weight than they deserve.

AFFIRMATION FOR THE DAY:
Everything that I see and *don't* see serves me completely.

BIG SPINS OF THE DAY:
Full Moon at 12° Scorpio: 3:10 A.M. PDT / 6:10 A.M. EDT
Moon Void of Course: 11:42 A.M. PDT / 2:42 P.M. EDT until tomorrow
Mercury conjuncts Sun: 9:06 P.M. PDT / 12:06 A.M. EDT (Thursday)

○◑◐●

THURSDAY

May 3

MOON IN SCORPIO/SAGITTARIUS
SUCCESS RATING: ★★

There's a very long Void of Course Moon today lasting until early evening. It's a blessing to have the Moon in this cycle so that you can take your time enjoying the energies that were introduced during yesterday's Full Moon.

Think of today as your opportunity to adjust and finish what you started. Keep your conversations light and your goals to a minimum. You're entering a new phase of energy, and the less you do to stir the pot right now, the less time you'll have to wait for things to settle down.

Tonight seek fun and folly through friends or food. The Sagittarius Moon wants you to feel worthy of abundance and expansion, so take it in! Avoid signing that important document until after the Void of Course, however, unless it's something that you've had planned for a while. It's not that there will be ill consequences if you do sign; it's just that your mind will be better equipped to think clearly later.

AFFIRMATION FOR THE DAY:
I invite stillness into my life so that
I may hear the Divine more clearly.

BIG SPINS OF THE DAY:
Moon Void of Course: until 3:48 P.M. PST / 6:48 P.M. EST
Moon enters Sagittarius: 3:48 P.M. PST / 6:48 P.M. EST

○◑◐●

FRIDAY

May 4

MOON IN SAGITTARIUS
SUCCESS RATING: ★★

Aim your arrows of wonder high, and shoot them toward the sky under this happy Sagittarius Moon. Do you recall how you used to dream about your future? Remember the hope and optimism you had when you were younger? Well, it's a good time to bring that energy to the present.

The most difficult part of dealing with this Moon is facing the reality of everyday duties when you feel so much more pleasure in wandering through the world, even if it's only in your mind. Find your personal bridge today, the one that allows you to bring your inner experience to the outer world. You'll be amazed by how easy it is to make the "garbage" disappear when you have all of your magic with you.

The planets are getting tense, so take an observer position and wait to see how things are unfolding before you leap too far in any one direction.

AFFIRMATION FOR THE DAY:
I am positively, absolutely,
undeniably embraced with pure love.

BIG SPINS OF THE DAY:
Moon in Sagittarius: All day and night

○◑◐●

SATURDAY

May 5

MOON IN SAGITTARIUS
SUCCESS RATING: ★★

This is a wonderful time to indulge in intellectual pursuits . . . it will be a great day if you teach, and even greater if you're a student. The planets are encouraging depth and growth while discouraging premature judgments based on old beliefs, so advance your knowledge today, but do mind your tongue. There's such high mental energy in the air that you could find yourself saying too much about taboo topics.

Worries could easily be magnified today if you let your mind wander too long without discipline. Remember that anxiety doesn't aid your situation—it simply keeps your thoughts in an unhealthy and unhelpful loop.

Squabbles and misunderstandings could prevail, so it's not the best day to sign anything. In fact, any agreements that are made today might have to be reviewed later. Find other ways to feed your mind instead.

AFFIRMATION FOR THE DAY:
I am not separate from the Divine, for that is impossible.

BIG SPINS OF THE DAY:
Mercury sextiles Uranus: 8:53 A.M. PDT / 11:53 A.M. EDT
Mercury squares Saturn: 3:55 P.M. PDT / 6:55 P.M. EDT
Moon Void of Course: 11:46 P.M. PDT / 2:46 A.M. EDT (Sunday) until tomorrow

○◑◐●

SUNDAY

May 6

MOON IN SAGITTARIUS/CAPRICORN
SUCCESS RATING: ★

The Moon slides into the stoic reign of Capricorn in the early-morning hours, and now key words such as *productivity, responsibility, duty, maturity,* and *tradition* take hold of your psyche. Even your dreams are likely to have some purpose to them! Today you're going to be required to resolve matters as efficiently as possible . . . it's almost as if you're being given the Capricorn Moon on this day because it's what's needed to bring you in for a smooth landing.

Venus is at odds with Pluto, and that can mean a power struggle, or a dispute between you and someone you love of either sex. The point is that there's a potential for conflict, and you have the foresight to avoid it. Use the grounding effect of this Moon to remain steady and on course. You'll know instinctively what to do, so trust yourself!

AFFIRMATION FOR THE DAY:
I am not afraid of money—
I attract it to me like bees to honey.

BIG SPINS OF THE DAY:

Moon Void of Course: until 2:21 A.M. PDT / 5:21 A.M. EDT
Moon enters Capricorn: 2:21 A.M. PDT / 5:21 A.M. EDT
Jupiter trines Saturn: 12:10 A.M. PDT / 3:10 A.M. EDT
Venus opposes Pluto: 7:03 P.M. PDT / 10:03 P.M. EDT

○◑◐●

MONDAY

May 7

MOON IN CAPRICORN
SUCCESS RATING: ★★

Today you have a great chance for success because it's the second day of the Capricorn Moon. You'll repeatedly find yourself at the right place at the right time without even planning it, and the day is filled with harmonious aspects (for the most part) that will help you stay on target and accomplish your tasks. Don't be fooled by a clumsy beginning . . . although Mercury starts an early-morning fight with Neptune and communications get a bit blurry, this will all pass by the afternoon.

This is a perfect day to get your car tuned up and your fluids checked. The Capricorn Moon loves it when you take preventive action because you're showing responsibility. Although there are better days to start a business, if you had something planned in advance that happens to land on this day, then have at it—you should be fine.

AFFIRMATION FOR THE DAY:
I acknowledge my judgments and lovingly release them.

BIG SPINS OF THE DAY:
Mercury squares Neptune: 7:29 A.M. PDT / 10:29 A.M. EDT

○◑◐●

TUESDAY

May 8

MOON IN CAPRICORN/AQUARIUS
SUCCESS RATING: ★★

Well, what a surprise: another adjustment day! This time you're adapting to the Moon's change from Capricorn to Aquarius and Venus's shift from Gemini into Cancer. This type of day simply means that moving right along with focus and a goal isn't necessarily an easy thing to do, as there are usually plenty of distractions calling for your attention.

Venus in Cancer represents a shift in your consciousness from the desire to be playful and carefree to the need to grow roots and nurture those around you. You may find yourself appreciating the tenderness that comes from compassion, so the first step in successfully navigating this energy is to give what you want to get.

Look around today, and notice who deserves special acknowledgment for his or her support or service . . . perhaps a kind note of thanks or even a raise would be an appropriate gesture. The best way to win favor is by *being* favorable.

There's an abundance of stimulation around you, thanks to the Sun's connection to Uranus. That's a hint to drive safely and keep your center—you can't catch the magic if you're flitting around all over the place! Stop the caffeine early today, and try a hot bath right before bedtime, since tonight's Mercury connection could very likely prevent you from sleeping soundly if you don't plan ahead.

AFFIRMATION FOR THE DAY:
I am the embodiment of harmony.

BIG SPINS OF THE DAY:
Venus enters Cancer: 12:28 A.M. PDT / 3:28 A.M. EDT
Moon Void of Course: 12:35 A.M. PDT / 3:35 A.M. EDT until
Moon enters Aquarius: 10:48 A.M. PDT / 1:48 P.M. EDT
Sun sextiles Uranus: 1:25 P.M. PDT / 4:25 P.M. EDT
Mercury sextiles Mars: 5:39 P.M. PDT / 8:39 P.M. EDT

○ ◑ ◐ ●

WEDNESDAY

May 9

LAST QUARTER MOON IN AQUARIUS
SUCCESS RATING: ★★

All Quarter Moons arrive a week after a Full or New Moon, marking the halfway point between the two. This means that now you have to review how you're doing and notice any obstacles that emerge in your path—they're your key. The more obstacles you find today, the greater the support you'll receive in clearing the way to your ultimate goal of peace. (Although you may have another specific objective in mind, peace is what it will ultimately bring you.)

The Sun is clashing with Saturn today, suggesting that you may have to make a decision between doing something that fully serves you and doing what that you think you *should* do. You'll recognize the need for such a choice when it emerges, and it will be helpful to remember that the best way to reconcile these two warring sides is to try to give each one a little bit of what it needs, but not at the same time. And don't enter into any official agreements today.

AFFIRMATION FOR THE DAY:
I feel peace with every breath.

BIG SPINS OF THE DAY:
Sun squares Saturn: 5:05 A.M. PDT / 8:05 A.M. EDT
Last Quarter Moon at 19° Aquarius: 9:26 P.M. PDT / 12:26 A.M. EDT (Thursday)

○◑◐●

THURSDAY

May 10

MOON IN AQUARIUS/PISCES
SUCCESS RATING: ★★

Hopefully, the early Moon-Neptune connection brought music to your dreams and set a peaceful tone for your day. Morning is the time to get your primary work done, and this may include clearing up a few miscommunications.

This is not the day to prove your authority, and it's certainly not the time to *dis*prove someone else's. It's likely that you have a few things on your mind that are bothering you, but you'll soon see how unfounded your worries are, thanks to a kind Jupiter connection. You may be tempted to take a leap into something new, but I'm honor bound to tell you to think twice before doing so.

There's more to this day and the opportunities within it than meets the eye, so give yourself some time to review everything before coming to a final decision. . . . Tonight do something that's pleasing to your senses.

AFFIRMATION FOR THE DAY:
The foods I love nourish me.

BIG SPINS OF THE DAY:
Moon Void of Course: 2:48 P.M. PDT/ 5:48 P.M. EDT until
Moon enters Pisces: 4:32 P.M. PDT / 7:32 P.M. EDT
Jupiter squares Uranus: 8:30 P.M. PDT / 11:30 P.M. EDT

○◑◐●

FRIDAY

May 11

MOON IN PISCES
SUCCESS RATING: ★★★

It's an all-day dreamy Pisces Moon, and nostalgia reigns supreme. Music, movies, and magic become high on your list of priorities as this watery Moon encourages you to come into your feelings.

Mercury has left the sign of Taurus today and entered its home—the flexible, playful, and communicative sign of Gemini. Notice how your mind seems to grasp ideas more quickly, and how much easier it is to express yourself with others. Everyone should be experiencing this effect, so your telephone may get an extra workout today. As you glide through this dreamlike experience, try using all that desire for communication to have a talk with your own *inner* voice. Chances are that it will have a lot to tell you . . . as long as your inner line isn't busy!

AFFIRMATION FOR THE DAY:
I use my words to offer support, compassion, and empowerment.

BIG SPINS OF THE DAY:
Moon in Pisces: All day and night
Mercury enters Gemini: 2:17 A.M. PDT / 5:17 A.M. EDT

○◑◐●

SATURDAY

May 12

MOON IN PISCES/ARIES
SUCCESS RATING: ★★

You'll be drifting through most of the day with the watery Pisces Moon. Don't be too discouraged if you don't have the amount of energy that you're used to, since most of this day will flow easily in the direction you choose. If you stay focused, you won't have any problems achieving what you want, although the afternoon holds some minor conflicts.

You may have to deal with the needs of someone close to you, but be careful not to fall too deeply into his or her drama. A clash between the Sun and Neptune may throw you into a fog, making this one of the worst days to engage in serious contractual agreements—it's worth waiting for your clarity to return, as this is a fast-moving connection.

This evening, the Aries Moon will toughen everyone up. Maintain strong boundaries during your interactions so that you won't have to use anger to rebuild them later.

AFFIRMATION FOR THE DAY:
I am made of light.

BIG SPINS OF THE DAY:
Moon Void of Course: 4:54 P.M. PDT / 7:54 P.M. EDT until
Moon enters Aries: 7:20 P.M. PDT / 10:20 P.M. EDT
Sun squares Neptune: 7:56 P.M. PDT / 10:56 P.M. EDT

○ ◑ ◐ ●

SUNDAY

May 13

MOON IN ARIES
SUCCESS RATING: ★

Hold on to your hat—and your tongue—as the fiery Aries Moon ignites your day. Under this Moon, you may be bursting with energy, but if you don't direct it, it may direct *you* . . . straight for a fight. Be very conscious of what you're doing today.

If you make Mother's Day plans, set them up for early in the day, during the adjustment period when the planets are still cooperating (Mars and Pluto are forming an aspect that's been known to cause wars). You can maneuver through this energy by staying aware of your feelings at all times . . . and they'll probably be intense. You may also want to keep an eye on the news to see other ways that this alignment could be manifested.

It would be ideal if could you kick back and read a great book, but there's little hope of that with this feisty energy in the sky. Since you're not likely to sit quietly for anyone today, go ahead and close your novel . . . and turn on the wrestling channel!

To everyone who's a mother, or to those who've mothered others in some way, take a moment to recognize and appreciate all that you are and all that you've been to the people who were lucky enough to experience your embrace.

AFFIRMATION FOR THE DAY:
Peace is what I am.

BIG SPINS OF THE DAY:
Mars squares Pluto: 8:11 A.M. PDT / 11:11 A.M. EDT

○◑◐●

MONDAY

May 14

Moon in Aries/Taurus
Success Rating: ★★

Okay, yesterday was an interesting one to say the least, but everything isn't over yet. Keep an eye on the news, and try to recognize how the world is responding to the tension between Mars and Pluto . . . it may help you understand what you're working with.

Most of the day will continue under the Aries Moon, but it will be winding down into Taurus tonight. This is the last day for Mars to be in Pisces, since it moves into its home of Aries tomorrow. Mars in Aries is a powerful mix of aggression and passion, and it will be important for you to harness and direct your desires so that you don't slip into anger as a replacement for motivation. Watching or playing sports can help channel this energy.

If you notice a little tension in the relationship department, don't worry—this is fast-moving energy that will go away (as does most annoying behavior) if you leave it alone.

Affirmation for the Day:
I am in constant communication
with my Divine Source.

BIG SPINS OF THE DAY:
Moon Void of Course: 5:25 p.m. PDT / 8:25 p.m. EDT until
Moon enters Taurus: 7:50 p.m. PDT / 10:50 p.m. EDT

○◑◐●

TUESDAY

May 15

MOON IN TAURUS
SUCCESS RATING: ★★★

Give attention to your body, and assess how it's feeling so that you can attend to its (often subtle) requests. The all-day Taurus Moon will help you focus on your physical needs, because this sign is all about what's tangible—if you can touch it, see it, hear it, or taste it, you're using the part of you that's endowed with the sensuality of the Bull. This effect is heightened since the Sun and Moon are both in Taurus, and working with it means that you'll have greater success navigating your day.

As if to offset this stronghold of Taurean energies, Mars moves into Aries today, a placement so dramatically different that it creates an interesting challenge. Now you have to figure out a way to appease the fiery push of Mars, while also allowing yourself to embrace the slow sensuality of the Moon and Sun in Taurus. The solution is pretty easy, however: Aggressively pursue your hot tub! Of course, if that's not literally feasible, the theory is still sound.

Use the extra energy you find today to focus on what pleases you. At the risk of encouraging complete hedonism, I suggest that you first tune in to your senses, and then direct Mars to fulfill their needs. You may find yourself helping others with a project or taking yourself off to the Bahamas—the form doesn't matter. What does count is that you first stop, then feel, and *then* act. Tomorrow is the New Moon, so get a list of your desires going.

AFFIRMATION FOR THE DAY:
I trust the wisdom of my body completely.

BIG SPINS OF THE DAY:
Mars enters Aries: 7:06 A.M. PDT / 10:06 A.M. EDT

○◐◑●

WEDNESDAY

May 16

NEW MOON IN TAURUS
MOON IN TAURUS/GEMINI
SUCCESS RATING: ★★★

New Moons occur when the Sun and Moon appear at the same point in space, and they represent a time of fresh beginnings. As the New Moon approaches, however, you tend to feel a bit depressed due to the absence of light on its face (it's only a metaphor, but that's what astrology is).

Today is a perfect time to take a moment to light a candle of intention. You certainly don't *need* a candle . . . in fact, you don't even need an intention. However, both do help you direct and focus your attention on yourself and your desires, if only for a moment—and that's what's important.

Since this particular New Moon is in Taurus, your desires will likely be more specific than usual. This sign immerses you into the physical world of your body, home, and work, making it easier to spot what's *not* there.

Get most of your tasks done in the morning (including your candle lighting), because the Moon goes Void of Course in the early afternoon and remains so until evening. It's not that you *can't* get much done during this time period . . . rather, it's that you probably won't feel like it.

AFFIRMATION FOR THE DAY:
All I want, all I need, and all I desire I have now.

MAY

BIG SPINS OF THE DAY:

New Moon at 26° Taurus: 12:28 P.M. PDT / 3:28 P.M. EDT
Moon Void of Course: 12:28 P.M. PDT / 3:28 P.M. EDT until
Moon enters Gemini: 7:35 P.M. PDT / 10:35 P.M. EDT

○ ◑ ◐ ●

THURSDAY

May 17

MOON IN GEMINI
SUCCESS RATING: ★★★

Not a bad day, not a bad day at all! . . . The Gemini Moon tickles your insides as you seek to make connections of all kinds. Use the power of yesterday's New Moon to guide you toward being at the perfect place at the perfect time, and notice how your mind is working in conjunction with your body as you encounter different experiences during the day. Your intuition is ripe, and you can easily trust yourself to make the decisions that must be made.

You may notice a subtle undercurrent of fear in the air, but it has nothing to do with your activities and a lot to do with the planetary tone. Saturn and Pluto are gearing up for a connection that tends to raise concerns, although this one—trust me—will not be as traumatic as when they were squabbling during 9/11. It's a great day to plan for the future, but if you're launching a business, you may want to delay the official opening until next month. I know that it sounds like a long time, but it would be better if the birth chart of your enterprise didn't have this particular aspect in it.

AFFIRMATION FOR THE DAY:
Fear cannot exist in the presence of love, and I am love.

BIG SPINS OF THE DAY:
None

○ ◑ ◐ ●

FRIDAY

May 18

MOON IN GEMINI/CANCER
SUCCESS RATING: ★★

Don't let the day's low Success Rating stop you from initiating deals and making plans—just try to avoid forging long-term commitments until you get out of this weirdness. There are communication issues you may encounter today, as well as mechanical troubles, all of which are designed to slow you down.

It's a metaphysical fact (I know it doesn't count as fact in the scientific community, but if you're reading this, *you'll* understand) that you create events outside of yourself so that you can use their reflection to take care of what's *in*side of yourself. So do it: Look around you and see what your reflections are trying to tell you.

The Moon slips into Cancer later tonight, so get into some cozy pajamas and snuggle up with your blankey . . . er . . . blanket. Dreams are waiting.

AFFIRMATION FOR THE DAY:
I am at peace in my stillness and in my activity.

BIG SPINS OF THE DAY:
Moon Void of Course: 5:58 P.M. PDT / 8:58 P.M. EDT until
Moon enters Cancer: 8:39 P.M. PDT / 11:39 P.M. EDT

MAY

○◑◐●

SATURDAY

May 19

MOON IN CANCER
SUCCESS RATING: ★★

You can now almost *feel* the push to get up and start moving. Maybe someone is really pushing you, or perhaps it's just your own inner list maker going wild—but today's energy would be best used for improving things around your home.

The Cancer Moon is a moody one, and that means that you're likely to encounter many different attitudes from everyone around you. Keep in mind that under the Cancer Moon, the urge is for security . . . so when people express their disapproval or disappointment about something, you can remember that they really just want reassurance. Depending on your mood, you may or may not be the one to give it to them, but remember that the same holds true for you. If you find yourself feeling a little worried about the same old issues, try offering your mind something different to observe (like someone else's problems).

Tonight a wonderful aspect encourages being with friends and loved ones. Get to bed early, as you may have trouble slowing your mind down for sleep.

AFFIRMATION FOR THE DAY:
Today I have an abundance of
support and encouragement to give.

BIG SPINS OF THE DAY:
Mercury opposes Jupiter: 10:31 P.M. PDT / 1:31 A.M. EDT (Sunday)

○◑◐●

SUNDAY

May 20

MOON IN CANCER
SUCCESS RATING: ★★

It's another all-day Cancer Moon filling you with imagination and fantasy, so use this energy to get creative in your home. Look at your walls, and picture yourself stepping outside your normal boundaries and into something new and different (if things get too out of hand, you may want to ask a friend or other household member what he or she thinks before running to the paint or furniture store). Due to a harsh aspect with Mercury, you may find that keeping your focus is a lot more difficult than you'd imagined. There's a great deal of activity in the air and potentially a lot of distractions coming your way, so it's important to keep a good attitude even when your nerves start to feel frayed. Don't ruin your day by blurting out what's on your mind—screen yourself first.

AFFIRMATION FOR THE DAY:
I am a well of creativity.

BIG SPINS OF THE DAY:
Mercury squares Uranus: 4:26 P.M. PDT / 7:26 P.M. EDT

HAPPY BIRTHDAY, GEMINI!

MAY 21–JUNE 21

Gemini is made up of the flexible characteristic known as *mutable* and the mental quality of Air. The sign is ruled by the planet Mercury, famously represented as both the messenger god and the trickster, suggesting that Gemini is both communicative and playful. There isn't much that people born under this sign can't do, thanks to their quick minds, but staying with something for too long is dangerously boring to them. Geminis give new meaning to the phrase "jack-of-all-trades, master of none," because there just isn't enough time in the day to learn everything and then *practice* it.

Geminis are represented by the Twins on the Zodiac wheel, and indeed for good reason—within them are two distinct personalities (although some would argue that there are many more than that!). One day, you might encounter someone who can't stop talking and connecting with you, and then the next, you could find the same person reticent and withdrawn. Each of the Gemini twins needs equal expression, and understanding this could save you from a lot of arguments. People born under this sign aren't bound by the roots of Taurus, and they don't have the warrior urges of Aries. They simply come prepared for change, which is why many Geminis have trouble keeping jobs. Some might call the Gemini a "walking oxymoron" because everything is simultaneously important to this sign, yet nothing really matters.

AFFIRMATIONS FOR GEMINI:
All the parts of me make me whole.
I am more than my mind.
It is safe to be in the present.

○◑◐●

MONDAY

May 21

SUN IN GEMINI
MOON IN CANCER/LEO
SUCCESS RATING: ★★★★

Today you're starting to pull out of a watery slump, and the planets are here to help. The Sun goes into Gemini for the next 30 days and activates all sorts of planetary communications. Notice how the world shifts from issues of security to those of connection . . . under this Leo Moon, you'll be experiencing the same thing as you pull your attention away from your worries and toward your heart.

If you can imagine it, you can have it today. Remember that you don't have to be preoccupied with thinking the perfect thought, since the Universe is much older and wiser, and it has a pretty good grasp of what you need. Relax and appreciate the break that this day is giving you.

AFFIRMATION FOR THE DAY:
I have the power to do anything I desire.

BIG SPINS OF THE DAY:

Moon Void of Course: 12:47 A.M. PDT / 3:47 A.M. EDT until
Moon enters Leo: 12:57 A.M. PDT / 3:57 A.M. EDT
Sun enters Gemini: 3:12 A.M. PDT / 6:12 A.M. EDT
Mercury sextiles Saturn: 3:48 A.M. PDT / 6:48 A.M. EDT

○◑◐●

TUESDAY

May 22

Moon in Leo
Success Rating: ★★★

The wonderfully optimistic Leo Moon is at your disposal today, giving you the classic choice of eating lemons or drinking lemonade. This Moon can accentuate the dramatic element in your life, so you have a choice of how you want to express yourself and what you want to emphasize. The morning starts off with good fortune and a feeling of expansion that you can use to coast through the rest of the day. The afternoon contains demands that may require you to focus, but remember that you're carrying a lucky charm (called *you*).

Carry yourself with a mix of humility and pride, and offer your sunshine to those who may need a gentle reminder that everything is going to be okay. The best way to teach is to show, so be what you believe in today . . . you'll be contagious!

Affirmation for the Day:
I am joy, and I extend myself to all I meet.

BIG SPINS OF THE DAY:
None

○◑◐●

WEDNESDAY

May 23

FIRST QUARTER MOON IN VIRGO
SUCCESS RATING: ★★★

Don't waste your time being critical of yourself today, since you have too much to do and are too important for such a petty display of nonsense. The Virgo Moon enters the scene this morning and moves on to make the First Quarter Moon, which is there to help you remove the clutter that's preventing your forward progress. You may not notice an inner craving to get organized—sometimes it's subtle—but if you pay attention, you'll find yourself recognizing every detail of your environment.

Sometimes the Quarter Moon in Virgo can be stressful, but if you flow with it, you'll see that it's simply another form of encouragement to clean house (not necessarily your *home*) and everyone in it! Sign important documents after the Void of Course Moon.

AFFIRMATION FOR THE DAY:
I organize my life with effortless pleasure and ease.

BIG SPINS OF THE DAY:

Mercury trines Neptune: 12:48 A.M. PDT / 3:48 A.M. EDT
Moon Void of Course: 6:09 A.M. PDT / 9:09 A.M. EDT until
Moon enters Virgo: 9:27 A.M. PDT / 12:27 P.M. EDT
First Quarter Moon 2° Virgo: 2:03 P.M. PDT / 5:03 P.M. EDT

MAY

○◑◐●

THURSDAY

May 24

MOON IN VIRGO
SUCCESS RATING: ★★★

Attention all Pisceans! Your ruling planet, Neptune, has stopped moving forward and is turning around for a six-month spin backward. Finally, you can stop pushing so hard and begin to relax in your inner sanctuary, where it's peaceful. Neptune keeps you in the flow of a creative, spiritual, dreamlike, and often confused state of mind. Now that the planet is moving backward, you'll be able to assimilate the lessons that it tries to teach you, such as how to be compassionate to yourself, how you can see that you're a part of everything around you, and how your thoughts affect your reality.

In general, Neptune turning backward is a gift that you can use to internalize the ethereal effects of this wonderful planet. Those of you who filter life through your mind may have trouble for the first couple of days, but the more intuitive types (the most likely audience that a book such as this would attract) should find the change quite enjoyable. However, I'd avoid signing any documents for fear of not having clarity.

AFFIRMATION FOR THE DAY:
My intuition is a finely tuned
work of art that guides me perfectly.

BIG SPINS OF THE DAY:
Neptune goes Retrograde: 6:09 P.M. PDT / 9:09 P.M. EDT
Venus trines Uranus: 11:42 P.M. PDT / 2:42 A.M. EDT (Friday)

○◑◐●

FRIDAY

May 25

MOON IN VIRGO/LIBRA
SUCCESS RATING: ★★

Okay, you're back on your feet again. Now, follow me: Take one step, then another, and move slowly until you can feel the rhythm of your steps. The slower you start out, the better your equilibrium will be throughout the day—keeping things balanced is the secret to preparing for the Libra Moon.

Aside from a few tempting distractions, you'll feel capable of completing a lot of work, since you have the focus of the Virgo Moon for most of the day. Remember that on the days that the Moon changes signs, you'll probably feel edgy and unfocused, so don't beat yourself up. Also, there's a Void of Course Moon this evening lasting for about four hours, so plan some real rest tonight. A good night's sleep makes for a terrific day tomorrow.

AFFIRMATION FOR THE DAY:
I love what I do!

BIG SPINS OF THE DAY:
Moon Void of Course: 5:44 P.M. PDT / 8:44 P.M. EDT until
Moon enters Libra: 9:17 P.M. PDT / 12:17 A.M. EDT (Saturday)

○◑◐●

SATURDAY

May 26

MOON IN LIBRA
SUCCESS RATING: ★★★

Charming and sweet, easy and balanced . . . that's what today is. (I bet you thought I was talking about myself—you're so kind). Most of you will be able to use the available rush of energy to bring beauty into your home, go out with the family to the park, or take the dog for a walk (be responsible and bring a plastic bag!). There's so much that you can do to make today feel perfect.

Libra Moons tend to bring out the urge to relate to others, but after a while you'll need an ivory tower to retreat to. Make sure to have some of your favorite things on hand: a book, knitting, and maybe a fashion magazine. It's been an active week with lots of adjustments required, so why not relax as much as possible today? (Unless, of course, there's a party that you're invited to!)

AFFIRMATION FOR THE DAY:
Yes is my favorite word.

BIG SPINS OF THE DAY:
None

MAY

○◑◐●

SUNDAY

May 27

MOON IN LIBRA
SUCCESS RATING: ★★

The scales of justice rule Libra—therefore, when one side is tipped, the other *must* respond in order to return things to balance. That means that if you've been overly nice, it may be time to bring out your naughty side, or vice versa.

Due to a conflict between Mercury (the planet of communication) and Pluto (the planet of power), you may have to step up and tell the truth if the circumstances require it. This energy is surrounding everyone, so it would be interesting to listen for some exciting news to hit the airwaves.

Tonight is dreamy and romantic, and movies, music, or any art form would be a good way to cap off your evening. Dreams may be powerful, so look for clues to what your subconscious mind might be trying to tell you.

AFFIRMATION FOR THE DAY:
I am beautiful.

BIG SPINS OF THE DAY:
Mercury opposes Pluto: 8:11 A.M. PDT / 11:11 A.M. EDT

○◑◐●

MONDAY

May 28

MOON IN LIBRA/SCORPIO
SUCCESS RATING: ★★★

Things are starting to ease up everywhere. There's a little irony in that statement, considering that the Moon is about to enter one of the heavier signs of the Zodiac (Scorpio), but it's true: You're beginning to breathe easier and feel lighter.

The feeling of oppression that's been lurking beneath the surface this entire month is starting to lift. You'll probably notice an obvious absence of angst, first in the people around you, and then in yourself. With the Moon and Mercury changing signs, this is a day of adjustments, so you may need some time to acclimate.

Don't make final decisions today unless you're completely clear about them, since there will be time for review tomorrow. Today take a dive into the imaginative, watery world of emotions . . . but be careful, as feelings do bruise.

AFFIRMATION FOR THE DAY:
My body reflects my thoughts,
and my thoughts are made of light.

BIG SPINS OF THE DAY:
Moon Void of Course: 9:17 A.M. PDT / 12:17 P.M. EDT until
Moon enters Scorpio: 10:12 A.M. PDT / 1:12 P.M. EDT
Mercury enters Cancer: 5:56 P.M. PDT / 8:56 P.M. EDT

○◑◐●

TUESDAY

May 29

MOON IN SCORPIO
SUCCESS RATING: ★★★

The depth of the Scorpio Moon supports you in seeing beneath the surface of everything around you. You become a natural investigator under this sign's rule, with plenty of options to explore. You may want to try some *self*-exploration, since it's much easier to do so under this Moon—and to handle what you find. Giving your inner secrets a bit of light is the best way to lose the heavy burdens that weigh you down.

If you can't open up to someone today, create an attitude that allows other people to share their secrets with you. It's just as effective as revealing your own, but a lot less risky. Respect the alliances you have—don't run to the gossip zone and violate your friendships. Part of making a good day even better is respecting the celestial energies around you.

AFFIRMATION FOR THE DAY:
I am not afraid to be alone,
because I know that is impossible.

BIG SPINS OF THE DAY:
None

○◑◐●

WEDNESDAY

May 30

MOON IN SCORPIO/SAGITTARIUS
SUCCESS RATING: ★★

A long Void of Course Moon dominates today, but it doesn't have to rule your choices. "Void of Course" means that the Moon is floating through space, making no connection to any other planet until it changes signs. In the same way that the Moon reflects the Sun's light, you reflect the Moon's behavior under these cycles, and you may feel that you, too, are free-floating without connection to anyone. Some people describe feeling dissociated under these Moons, while others report that nothing seems different—the reason why is in everyone's personal birth chart. Some individuals really aren't conscious of the Moon's effect on them and function fine during these strange "Void" periods.

So, if you feel good today, do your business as usual, but if you're one of those who feels a little left of center, you might want to wait until tomorrow to take on anything new and just work on what you didn't finish yesterday. There's a Full Moon tomorrow, so treats are on the way (finally).

AFFIRMATION FOR THE DAY:
The guidance I follow is Divine
and always there when I need it.

BIG SPINS OF THE DAY:
Moon Void of Course: 10:12 A.M. PDT / 1:12 P.M. EDT until
Moon enters Sagittarius: 10:07 P.M. PDT / 1:07 A.M. EDT (Thursday)

○◑◐●

THURSDAY

May 31

FULL MOON IN SAGITTARIUS
SUCCESS RATING: ★★★★

I don't want to take away any of the magic that you already had planned for this Full Moon, but if you're calling it a "Blue Moon," you're technically incorrect. You probably learned that a *Blue Moon* meant the second Moon in the same month, because of someone's (specifically, James Hugh Pruett's) misinterpretation of the original *Maine Farmers' Almanac* that explained the whole mess. Actually, Blue Moons occur when there are four Full Moons in one season instead of the usual three—so this one doesn't qualify. But if you send me a small contribution, I'll consider dubbing this "Moon Blue." (For the record, there's a real one in 2008.)

Today *is* a Full Moon (Blue or not), and that means that you can revel in the extreme possibilities that are known to belong to the Sagittarian clan! Hovering at about 10 degrees of Sagittarius, this Moon brings high emotional tides that you can use to surf toward big rewards. Full Moons are about receiving the gifts that you planted in your heart at the New Moon.

Don't be surprised if people around you are acting as if they could become werewolves in a matter of hours, as this is just the nature of the first part of any Full Moon. When it's in Sagittarius—the feisty Fire sign—things just seem magnified. Tonight get some rest, since you're in for an even bigger day tomorrow.

(**Important note:** Mercury returns to this day, so take notes and review the section in this book on the Mercury Retrograde. When the planet travels backward later on, it will eventually revisit the issues of today, and it's helpful to notice any events that grabbed your attention.)

AFFIRMATION FOR THE DAY:
I am willing to see and receive the gifts of my past.

BIG SPINS OF THE DAY:
Full Moon 10° Sagittarius: 6:04 P.M. PDT / 9:04 P.M. EDT

Thought for the Month

On Longing

One day, a realization hit me while surfing through my television guide, as I gazed with astonishment at the number of "reality shows" in existence. I have nothing against any particular form of entertainment, but for some reason, while reading over this glut of "real TV," I starting thinking about my own desire to create more—of *everything*. I wanted more money, more time, more health, more energy, more room, more clothes, more hair . . . it was a list that kept perpetuating itself, regardless of the achievement of my goals. In other words, when I made more money, I *wanted* an even greater amount, and it seemed that anything I accomplished instantly generated the question "What's next?" I embodied the stereotype of the hunter who loves the hunt, but nothing more.

When I applied this idea to my spiritual life, I noticed that throughout the course of a week, I'd received incredible moments of grace—times when what I needed suddenly appeared, or close calls where disaster could have struck, but didn't. In addition, whenever I needed an answer to a personal question, it would come. I was continually surrounded by this kind of support, yet my daily complaint was that just the opposite was the case: I moaned about not feeling at all connected to that incredible Spirit.

This Thought for the Month is about recognizing that perhaps the longing for more is really about our deeper belief that we don't deserve what we desire. Maybe we keep searching because we feel that at any moment, it could all be taken away. As the next month progresses, if you feel that familiar desire for something new in your life, take just a second to affirm: *What I am really seeking is already here—and it has no conditions or limits.*

JUNE 2007
SUMMARY

What makes June remarkably different from May is the choice factor. This month carries the Sun in Gemini for the first 21 days, before the introduction of Cancer. Now if you aren't familiar with Gemini, it's the sign of *multi*-everything: multifaceted, multitalented, multidimensional, and—lest we forget—multi-personality. It lets you choose from a plethora of options. In addition, under Gemini's rays, you long for communication, information, people to talk to, and minds to merge with, like a sponge seeking water.

The big news in June is the third and final opposition of Saturn and Neptune. These two planets had this meeting originally in August 2006, then in February 2007, and now they're back again for their last run. Saturn in Leo relates to your leaders (Saturn is authority and Leo is royalty), and with these two planets fighting, there's going to be disillusionment (Neptune) in that leadership, and heads may roll! You'll finally have a clear idea about the end of the story that started in August of last year.

June is filled with planets—five out of ten—in the Fire signs (Aries, Leo, and Sagittarius). The element of Fire is about inspiration and motivation, so there should be plenty of both on hand. And while we're on the topic of heat, the first day of summer (also called the Summer Solstice) is June 21—that's the day that the Sun enters the watery sign of Cancer, which may help with the overabundance of Fire.

This month is also host to the second Mercury Retrograde of the year, starting on June 15 in the sign of Cancer (a particularly psychic placement for this planet).

June's main events:

June 5: Venus enters Leo
June 14: New Moon 24° Gemini
June 15: Mercury goes Retrograde
June 21: Summer Solstice (Sun enters Cancer)
June 23: Uranus goes Retrograde
June 24: Mars enters Taurus
June 25: Saturn opposes Neptune
June 30: Full Moon 8° Capricorn

◐

○◑◐●

FRIDAY

June 1

MOON IN SAGITTARIUS
SUCCESS RATING: ★★★★

June welcomes you warmly and then tantalizes you with the promise of a good time! Under an all-day Sagittarius Moon, there's excitement in the air and a feeling of adventure that urges you to quest for more knowledge, travel, and fun. Hopefully, you won't be tempted to indulge the less attractive side of Sagittarius that's prone to gossip and idle chatter—usually you'll find yourself engaging in such activities when it feels as if your circumstances have imprisoned you.

Believe that you're in the right place at the right time, and let your magic brighten things up. Consider yourself a flame today, and look upon the people you encounter as candles . . . light them and move on. You won't sit with any one feeling for too long, so don't fret about the more difficult moments of the day.

You could be filled with delicious feelings of accomplishment today. Say yes to signing contracts and making agreements, since June is attempting to lift the barrier that's impeded you for almost two months! And tonight, big dreams await you.

AFFIRMATION FOR THE DAY:
I embrace myself first and
then extend my support as needed.

BIG SPINS OF THE DAY:
None

○◑◐●

SATURDAY

June 2

MOON IN SAGITTARIUS/CAPRICORN
SUCCESS RATING: ★★★

The Moon prepares you for its entrance into Capricorn this morning by slowing you down and directing your attention to your surroundings. If today doesn't seem quite as bright as yesterday, it's only because the Capricorn Moon seems heavier in contrast to the Sagittarius one—but it's only in contrast. In reality, this Moon will help you look at the areas of your life that need improvement.

Under Capricorn's guidance, you won't be tempted to gloss over your world with Pollyanna-like euphemisms, but will instead be more likely to accept what you see at face value. You can't fix what you won't let yourself see, so don't confuse this process with depression, even though they may feel the same. Clearing out old mental cobwebs is the first step toward creating fresh new ideas.

Avoid verbal disputes tonight. Being agreeable in the moment isn't giving in . . . it's just allowing peace to exist in your space until things become clearer.

AFFIRMATION FOR THE DAY:
The reflections that I see around me serve to represent the judgments that exist within me, allowing me to release them.

BIG SPINS OF THE DAY:
Moon Void of Course: 4:29 A.M. PDT / 7:29 A.M. EDT until
Moon enters Capricorn: 8:10 A.M. PDT / 11:10 A.M. EDT

○ ◑ ◐ ●

SUNDAY

June 3

MOON IN CAPRICORN
SUCCESS RATING: ★★★

Under the Capricorn Moon, you're protected from intense feelings, since this sign gives you the ability to build walls around any extreme emotion. Today you may find that your sensitivity levels have increased (therefore building a thicker wall) because of the actions of someone close to you. Be aware of your reactions—it will be easy to stuff them behind your emotional barricade, only to have them reemerge to bite you later.

Luckily, you won't be short on things to do (you know what they say about idle hands). This is a high-energy day, so you'll have a lot to focus on and accomplish if you put your mind to it. Later this evening, your spirits should lift, and you may even get a surprise . . . but remember not to show too much excitement, since you have a duty under this Moon to remain stoic (just kidding!).

AFFIRMATION FOR THE DAY:
My feelings are safe and supportive,
and it is easy to express them.

BIG SPINS OF THE DAY:
None

○◑◐●

MONDAY

June 4

MOON IN CAPRICORN/AQUARIUS
SUCCESS RATING: ★★★

The mature Capricorn Moon guides you through the better part of the day, encouraging you to focus on productivity and accomplishments. Try to aim your intentions at completing leftover tasks so that you can revel in the knowledge that your responsibilities have been tended to. Successful navigation through a Capricorn Moon is achieved only when you've used it to create tangible progress—shirking any duties just won't feel good.

Mars is making a jolting connection to Jupiter, which means that energy will be high and the heat will be on! Try to maneuver through this day with perspective so that you don't take on more than you should and ignore your responsibilities. Watch your attitude, and keep it positive . . . you don't want to inadvertently burn any bridges due to impatience or your high-speed pace.

As the Moon shifts into Aquarius midday, there's a chance of irritability with a co-worker or classmate, so try to stay grounded until you feel back at your center. Contracts that you sign today should be fine, but you might be prone to accept more responsibility than you should, so remember to be willing to negotiate.

AFFIRMATION FOR THE DAY:
I breathe in patience today.

BIG SPINS OF THE DAY:
Mars trines Jupiter: 7:58 A.M. PDT / 10:58 A.M. EDT
Moon Void of Course: 2:45 P.M. PDT / 5:45 P.M. EDT until
Moon enters Aquarius: 4:16 P.M. PDT / 7:16 P.M. EDT

○◑◐●

TUESDAY

June 5

MOON IN AQUARIUS
SUCCESS RATING: ★★★★

The big news of the day is that the planet of love, Venus, is entering the royal sign of Leo. Although you may have to wait a day or so to feel the effects, you'll have plenty of time to bask in them: Venus will remain in Leo for a whopping 99 days, thanks to its retrograde motion next month. You might plan on changing your look, especially your hair, as well as welcoming a renewed interest in being noticed. However, Venus in Leo is about so much more than personal appearance. Romance will also take on a special quality, and Leos around the world will be awakening the part of them that's felt underappreciated so that it can gain new ground. Be ready to leave bigger tips for people in the service industry and engage in random acts of kindness, as this placement gives new meaning to the word *generosity*.

With today's Moon in Aquarius, the world will look like your oyster. As you seek to find the pearl, the day could feel so expansive that you might overextend yourself and lose your boundaries. Excesses *should* be monitored, although I hate to suggest that you withhold your natural expression. . . . Go ahead and be all that you can be, but do so consciously.

AFFIRMATION FOR THE DAY:
I am limitless—as part of the Divine, I could be nothing less.

BIG SPINS OF THE DAY:
Venus enters Leo: 11:00 A.M. PDT / 2:00 P.M. EDT
Sun opposes Jupiter: 4:13 P.M. PDT / 7:13 P.M. EDT

JUNE

○◑◐●

WEDNESDAY

June 6

MOON IN AQUARIUS/PISCES
SUCCESS RATING: ★★★★

There's plenty of time today to inhale the changes from yesterday, but you'll want to get your primary workload done before the day's end, since the Moon in Aquarius guides you above any emotional distractions. Like an eagle looking down at the terrain, you'll have the overview that you need to organize your day, and you'll also possess the wisdom to respond to the requests that others may make.

People from your past could put in an appearance, so look your best . . . you don't want them to think that you've been slacking off (or do you?). Sign important documents to your heart's content—that is, until the Moon goes Void of Course tonight.

The Moon enters Pisces late in the evening and promises a lush night of dreams, but you have to go to bed in order to get them! Try cutting out the stimulants early so that your sleep is restful and productive.

AFFIRMATION FOR THE DAY:
My foresight is 20/20.

BIG SPINS OF THE DAY:
Moon Void of Course: 6:48 P.M. PDT / 9:48 P.M. EDT until
Moon enters Pisces: 10:25 P.M. PDT / 1:25 A.M. EDT (Thursday)

○◑◐●

THURSDAY

June 7

MOON IN PISCES
SUCCESS RATING: ★★★

Moving from an Aquarius Moon to a Pisces one is sometimes startling: The Aquarius Moon tends to keep you more objective, while the watery nature of Pisces is inclined to bring you closer to your inner imaginative world. Today may heighten your intuition, and you could be asked to follow hunches that may or may not make sense.

The world is your reflecting pool, so look out and see what that reflection is. Are you happy? Sad? Or perhaps you're immersed so deeply in your work that you don't realize you're using it as a shield against feeling vulnerable. Whatever it is you're doing today, use it to understand your emotions. This Moon celebrates your inner world, and if you aren't accustomed to looking in that direction, you may just need a little external encouragement—you'll see what I mean.

Signing important documents or launching a new business is fine if your insides are in agreement, but if you have a nagging fear, just wait it out. You'll be in a much clearer position after the weekend.

AFFIRMATION FOR THE DAY:
I'm in the flow and am being directed perfectly to my next destination.

BIG SPINS OF THE DAY:
None

○◑◐●

FRIDAY

June 8

LAST QUARTER MOON IN PISCES
SUCCESS RATING: ★★★

The Last Quarter Moon is the final clash between the Sun and Moon before they form the New Moon next week. That means you have one week to get yourself back on track.

Since Pisces rules addictions, use this time to initiate the changes you've wanted to make to old habits. If you're depressed, don't worry—this is the opportunity to release anything that's in the way of remembering who you really are. Friends will probably prove helpful today, so let them assist you. Remember, you don't always have to be the one giving.

Health concerns that may be in your life (including people around you who might be ill) could also get some extra help during this cycle. You're still under the Pisces influence until this evening, so emotional issues may seem harder to slough off than usual . . . let your inner feelings come through.

AFFIRMATION FOR THE DAY:
I surrender my life to the greater love of the Divine.

BIG SPINS OF THE DAY:

Last Quarter Moon 17° Pisces: 4:44 A.M. PDT / 7:44 A.M. EDT
Moon Void of Course: 10:53 P.M. PDT / 1:53 A.M. EDT (Saturday) until tomorrow

○◑◐●

SATURDAY

June 9

MOON IN PISCES/ARIES
SUCCESS RATING: ★★

Use the incoming Aries Fire to shake off the murky effects of the Pisces Moon. The Aries Moon shifts your focus from the past and aims you toward the future. Like the Ram that symbolizes this sign, you'll be able to put your head down, horns out, and charge out of the doldrums that may have chained you.

The Sun is forming an electric position in relation to Uranus, which means that you could find yourself moving excessively fast. Try to stay grounded by taking a breath before each new project that you start. In general, this is an astrologically friendly day, but that may not be enough to prevent you from being careless. Please heed this warning: *Slow down!*

Let the day unfold for you according to its own schedule. What the Aries Moon lacks in patience, it makes up for in common sense, so be sure to use it. With that in mind, go have a good time and give the economy the boost it needs—spend money!

AFFIRMATION FOR THE DAY:
I am successful and abundant,
and it shows in all areas of my life.

BIG SPINS OF THE DAY:
Moon Void of Course: until 2:28 A.M. PDT / 5:28 A.M. EDT
Moon enters Aries: 2:28 A.M. PDT / 5:28 A.M. EDT
Sun squares Uranus: 1:08 P.M. PDT / 4:08 P.M. EDT

○◑◐●

SUNDAY

June 10

MOON IN ARIES
SUCCESS RATING: ★★

You should be resting today, but there's a good chance you can't sit still. With the Aries Moon in full swing, you'll very likely have a buzz of nervous energy that's trying to get you to go out to the park, or at least the garden. It's an active day, but it has enough of Saturn's grounded energy to prevent you from being too irresponsible. The purpose factor will be in full bloom tomorrow, so play while you can.

Check out the news every now and then, since things could be getting interesting as Neptune and Saturn pull closer together. This is their third and final time being together, finishing up something that was started back in August of 2006.

It's a great day for creative expression, so don't forget about dancing, music, art, and all the pleasures available at your banquet of life. And speaking of food, go ahead and cheat on your diet . . . your secret is safe with me.

AFFIRMATION FOR THE DAY:
There is an endless stream of energy running through me, and I use it as I desire.

BIG SPINS OF THE DAY:
None

○◑◐●

MONDAY

June 11

MOON IN ARIES/TAURUS
SUCCESS RATING: ★★

The Moon moves into Taurus early in the morning, and you'll probably notice your attention shifting to your body. The Taurus Moon is also your call to notice your physical surroundings, including money and material goods. The "desire to acquire" is big under this Moon as you seek to satisfy your needs.

Today's planets are shouting at you to accomplish your goals, and work will be a major focus. If you're unemployed, your drive to look for a job will gain momentum, and if you're already working, your motivation to produce results will be equally enhanced.

It's a great day to get tangible results, especially if you reward yourself with a massage or a long, hot bath. Keep your attention on your intuition . . . your body will tell you if something isn't right.

AFFIRMATION FOR THE DAY:
I love and accept my physical body, and I shower it with gratitude for the myriad ways it supports me.

BIG SPINS OF THE DAY:
Moon Void of Course: 12:58 A.M. PDT / 3:58 A.M. EDT until
Moon enters Taurus: 4:30 A.M. PDT / 7:30 A.M. EDT
Sun sextiles Mars: 3:25 A.M. PDT / 6:25 A.M. EDT
Sun sextiles Saturn: 12:39 P.M. PDT / 3:39 P.M. EDT
Mars trines Saturn: 3:43 P.M. PDT / 6:43 P.M. EDT

○◑◐●

TUESDAY

June 12

MOON IN TAURUS
SUCCESS RATING: ★★

Get focused, and accomplish those tasks in the early part of the day. The Moon will move Void of Course this evening (lasting until tomorrow morning), and by then, you may find yourself increasingly distracted by everything around you and unable to focus on work or a project.

Don't succumb to the loudest "squeaky wheel" by attending to a situation that wasn't on your list of things to do. Try to move in the direction of your river . . . swimming against the flow of the current just creates stress, and you need to keep that at a minimum today.

You might want to end your workday early and retreat to the comfort of your couch (or bathtub), since there will be plenty of time to catch up later. A New Moon is coming, which can introduce a slight feeling of depression, but if you know about it, you can ride it out by relaxing and breathing through it.

AFFIRMATION FOR THE DAY:
There is nothing that can prevent
me from experiencing peace.

BIG SPINS OF THE DAY:
Moon Void of Course: 4:18 P.M. PDT / 7:18 P.M. EDT until tomorrow

○◑◐●

WEDNESDAY

June 13

MOON IN TAURUS/GEMINI
SUCCESS RATING: ★★★

The Moon enters communicative, flexible, and lighthearted Gemini early today, and you'll find yourself moving a little slower than usual due to the early change in signs. This day will probably have a surreal quality to it, which it can be fun to enhance with music or perhaps your favorite movie.

I wouldn't count on having a clear direction, as it may be difficult for you to focus. The Gemini Moon can bring out your desire to connect with others, but it can also bring out the "other" Twin who's more moody and antisocial. You probably won't have any control over which part of you is emerging, so look around: If people are running from you, there's a good chance that your Mr. Hyde is coming through. There's no need to feel bad—just ride it out, as things will find balance in their own time. I'd avoid signing important documents today if possible.

AFFIRMATION FOR THE DAY:
I love all the different expressions of me.

BIG SPINS OF THE DAY:
Sun trines Neptune: 12:30 A.M. PDT / 3:30 A.M. EDT
Moon Void of Course: until 5:25 A.M. PDT / 8:25 A.M. EDT
Moon enters Gemini: 5:25 A.M. PDT / 8:25 A.M. EDT
Mars sextiles Neptune: 1:36 P.M. PDT / 4:36 P.M. EDT

○◑◐●

THURSDAY

June 14

NEW MOON IN GEMINI
SUCCESS RATING: ★★

Happy New Moon! Every month has a moment when the Moon positions itself between the Earth and the Sun in such a way that it appears as a dark orb in the sky. It's a time of newness; there's a feeling of rebirth in the air; and it's an opportunity to come into the present moment. This is a fabulous chance to forgive your past and remember that you can't be a victim of any circumstance, because you're more than the details of your life.

Use the New Moon today to jot down everything that you want to release, and then write out all that you desire as if you already had it. Your brain is particularly receptive under a New Moon, and this is the last day before Mercury goes retrograde, so you'll have a chance to refine your goals and finish what's been left undone. Be sure to get out a candle to symbolize the light that's come to completion, and invite the support that you know is all around you.

AFFIRMATION FOR THE DAY:
Fear is the shadow that cannot exist in my light.

BIG SPINS OF THE DAY:
New Moon at 24° Gemini: 8:14 P.M. PDT / 11:14 P.M. EDT

○◑◐●

FRIDAY

June 15

MOON IN GEMINI/CANCER
MERCURY RETROGRADE BEGINS
SUCCESS RATING: ★★

Far too many warnings about the infamous Mercury Retrograde exist, I'm afraid. And since they're unfounded and produce only dread, you won't be hearing them from me. Most of this alarm is the result of ignorance and our desire to have a scapegoat for our irresponsible choices (please refer to the section at the beginning of the book on this subject).

That said, today begins Mercury's backward journey, which just means that you'll be allowed a chance to review the past few weeks and be given heightened intuition, as well as clearer insight into your motives and actions. The real activity doesn't happen until the planet builds up momentum (it slows down to a stop before going in reverse), so move slowly and let yourself adjust to this new cycle.

This is the time when things begin to break down because of your unwillingness to emulate Mercury's cycle. Stop, take a look, and then start moving—it's easy if you just tune in to the energy around you. And if you won't stop on your own, the Universe will be happy to do it for you.

Most of the day brings in the energy of the Cancer Moon, and attention on home and family may seem enhanced. This Moon does tend to bring up insecurities, so be the person in the world reflecting stability and reason, and you'll get what you give.

AFFIRMATION FOR THE DAY:
I use the planets to reflect my consciousness, not to *be* my consciousness.

BIG SPINS OF THE DAY:
Moon Void of Course: 2:59 A.M. PDT / 5:59 A.M. EDT until
Moon enters Cancer: 6:46 A.M. PDT / 9:46 A.M. EDT
Mercury goes Retrograde 12° Cancer: 4:33 P.M. PDT / 7:33 P.M. EDT

○◑◐●

SATURDAY

June 16

MOON IN CANCER
SUCCESS RATING: ★★

You'll probably feel that you're more centered today after yesterday's mammoth changes in tone, but you still may want to move slowly. The Cancer Moon is unpredictable: Sometimes you feel great under it, and other times you just don't (can you say "moody"?). This also holds true for people around you, so it's best to avoid being too harsh if someone's negative vibe is getting to you. Letting others find their balance before reacting is one gift you can offer with little effort.

By the afternoon, the Moon's contact with Uranus will have lit the fuse, and energy should be abundant. Someone from your past may irritate you, so the better you take care of yourself in the morning, the better you'll be able to deflect any annoyance.

AFFIRMATION FOR THE DAY:
My home is filled with a loving
force that penetrates any wall.

BIG SPINS OF THE DAY:
None

○◑◐●

SUNDAY

June 17

MOON IN CANCER/LEO
SUCCESS RATING: ★★

The groggy feeling that you probably have this morning will be gone by noon as the Moon prepares to enter the more optimistic sign of Leo. Let your own pace dictate the speed of your day . . . there's no need to force yourself to perform at any level other than your own.

The Leo Moon is the perfect placement for the celebration of Father's Day, because the myth of this sign is about the quest for the father. Leo reminds you to find the part of you that protects and defends your choices, as a paternal figure would. If you're engaged in celebrating your own pop today, remember to appreciate the pressure that all dads endure in a culture that doesn't make it easy for them to show how they feel. Simultaneously, recall your inner father—a voice that supports you in all your endeavors—and use this day to strengthen that part of you.

You may feel the intensity of an upcoming connection with the Sun and Pluto just below the surface of your consciousness. If symptoms such as slight paranoia, an increase in the desire for a good mystery, or fantasies of empowerment enter your mind, then you're simply in tune with the song of the Universe.

Be the observer today, and watch how you adjust. Wonderful things are coming, and you're the magnet for them.

AFFIRMATION FOR THE DAY:
I make the decision to trust everyone in my life, because in doing so, I affirm my own trust.

BIG SPINS OF THE DAY:
Moon Void of Course: 12:40 A.M. PDT / 3:40 A.M. EDT until
Moon enters Leo: 10:25 A.M. PDT / 1:25 P.M. EDT

○◐◑●

MONDAY

June 18

MOON IN LEO
SUCCESS RATING: ★★

Get up, get out, move your arms, and shout! Okay, don't shout *at* anyone, but do shake away any residual worries and woes that you brought with you from yesterday. This is a great day, full of wonderful opportunities, thanks to the spirited connections that the Moon is making. Although the Leo Moon wants you to be proud, don't hold your head up so high that you can't see the people around you, especially the ones who've been there for you with few complaints or expectations.

Be generous and tip big. You know that it's all about adding your light to the light around you, so be the one who reminds everyone else that happiness is a choice. It's not about what you say today—it's about who you are.

The connection of Saturn and Neptune prevent this day from being a good one to sign big contracts, but it won't be long before the planets' impact peaks and quickly diminishes. Until then, avoid launching a new business or other venture.

AFFIRMATION FOR THE DAY:
I see the love that I have inside
of me in everyone around me.

BIG SPINS OF THE DAY:
Sun opposes Pluto: 11:46 P.M. PDT / 2:46 A.M. EDT (Tuesday)

○◑◐●

TUESDAY

June 19

MOON IN LEO/VIRGO
SUCCESS RATING: ★★★★

Venus and Jupiter are making their second and last alignment of this kind for the year. It's a fast-moving connection, and every opportunity should be seized to make the most of it. If there's something that you're trying to achieve, go for it today—especially if it involves another person. Venus and Jupiter are both planets that have traditionally represented success in matters dealing with the heart, and that includes all that you desire. Ask for what you want today . . . everyone else is under this same influence, so if you don't speak up, someone else just might.

The Moon will shift into the more humble sign of Virgo this afternoon, so leap big in the morning and sort everything else out later. Saying "Good luck" would be unnecessary, since you already have plenty of it today! Now get an early start, and keep your eyes open for a few excellent opportunities.

AFFIRMATION FOR THE DAY:
My essence extends into eternity.

BIG SPINS OF THE DAY:
Moon Void of Course: 2:22 P.M. PDT / 5:22 P.M. EDT until
Moon enters Virgo: 5:46 P.M. PDT / 8:46 P.M. EDT
Venus trines Jupiter: 3:48 P.M. PDT / 6:48 P.M. EDT

○◑◐●

WEDNESDAY

June 20

MOON IN VIRGO
SUCCESS RATING: ★★★

The Virgo Moon tends to bring out your inner hermit and organizer. You may still be riding the high from yesterday's planetary alignments and could even be feeling them more intensely today. There's no denying that there's passion in the air, and this can apply to anything in your life that you care about, including work, art, a particular person, or the well-being of small animals. If you've been trying to conceive an idea or a baby, this cycle is one of the most fertile you can find, so plant your seeds!

This is the last day for the Sun to be in Gemini, moving toward the official first day of summer tomorrow. Act as if you were relocating and get your things organized so that the transition can be smooth and nothing gets broken in transit.

If you're still feeling blocked or limited, with a general undertone of depression, you're experiencing the Saturn-Neptune alignment. Use it to purge unhealthy thoughts, and remind yourself that it's helping you sort through a persistent confusion. . . . Things will untangle in time.

AFFIRMATION FOR THE DAY:
I am the embodiment of creativity.

BIG SPINS OF THE DAY:
None

Happy Birthday, Cancer!

JUNE 21–JULY 22

Cancers don't have friends . . . they have *family members*. If you're lucky enough to be embraced by a person born under this sign, you can bet that you'll always have a shoulder to cry on, a cheerleader to encourage you onward, and a personal comedian to help you keep the proper perspective during your most difficult challenges.

You won't find a more devoted caregiver than a Crab. This sign is the most imaginative of the Zodiac, drawing on inner lunar magic. Cancers can make you laugh or cry through their ability to connect right to your own emotions. When they're consciously aware, they're wise and intuitive and know how to gently give support where it's needed. However, if Cancers let their insecurities rule them, they can be moody and controlling, believing that they know best about your well-being. But that's only to be expected from the Zodiac's matriarchs (whether male or female)—they certainly had lots of training. As children, Cancers had their own controlling figure to confront, and they often continue having to contend with her as adults.

The tough-shelled Crab is an awesome ally, one who can bat big, watery eyes and melt the heart of the most ferocious beast. Ultimately, Cancers must learn how to give themselves the nurturance that they so readily provide for others. Lucky for them, they're good with money . . . but don't expect them to reveal how much they have! Money is one security blanket that Cancers won't leave behind.

AFFIRMATIONS FOR CANCER:

I am grateful for my depth of feeling.

I can care for others by caring for myself.

I am loved deeply and profoundly, and it shows everywhere around me.

○◐◑●

THURSDAY

June 21

SUMMER SOLSTICE
SUN IN CANCER
MOON IN VIRGO
SUCCESS RATING: ★★★

The Sun leaves the dualistic sign of Gemini today and brings us into summer. For the next 30 days, the family, home, and security issues of Cancer will take the front seat. Be aware that since the Sun is changing signs, this is a transition day, and it's always a good idea to move just a little slower than usual so that you can keep the right amount of balance throughout your day.

Mars and Pluto are adding some jet fuel to the mix, and you may find that the level of your desires is at an all-time high. Use this surge of energy to set in motion some of the things that you've wished for, since nothing can prevent you from achieving your dreams. Direct your attention toward what you want, and see yourself as a magnet drawing it toward you. Be careful, though: You're hot, and you could burn innocent bystanders along the way.

One of the negative sides of a Mars-Pluto connection is anger. You may see a show of it reflected in the events of the world—the news could be interesting and include some intense images. This is a fast-moving set of planets, so if there's something that you want, go and get it. Show the world what's possible!

AFFIRMATION FOR THE DAY:
My desires are small reflections of the grandeur that is truly available to me.

BIG SPINS OF THE DAY:
Mars trines Pluto: 6:33 A.M. PDT / 9:33 A.M. EDT
Sun enters Cancer: 11:07 A.M. PDT / 2:07 P.M. EDT
Moon Void of Course: 11:50 P.M. PDT / 2:50 A.M. EDT (Friday) until tomorrow

○◑◐●

FRIDAY

June 22

FIRST QUARTER MOON IN LIBRA
MOON IN VIRGO/LIBRA
SUCCESS RATING: ★★

The tide is changing, and there's no question that this day is signaling a shift in the air. Although it's not as ominous as it sounds and certainly nothing you haven't felt before, this First Quarter Moon is bringing your attention to the areas of your life that may need some adjustment.

There's nothing you can do but observe yourself and notice what activities are calling you. You're leaving the self-critical Virgo Moon and are being asked to lift your head up and recognize the things in your life that aren't in balance. Perhaps you've been working too many hours and neglecting your own time . . . or you may have been investing *too* much time in personal matters. Whatever the situation, today calls for you to fix what's broken.

AFFIRMATION FOR THE DAY:
I accept that the outer world is reflecting my inner one, and I use this information to support myself.

BIG SPINS OF THE DAY:
Void of Course Moon: until 4:44 A.M. PDT / 7:44 A.M. EDT
Moon enters Libra: 4:44 A.M. PDT / 7:44 A.M. EDT
First Quarter Moon 1° of Libra: 6:16 A.M. PDT / 9:19 A.M. EDT

○◑◐●

SATURDAY

June 23

MOON IN LIBRA
SUCCESS RATING: ★★

Uranus is the planet that rules big change, and today it stops in its tracks and begins its yearly journey backward through the Zodiac, a trek that will last for the next five months. Aquarians will probably feel the effect of this motion, since they're being asked to go inside and approach life through their hearts rather than their minds (no easy feat).

You may notice a lot of attention being paid to scientific breakthroughs and advancements in technology, since Uranus is allowing our higher minds to refine ideas that have already been presented. On a personal level, this retrograde motion may require a day of adjusting—you may feel tired or even unimaginative as your creative mind changes course. The all-day Libra Moon will help make this a fun day anyway, so get together with some friends and keep the conversation light.

(**Special note:** Venus, the planet of love and appreciation, will be moving backward next month and will revisit this day before going forward again. Begin taking notes about which issues are arising so that you can reference them when Venus makes her encore. Don't worry—I'll remind you!)

AFFIRMATION FOR THE DAY:
I am a part of an endless light whose source is love.

BIG SPINS OF THE DAY:
Uranus goes Retrograde: 7:43 A.M. PDT / 10:43 A.M. EDT

○◑◐●

S U N D A Y

June 24

MOON IN LIBRA/SCORPIO
SUCCESS RATING: ★★

I hope that you're not tired of adjusting, because Mars is leaving Aries today and entering the earthbound sign of Taurus, which may take you a day or two to get used to. While in Aries, Mars kept your defenses and energy high so that you could face the challenges that came your way. In fact, Mars in that alignment loves a challenge so much that you might have found yourself causing trouble just to satisfy an urge.

Now the planet immerses you in the material world. Financial issues may become your focal point, or you could find that money has already driven you for way too long. However you deal with Mars, one thing is for sure: Your attention will be focused on your surroundings—your body, your comfort, and your security. The dramatic shift in energy from Aries to Taurus might zap some of your energy, but don't fret . . . you may just have to linger around the hot tub for a couple of days, with intermittent breaks for big meals. And speaking of eating, your lust for food may spike (just go with it).

AFFIRMATION FOR THE DAY:
My body knows exactly what to do.

BIG SPINS OF THE DAY:
Moon Void of Course: 12:23 P.M. PDT / 3:23 P.M. EDT until
Moon enters Scorpio: 5:27 P.M. PDT / 8:27 P.M. EDT
Mars enters Taurus: 2:27 P.M. PDT / 5:27 P.M. EDT

○ ◑ ◐ ●

MONDAY

June 25

MOON IN SCORPIO
SUCCESS RATING: ★

This is the last clash of Saturn and Neptune (see February 28), and you may already feel its effects and resolutions coming through. It's wonderful that I'm writing this prior to gaining any knowledge of the first hit back in August 2006, as I'm only able to ground my interpretation in what the planets represent (including their history). From what I can see based on past events, right now we're probably learning how to adjust to an economic pinch and the development of vaccines for new diseases.

This clash between control (Saturn) and freedom (Neptune) can bring an end to a cycle of tyranny somewhere in the world. Perhaps your own political divide is changing for the better . . . it's certainly hard to know, but by the time you're reading this, you can put it together. Someplace there's a structure being torn down, either literally or figuratively.

It's certainly not a time when you want to launch a business, but this relationship between Saturn and Neptune will not be back for many years, so all you have to do is wait a few days for its impact to weaken considerably. Don't let the Scorpio Moon conjure any fears in you, but rather, use your deeper radar to find the truth—which is always simple and supportive.

AFFIRMATION FOR THE DAY:
I choose to see my life from the highest perspective.

BIG SPINS OF THE DAY:
Saturn opposes Neptune: 8:55 A.M. PDT / 11:55 A.M. EDT

○◑◐●

TUESDAY

June 26

MOON IN SCORPIO
SUCCESS RATING: ★

Schedule meetings and important events for the first part of the day, and leave the afternoon open. There's an unusually long Void of Course Moon today, and although this is a great time to finish what hasn't been completed, it's not always the best occasion to start something new.

You might need some time alone so that you can release any stress that may have accumulated. This is the kind of day when it seems as though everyone needs something from you, yet no one has what *you* want.

The fun part of the Scorpio Moon is that it takes you on a personal, inner journey to discover aspects of yourself that you haven't seen for a while. Go on that internal voyage today, since a little fresh air on the inside does a world of good.

Try to avoid signing anything that's binding (like a contract), and use today to review your course. Things will get lighter soon—you have my word.

AFFIRMATION FOR THE DAY:
I love looking within.

BIG SPINS OF THE DAY:
Moon Void of Course: 1:24 P.M. PDT / 4:24 P.M. EDT until tomorrow

○◑◐●

WEDNESDAY

June 27

MOON IN SCORPIO/SAGITTARIUS
SUCCESS RATING: ★

Newsworthy alignments take the stage as the planets shake things up a bit. Keep your eyes on world events for the next couple of days just so that you can understand the tone affecting the globe. Mars is closing in on Saturn and can make achieving even the smallest feat feel as though it were an uphill battle.

As the Moon slips into Sagittarius, you'll begin to be more optimistic, but this could be the kind of day that almost seems to work against your progress. If you're swimming upstream, you aren't paying attention to the flow, so get yourself into alignment with the forces around you. If you decide that nothing seems to be working, then *stop* working. Use this cycle to hone your intuition, since it's rarely wrong.

AFFIRMATION FOR THE DAY:
I accept everything that comes my way with open arms, because I know that it is here to serve me.

BIG SPINS OF THE DAY:
Moon Void of Course: until 5:25 A.M. PDT / 8:25 A.M. EDT
Moon enters Sagittarius: 5:25 A.M. PDT / 8:25 A.M. EDT

○◑◐●

THURSDAY

June 28

MOON IN SAGITTARIUS
SUCCESS RATING: ★

It's a very important day for you Mercury Retrograde watchers! The planet is making what's known as an Inferior Conjunction to the Sun (say what?). During every Retrograde, at some point Mercury will be at the same degree as the Sun, and this turns everything around symbolically. Our minds are reactivated under this aspect, and we can begin to think about moving forward (as opposed to dwelling on the past).

Misunderstandings are more easily corrected today. If you have something that you need to talk about, you may want to start doing so, since people will be more receptive than usual. There's a little frustration building—a push-pull of some kind—but don't undermine your chance to have a good chat by being stubborn.

Remember to watch the news in order to get information you can use to reflect on what kind of energies are dominating.

AFFIRMATION FOR THE DAY:
My words flow through me lovingly and accurately, communicating exactly what I meant them to.

BIG SPINS OF THE DAY:
Mercury conjunct Sun: 11:40 A.M. PDT / 2:40 P.M. EDT

JUNE

○◑◐●

FRIDAY

June 29

MOON IN SAGITTARIUS/CAPRICORN
SUCCESS RATING: ★

When there's a Void of Course Moon in the middle of the day, it's best to look around and see what things in your life could use a bit of tidying up . . . after all, it's better than sitting around feeling listless. There's a Full Moon tomorrow, and you'll appreciate having done a little prep work today so that nothing is lingering.

Accomplishments seem to matter under this Full Moon, so don't be surprised if it appears that everyone's sense of humor has gone missing. Be brave today, make people laugh, and remember not to take yourself or your situation too seriously. Give the world a smiling face, and remind people that they're more than what they do.

Since the Full Moon is early tomorrow, you might want to light a candle tonight with a special intention to see all the beautiful gifts that are coming your way.

AFFIRMATION FOR THE DAY:
My smile shines through any
expression that my face is wearing.

BIG SPINS OF THE DAY:
Moon Void of Course: 10:08 A.M. PDT / 1:08 P.M. EDT until
Moon enters Capricorn: 3:06 P.M. PDT / 6:06 P.M. EDT

○◑◐●

SATURDAY

June 30

FULL MOON IN CAPRICORN
SUCCESS RATING: ★

Feel the power of the Full Moon, and watch the world around you as it shows its extremes of expression. Sometimes it seems as though nothing is neutral on a Full Moon, since your emotions tend to expand and your rational mind takes a temporary backseat. Today brings an intense ending to a month that started out with ease, which may cause you to wonder what all these serious issues are doing in the mix.

Today wouldn't be a good time to sign an agreement or launch a business because of the lack of clarity that's typical of a Venus-Neptune clash. Your romantic life may also take a hit as you struggle to find the meaning in your connections.

Under the Capricorn Moon, everything is about purpose, but it only lasts one more day. Try not to take the harsher realities of the day too seriously—after all, there's a part of you that remembers the transitory nature of everything.

AFFIRMATION FOR THE DAY:
What I truly desire is already here.

BIG SPINS OF THE DAY:
Full Moon at 8° Capricorn: 6:50 A.M. PDT / 9:50 A.M. EDT
Venus opposes Neptune: 8:32 A.M. PDT / 11:32 A.M. EDT

Thought for the Month

The Blindness of Love

Although the expression "Love is blind" is often used to excuse someone who's romantically involved with an unkind or unattractive person, its implication can certainly stretch to include all areas of love. The phrase could also be seen as a spiritual directive asking us to love others, in spite of their appearance or actions.

Let's play a game. Next time you run into a stranger or someone with whom you have a limited opportunity to exchange words, such as a bank or grocery-store clerk, pretend that you've known him or her since birth. Imagine that you have that same "love-is-blind" feeling for this individual that you have for your dog, cat, or childhood friend. You don't have to say anything, since you just have this "inner familiarity" of having known him or her all your life. Age, race, or gender doesn't matter . . . for just a few seconds, you're in the other person's energy as if you'd known each other forever.

The point of this little exercise may seem clear to most of you, but in that moment of practicing blind love for a stranger, what's really happening is that you're actually practicing feeling it for yourself. We tend to forgive our old friends and family members their idiosyncrasies, but we rarely give ourselves the same level of compassion when we find that we acted inappropriately or made some kind of mistake. Just think about the last time you stayed awake all night reviewing some action that you regretted.

It's time to start extending compassion to others—if for no other reason than to become accustomed to extending it to yourself.

JULY 2007
SUMMARY

The first weekend of July introduces a Venus-Pluto alignment that's heralded as one of the sexiest aspects around, and it's supported by a couple of other nice connections that could set the tone for many of you to fall in love this month. Although July doesn't host any of the big planetary changes that June did, it doesn't lack for events—in an almost Libra-like fashion, July giveth . . . and it taketh away.

For starters, this month brings an end to the Mercury Retrograde on the 9th. Although many of you will celebrate the direct motion of the planet, it can cause chaos if you push thoughtlessly forward. On the 14th, July hosts a New Moon at 22° of Cancer, and it simultaneously introduces Venus into the sign of Virgo. That makes the week of July 8 a powerful one—you get to feel sexy, put your head on straight, and then turn prudish and worry about money (just kidding). The Sun will enter Leo on the 22nd, and everyone in your life who was born under that sign will start feeling happier, since they finally get to rest. That's because they know that over the next month, there's at least one day reserved for them to receive undivided attention! (That's kind of a joke.)

In the "taketh-away" department, July will be the month that brings Venus out of her forward motion and sets her to spin retrograde in Virgo. If you're in the beauty industry, this is the time to market your business to play on customers' feeling not attractive enough . . . your sales will soar!

July highlights:

July 8: Venus trines Pluto
July 9: Mercury goes direct
July 14: New Moon at 22° Cancer; Venus enters Virgo
July 22: Sun enters Leo
July 27: Venus goes Retrograde
July 29: Full Moon at 7° Aquarius

○◑◐●

SUNDAY

July 1

MOON IN CAPRICORN/AQUARIUS
SUCCESS RATING: ★

The first day of July greets you with an underwhelming all-day Void of Course Moon. It looks as if this is a perfect way to send the message that you need to rest and take in the upcoming month with a relaxed and open mind. It's not as if there isn't a lot of activity in the air—there is, but this is the sort of day that's better met with openness, rather than defensive preparedness.

Venus is holding hands with Saturn, suggesting a quality of caution and maturity when it comes to matters of the heart. In addition, Mercury's connection with Mars points to the possibility of irritability, especially if you don't do something to stimulate your mind. The solution is pretty clear: A ride to the mountains or a nice long walk in the park will probably help you shake off the day's tired feeling and provide the stimulation you need to feel connected. The Aquarius Moon takes flight late tonight, so an early bedtime will ensure a positive outlook.

AFFIRMATION FOR THE DAY:
Everything I do has a purpose that is often much more important than I can see.

BIG SPINS OF THE DAY:
Moon Void of Course: 1:46 A.M. PDT / 4:46 A.M. EDT until
Moon enters Aquarius: 10:25 P.M. PDT / 1:25 A.M. EDT (Monday)
Venus conjuncts Saturn: 7:41 A.M. PDT / 10:41 A.M. EDT
Mercury sextiles Mars: 12:07 P.M. PDT / 3:07 P.M. EDT

○ ◑ ◐ ●

MONDAY

July 2

MOON IN AQUARIUS
SUCCESS RATING: ★★★

Hopefully, you got to rest after yesterday's long Void of Course, and you're ready to take the world by storm. You're coming into a lucky cycle (I can't believe I finally get to say that!), as the Sun and Jupiter make an alliance, along with a few other participants. Remember that you're still under the Full Moon influence of last Saturday, and this is just about the time when the gifts should start pouring in (my contact information is somewhere at the back of the book if *you* feel like giving).

Things are really lightening up, and with the help of the Aquarius Moon, you're able to see your life from the perspective of the eagle, high off the ground. Enjoy yourself today, but get some things done . . . you know how self-critical you are when you haven't been productive. Agreements made today are in the safe zone.

AFFIRMATION FOR THE DAY:
Today I stop harming myself with critical thoughts and replace them with supportive, encouraging ones.

BIG SPINS OF THE DAY:
None

○◑◐●

TUESDAY

July 3

MOON IN AQUARIUS
SUCCESS RATING: ★★★

More of yesterday's magic is in the air today as the Aquarius Moon takes hold and reminds you to break some rules and have a little fun. The morning should be a smoother ride than the afternoon, so if you have work to do or meetings to attend, try to schedule them before noon.

A few minor problems may greet you in the afternoon, but you're given the opportunity to bite your tongue and take a higher road. An authority figure in your life may seem to be picking on you, but trust me—you can make the situation worse than it is by turning it into a drama. Choose your battles wisely today. You can have an amazing time, or you can make being a victim the theme of the day . . . you *do* have a choice in the matter.

A shopping spree won't hurt anything, but a long, hot bath is cheaper and will have longer-lasting effects. Dreams should also prove very powerful tonight if you can get your mind to slow down.

AFFIRMATION FOR THE DAY:
I am the perfect size: infinite.

BIG SPINS OF THE DAY:
Moon Void of Course: 11:03 P.M. PDT / 2:03 A.M. EDT (Wednesday)

○◑◐●

WEDNESDAY

July 4

MOON IN AQUARIUS/PISCES
SUCCESS RATING: ★★★

It's a wonderful day to use the metaphor of independence, since the Sun is leaving the *independent* sign of Aquarius and entering the more *dependent* Pisces. I'm not describing Pisces this way in a negative sense, but it *is* more difficult for the sign to keep the emotional distance that Aquarius does. With that in mind, let today be a reminder that even though you're under the compassionate energy of the Pisces Moon, you can sense the hearts of those around you and still maintain your own identity. In other words, you don't have to solve everyone's problems—you may *feel* them, but you don't have to *fix* them. And if you understand that one, you've claimed your real independence!

The Pisces Moon often brings a resurgence of people from your past . . . perhaps you've traveled to see them, or vice versa. In any case, view these individuals as reflections of how you've grown. Also, control your use of alcohol or other substances today.

AFFIRMATION FOR THE DAY:
My feelings are part of me, and I support them completely.

BIG SPINS OF THE DAY:
Moon enters Pisces: 3:53 A.M. PDT / 6:53 A.M. EDT

○◑◐●

THURSDAY

July 5

MOON IN PISCES
SUCCESS RATING: ★★★

Love is in the air, so take a deep breath! For those of you seeking a romantic partner, your chances of finding one are greatly increased today, and for those of you who'd like to fall in love with what you're doing, your odds of that also good.

A day such as this isn't always about love (although it's easy to relate it to the excitement that comes from a wonderful encounter)—it can be about appreciating where you are and what you have. You have the opportunity to view your situation through the window of gratitude, or to see it as something that's being done *to* you by forces beyond your control—the choice is yours. The energy to be empowered *or* to be victimized are both in today's sky . . . only you can choose which you want to embrace. (*Hint*: It's not the second one.)

AFFIRMATION FOR THE DAY:
I see the beauty that is me reflected in all of life.

BIG SPINS OF THE DAY:
None

○◑◐●

FRIDAY

July 6

MOON IN PISCES/ARIES
SUCCESS RATING: ★★★

The transition from Pisces to Aries is one of the most obvious changes in the Zodiac. In Pisces, you merge with the world around you and are inclined to follow the lead of the strongest energy. In Aries, you tend to just *do,* without noticing if you're following or leading. . . . Today you'll begin your forward launch.

The best thing you can do is to shake off what remains of the heavy energy that you felt yesterday. What made you cry tears of compassion then will have no effect on you today. Aries is the warrior sign, and when the Moon is in it, you *become* a warrior. So go out and act on this energy: Hunt down food at the grocery store, ambush your co-workers at the watercooler, or take a long walk . . . just do *something* to get this Aries Moon hopping! You may want to cool things down in the afternoon, since it looks as though misunderstandings could be prominent.

AFFIRMATION FOR THE DAY:
I am invincible!

BIG SPINS OF THE DAY:
Moon Void of Course: 3:09 A.M. PDT / 6:09 A.M. EDT until
Moon enters Aries: 7:57 A.M. PDT / 10:57 A.M. EDT

○◑◐●

SATURDAY

July 7

LAST QUARTER MOON IN ARIES
SUCCESS RATING: ★★★

An uninterrupted, all-day Aries Moon shakes the sky today, and heaven help the person who tries to control your energy or tell you what to do. The irony is that you may find *yourself* trying to be bossy under this influence, too, and the result could be a day filled with finger-pointing, power-pushing, and impatient people walking around with no sports on TV to divert their aggressions.

You certainly could stay home if you like . . . although if the Sun is out, you can forget that idea. Aries Moons make you yearn to be active, and the Sun is an irresistible magnet. There's nothing in your way today to prevent you from having a great time (thank goodness!), provided that you clear any obstacles that this Last Quarter Moon may present. Go play, and leave the mess for everyone else to pick up.

AFFIRMATION FOR THE DAY:
My power is pure, and I use it to support my life fully.

BIG SPINS OF THE DAY:
Last Quarter Moon 15° Aries: 9:54 A.M. PDT / 12:54 P.M. EDT

○◑◐●

SUNDAY

July 8

MOON IN ARIES/TAURUS
SUCCESS RATING: ★★★

Mercury, the planet of thinking, has been reducing its speed to a crawl as it prepares for the process of moving forward again. During this slowdown, you may feel a little stuck or less mentally sharp than usual. The effect may inhibit your ability to think clearly and could actually incite a mild depression, but it won't last long.

The Moon is supporting your slower pace by entering the sign of Taurus. You may find yourself placing attention on your body and removing attention from your mind. To further aid you in decelerating is Venus, who's playing a very sexy role with Pluto and is making your sensual side sing (luckily, no one can hear it but you!).

You may find yourself irresistibly attracted to the idea of soaking in a hot bath, getting a massage, or engaging in any other form of physical activity that reminds you that it's good to feel your body.

AFFIRMATION FOR THE DAY:
I transcend all of my limitations.

BIG SPINS OF THE DAY:
Moon Void of Course: 6:06 A.M. PDT / 9:06 A.M. EDT until
Moon enters Taurus: 10:54 A.M. PDT / 1:54 P.M. EDT
Venus trines Pluto: 6:04 P.M. PDT / 9:04 P.M. EDT

○◑◐●

MONDAY

July 9

MERCURY RETROGRADE ENDS
MOON IN TAURUS
SUCCESS RATING: ★★

The all-day Taurus Moon will allow you to feel the effects of today's big event: Mercury moving forward. I'll try not to lecture you too strongly if you're among the millions of people who celebrate this event. After all, it makes sense that our culture, which worships pushing ahead, would shun a planet that suggests you turn inward. Whatever your beliefs about the Mercury Retrograde, however, the fact remains that it's over tonight.

Now, don't forget that Mercury must once again—for the third time this cycle—retrace the same path over which it just went backward. That means that you'll definitely see conclusions to your stories, get a chance to complete what wasn't finished, and have the opportunity to change your mind about decisions that were made.

Make this a day that celebrates your comforts, but move slowly . . . there's always that issue of needing to acclimate before you feel completely centered.

AFFIRMATION FOR THE DAY:
Fear cannot exist in me—I am
love, and love is fear's opposite.

BIG SPINS OF THE DAY:
Mercury Retrograde ends: 7:10 P.M. PDT / 10:10 P.M. EDT

○◑◐●

TUESDAY

July 10

MOON IN TAURUS/GEMINI
SUCCESS RATING: ★★

Respect the final hours of the Taurus Moon by moving slowly and sensually, as if you love being in your body. Also, note that the Moon will be Void of Course until the afternoon, so if you have old business to take care of, do so early.

Later in the afternoon, the Moon will enter the lighthearted sign of Gemini and will help ignite your mind, which has probably been feeling like slush. Clearly, this isn't the day to make big decisions . . . not only are you prone to rub people the wrong way, but your logic might be skewed as well.

Don't let the more depressed side of Gemini take over your mood—if you're down, let the feeling pass. The shift *is* coming, so just ride it out. Talking to friends and family members is a great way to get your head turned back so that you're looking in the right direction.

AFFIRMATION FOR THE DAY:
In you, I see the part of me that calls for love.

BIG SPINS OF THE DAY:
Moon Void of Course: 9:54 A.M. PDT / 12:54 P.M. EDT until
Moon enters Gemini: 1:10 P.M. PDT / 4:10 P.M. EDT
Sun trines Uranus: 10:33 P.M. PDT / 1:33 A.M. EDT (Wednesday)

○◑◐●

WEDNESDAY

July 11

MOON IN GEMINI
SUCCESS RATING: ★★★

All right, you're coming back and very likely feeling lighter than you have in a while. The Gemini Moon is in full swing and calls upon you to make connections with like-minded friends. The excitement of yesterday's Sun-Uranus alignment has carried over into today, and you may feel empowered to break the rules that need to be broken.

You're always cautioned to stay grounded and keep hold of common sense, so buckle your seat belt, look both ways before crossing the street, and—whatever you do—*don't* step on the sidewalk cracks (I'm kidding).

Books and magazines could provide good fodder for your mind, but don't substitute gossip for mental stimulation. You may find that sleep is elusive due to the Moon's interaction with Uranus, so cut out the stimulants early tonight, and try to keep your mood in balance.

AFFIRMATION FOR THE DAY:
I am grateful for the gifts in my life—
those I can see and those I cannot.

BIG SPINS OF THE DAY:
None

○◑◐●

THURSDAY

July 12

MOON IN GEMINI/CANCER
SUCCESS RATING: ★★★

The morning holds the last hours of the Gemini Moon prior to its shift into Cancer. Wrap up your work early, and use the afternoon to plan the new colors for your favorite room. Cancer Moons conjure up the artist within you, as well as a longing for security . . . satisfy your urges with a childlike treat.

You may find yourself struggling with someone over issues of power. Your opponent could be a boss, colleague, or teammate, but it's important not to lose your cool. The emotions of the morning will balance out, and by tonight, you'll be feeling a tender connection to your inner self.

There's nothing preventing you from launching a successful endeavor . . . just try to avoid doing so during the Void of Course Moon.

AFFIRMATION FOR THE DAY:
I choose to live my life with confidence and empowerment, even in the midst of uncertainty.

BIG SPINS OF THE DAY:
Moon Void of Course: 2:13 P.M. PDT / 5:13 P.M. EDT until
Moon enters Cancer: 3:40 P.M. PDT / 6:40 P.M. EDT

○ ◑ ◐ ●

FRIDAY

July 13

MOON IN CANCER
SUCCESS RATING: ★★

It's the day before the New Moon, and, as always, I'm reminding you about the possible feelings of hopelessness that can emerge. As the Moon readies itself for a new cycle, you can follow suit and prepare to release the past and bring your attention to the present.

The Moon in Cancer paints your world in an array of colors, some much brighter than others. Take a look at the canvas around you, and use the images it holds as a way to understand how you're feeling. For example, if you see a homeless person on the street and have pity for him, there may be a part of *you* that feels homeless . . . and so forth.

The Cancer Moon is the perfect time to address the parts of your life that need to be nurtured. Tomorrow's New Moon will accelerate this activity, and you may find that you have a long list of changes you'd like to see in your life. These Moons can incite worries related to security and safety, so use your concerns to compose a list of desires.

Since tomorrow's New Moon occurs very early in the morning, send out your intentions tonight—that will give you time to empower them while you sleep.

AFFIRMATION FOR THE DAY:
All my thoughts are expansive because they reflect me.

BIG SPINS OF THE DAY:
None

○◑◐●

SATURDAY

July 14

NEW MOON IN CANCER
MOON IN CANCER/LEO
SUCCESS RATING: ★

An all-day Void of Course Moon occurs just after the New Moon and makes it possible for you to fully absorb the lunar energies. Venus will enter the meticulous sign of Virgo and activate your discriminating mind, helping to eliminate any fogginess that you may be feeling—fog has *no* chance when Venus in Virgo is on the scene. Your specific and distinct preferences will begin to emerge, helping you sort through any mess that may be in your path, so discard things that are no longer useful to you.

This effect will grow in strength over the next few days . . . allow yourself some time to adjust. Until Venus gets a chance to fully enter your consciousness, try to avoid any legal agreements or documents, as you'll want to make sure that you have a strong footing. Let the New Moon start reflecting some of the Sun's light before you begin anything new. When you see a sliver of it, that means you're getting a green light.

AFFIRMATION FOR THE DAY:
I embrace my preferences and recognize that they are temporary inclinations, not declarations of judgment.

BIG SPINS OF THE DAY:
New Moon at 22° Cancer: 5:04 A.M. PDT / 8:04 A.M. EDT
Moon Void of Course: 5:04 A.M. PDT / 8:04 A.M. EDT until
Moon enters Leo: 7:44 P.M. PDT / 10:44 P.M. EDT
Venus enters Virgo: 11:24 A.M. PDT / 2:24 P.M. EDT

○ ◑ ◐ ●

SUNDAY

July 15

MOON IN LEO
SUCCESS RATING: ★★★★

Fire signs dominate the celestial scene as the Moon in Leo holds hands with Jupiter in Sagittarius. Optimism will be hard to squelch today, so don't waste time in bed—get up and get your day going!

The day after the New Moon is packed with power, and you're a walking bundle of inspiration. Don't let the Leo Moon trick you into becoming a drama king or queen; instead, choose your overreactions wisely, and don't waste them on spilled milk. This is one of the few days when you get to shake off your worries and fears and replace them with an unquestionable truth: *You are very special and deserve a good life.* Spread that thought throughout your body, and share it with those around you who aren't feeling it yet.

Make sure that you wind down early today. There's so much energy in the air that it may be hard for you to fall asleep . . . but your presence is so important at school or the office that you must get some rest.

AFFIRMATION FOR THE DAY:
I am the reflection of pure delight.

BIG SPINS OF THE DAY:
None

○◑◐●

MONDAY

July 16

MOON IN LEO
SUCCESS RATING: ★★★

There's another beautiful day on the celestial horizon as the Moon in Leo dominates the sky. Today the Moon is touching all the big celestial players, which is always a clue that some important events could occur. It connects with Uranus first thing in the morning, and that can activate your inner rebel. Thoughts of playing hooky are fine if you don't have responsibilities to attend to . . . but by the looks of things, you probably do!

Later, the Moon hits Neptune, and the fog returns with regard to some past person or event that must be taken care of. Your energy level could take a hit from midmorning until later in the afternoon, when the Moon touches Saturn. That's when you'll start to feel good if you achieved any of your personal goals, and maybe *not* so good if you didn't—Saturn is so demanding!

Tonight you'll want to reward yourself with an intimate chat, the kind that reminds you that you're not alone in what you see.

AFFIRMATION FOR THE DAY:
I am always empowered by love—inside and out.

BIG SPINS OF THE DAY:
Moon Void of Course: 8:55 P.M. PDT / 11:55 P.M. EDT until tomorrow

○◑◐●

TUESDAY

July 17

MOON IN LEO/VIRGO
SUCCESS RATING: ★★

The Moon changed signs from the optimism of Leo to the humility of Virgo in the wee hours of the morning. The hope of the Virgo Moon is that you can now lower your head just a bit and look at any mess you might have made while dancing around shamelessly under the Leo Moon.

For those of you who confuse Virgo with a schoolmarm who never smiles, you're quite mistaken. This is one of the funniest signs of the Zodiac, with a dry wit that's as quick as it is smart. That particular quality is in you today . . . and you might need it, as the world may be a little depressed due to something in the news. Of course, I could say that about almost any day, but today holds a little tension that may permeate your psyche.

The best course of action under a Virgo Moon is to use the sign's qualities of service and detail management to get through the day. Help a colleague in need of your support, give extra attention to your pets (Virgo rules small animals), and bring some sort of organization to an area in your life that needs it (I'm sure there's a bill that you've been ignoring). Any extra effort you put in now gives you an edge when tomorrow comes, since it may not hold the clarity of today.

AFFIRMATION FOR THE DAY:
I am perfect, as is everyone I see.

BIG SPINS OF THE DAY:
Moon enters Virgo: 2:40 A.M. PDT / 5:40 A.M. EDT

○◑◐●

WEDNESDAY

July 18

MOON IN VIRGO
SUCCESS RATING: ★★

If you find that you're being critical to the extreme, then you aren't taking care of yourself. Sure, there are probably many things you see that are out of place in your life, and people are never going to step up to the plate the way that you do. But if you're complaining about it, that means you've assumed too much responsibility and don't know how to get back to your center.

If the above paragraph describes how you're feeling, then pull yourself inward and spend some time alone . . . you'll be fine in a short while. However, if this description sounds more like your colleague or housemate, then he or she may be acting out in response to your repressed anger, and you *still* need to spend some time alone.

Because the Virgo Moon is focused on the details of the physical world, and that world will invariably need some work, you won't always know when to stop. Today take a few moments to get a little distance from your everyday environment—it will make a vast difference in how you perceive what's going on.

AFFIRMATION FOR THE DAY:
My wholeness is guaranteed and
is not dependent on what I do.

BIG SPINS OF THE DAY:
None

○◑◐●

THURSDAY

July 19

MOON IN VIRGO/LIBRA
SUCCESS RATING: ★★

A Void of Course Moon dominates the morning with its usual suggestion of slowing down and finishing things up. You may find that your mind is working hard—reviewing, worrying, and repeating awful songs that you can't get out of your head . . . well, it's all part of the change from Virgo to Libra. It's almost as if your mental battery has to burn itself out so that it can be recharged with Libra's balanced perspective.

It certainly looks as if this is a day where actual productivity may have to take a backseat. There are just too many distractions, and at least one of them looks pretty important. Let this day guide you to your perfect place, and then stay open to the unexpected.

If you find that you're being asked to prove something to someone, don't ruin your day by worrying—you'll do just fine. Tonight get together with your pack of like-minded friends to complain and get it all out. Enough of the nice-guy stuff for today . . . tomorrow you can send your apologies!

AFFIRMATION FOR THE DAY:
I take responsibility for how I see the world and recognize that I can change my perspective at will.

BIG SPINS OF THE DAY:
Moon Void of Course: 6:45 A.M. PDT / 9:45 A.M. EDT until
Moon enters Libra: 12:54 P.M. PDT / 3:54 P.M. EDT

○◑◐●

FRIDAY

July 20

MOON IN LIBRA
SUCCESS RATING: ★★★

You'll probably be welcoming back your energy today, as the planets are holding steady. The Libra Moon dominates the day, and you'll be compelled to dress up rather than down, due to the sign's love of the beautiful. In addition, friends and colleagues will prove more willing to be cooperative (although there's always that one exception).

A special connection between Mars and Uranus could prove helpful in giving you an extra dose of energy, but you have to be careful with these two. Mars is aggressive, and Uranus is surprising, so accidents could happen when they come together . . . but *only* if you aren't grounded. (Of course, this doesn't apply to rides on planes or other commercial forms of transportation where you're not the driver.)

The positive part of this alignment is that you'll feel free to approach anything and accomplish whatever you put your mind to. However, you won't have much tolerance for authority—so just leave if things get too intense, and don't express your feelings without screening them.

AFFIRMATION FOR THE DAY:
I am a source of light, which I shine everywhere I go.

BIG SPINS OF THE DAY:
Mars sextiles Uranus: 3:13 P.M. PDT / 6:13 P.M. EDT

○◑◐●

SATURDAY

July 21

FIRST QUARTER MOON IN LIBRA
SUCCESS RATING: ★★

Most of today should go smoothly under this Libra Moon, but you may notice that stress is singing a subtle tune just below the surface of the day. On the one hand, you'll want to feel the carefree nature of this airy Moon . . . but on the other, you may be constantly presented with reasons to stray from your course.

Remember that Libra's ultimate motive is to be fair and balanced. Any disruptions in the day require your attention to bring things back to order, so it would be in your best interest to address any challenges the moment you see them. Don't run off to the mall at the first sign of freedom; instead, look around and make sure that all your emotional hatches are secured and your duties for the day are completed.

The First Quarter Moon occurs late tonight (early tomorrow on the East Coast), so you should be able to get through most of the day unchallenged.

AFFIRMATION FOR THE DAY:
My life is in perfect balance,
regardless of what my perception of it is.

BIG SPINS OF THE DAY:
First Quarter Moon at 29° Libra: 11:30 P.M. PDT / 2:30 A.M. EDT (Sunday)
Moon Void of Course: 11:30 P.M. PDT / 2:30 A.M. EDT (Sunday) until tomorrow

Happy Birthday, Leo!

JULY 22–AUGUST 23

Leo is arguably one of the most misunderstood signs of the Zodiac, carrying a bad rap for its supposed ego and self-centeredness. What's really going on with Leos, however, is a search for acceptance, love, and the kind of support that they *didn't* experience in childhood. It may take a lifetime for people born under this sign to realize that the approval they so desperately want must come from within.

These Lions have magic around them, and they can shine that glorious sun on you, creating optimistic feelings of hope and safety. In Leo's light, you feel special, chosen, and—most of all—*loved* . . . that's the spell of this sign. But for every ray of light, a shadow is cast, for as brightly as Leos may shine on you, they can take that radiance away, leaving you in a cloud of overcast gloom! Suddenly, the glow that you were basking in turns bleak and cool, the ongoing inspiration is gone, and what seemed like a dream is now a nightmare. This can happen when a Lion has been hurt, offended, or even worse, *ignored!*

Leos often have the loudest, most contagious laugh and fit the archetypal image of a king or queen such as Henry VIII or Victoria. And don't let a detached exterior fool you: Lions are watching every nuance and glance, making note of who's safe and who isn't, because behind that roar is truly a kitten. Leo is a very generous sign, with the charismatic Fire energy that asks the question: *Have you hugged your Leo today?*

AFFIRMATIONS FOR LEO:

I support myself in everything I do.

I only need my own approval, and I give it to myself freely and unconditionally.

There is plenty of love to give to everyone.

○◑◐●

SUNDAY

July 22

SUN IN LEO
MOON IN LIBRA/SCORPIO
SUCCESS RATING: ★★

This is the last day of the Cancer Sun cycle, so if you have a friend who was born under that sign whom you haven't wished a happy birthday, you've probably missed your chance. Technically, the Sun enters Leo at 10 P.M. on the West Coast but not until 1 A.M. in the East, so your calendars may vary as to when the first day of the sign is. But as you know, *every* day is Leo Day (at least according to your wonderful Lion friends!).

For most of today, the Sun will remain in Cancer and the Moon will be in Scorpio. You'll have one last day of emotional tides before the optimistic and royal sign takes hold, so this is a perfect time for your feelings to come out in full bloom. Allow yourself to review the last 30 days; and release any hurt feelings, forgive any thoughtless acts, and embrace all of the kindness that you've felt.

You're free to pursue anything that you want . . . just stay in touch with your feelings and let them guide you. Tomorrow kicks off a brand-new cycle, along with a few birthdays that you'd *better* not forget!

AFFIRMATION FOR THE DAY:
I release all pain and hurt from my awareness
and replace them with peace and love.

BIG SPINS OF THE DAY:
Moon enters Scorpio: 1:19 A.M. PDT / 4:19 A.M. EDT
Sun enters Leo: 10:00 P.M. PDT / 1:00 A.M. EDT (Monday)

○◐◑●

MONDAY

July 23

MOON IN SCORPIO
SUCCESS RATING: ★★

Scorpio Moons can bring you some serious perspective. After all, this is the sign of the natural investigator, who loves to direct your gaze under all the nooks and crannies in order to uncover any possible problems. This means that the way you listen will be accentuated today, as well as how you process what you hear.

The Scorpio Moon wants you to look for clues that may help you understand who you are, and some of those clues lie in the secrets of others. Today you may be the one whom people seek out to share their inner world—and you, in turn, will guard their confessions with your life, because you understand the importance of keeping a confidence.

There's lots of energy available for you today, along with a great deal of determination to accomplish anything that you need to. It's your responsibility to wield this power at appropriate times. Don't hold people to their word; hold them to their intentions.

AFFIRMATION FOR THE DAY:
All of my fears vanish in the face of the truth I hold.

BIG SPINS OF THE DAY:
None

○◑◐●

TUESDAY

July 24

MOON IN SCORPIO/SAGITTARIUS
SUCCESS RATING: ★

A long Void of Course Moon lasting all morning frees you up to pursue your leftover projects from yesterday. There's a good chance that "chipper" will not be an adjective used to describe your mood, but you won't mind. Your goal will be to make sure that whatever you require for your well-being is in place. Here's a hint: *What you need isn't anything that's outside of you.*

Be a good friend today by helping those who can't remember that everything is really going to be fine. You can start by being "fine" yourself and releasing any undercurrents of anger that you may be carrying. It's important to remember that holding grudges only keeps you from feeling peace and gives way too much power to your circumstances, and not to you.

As the day progresses, the Moon will find its way into Sagittarius and could illuminate an otherwise gloomy Tuesday. A clash between Mars and Neptune may zap your energy, but it's really a good excuse to withdraw and relax—by the end of the day, home will feel like a perfect retreat. If you can help it, avoid signing important documents or making major purchases.

AFFIRMATION FOR THE DAY:
I safely surrender my life into the hands of the Divine.

BIG SPINS OF THE DAY:
Moon Void of Course: 3:32 A.M. PDT / 6:32 A.M. EDT until
Moon enters Sagittarius: 1:31 P.M. PDT / 4:31 P.M. EDT
Mars squares Neptune: 4:10 P.M. PDT / 7:10 P.M. EDT

○◑◐●

WEDNESDAY

July 25

MOON IN SAGITTARIUS
SUCCESS RATING: ★★

Inspiration may be back in your life, and the feeling of well-being could be a lot closer than it was yesterday. The Moon is fully into Sagittarius and very close to Jupiter, allowing you to notice just how special you are and appreciate how luck has a way of finding you, even when you doubted that it could.

It's Venus's turn to have a go at spinning backward. After all, she hasn't done so since December of 2005 . . . and, well, every other planet has to go retrograde, so why should she be left out? When Venus slows down, your drive to feel appreciated seems to speed up. You may not know it, but you tend to compensate for Venus's deceleration by looking for your sense of worth out in the world. Shopping is certainly one way to satisfy this longing—as is changing hairstyles or seeking romance.

However you deal with the upcoming changes, it's best to be the observer of your life and watch the different forms that your urges take, without really attaching significance to any of them. Today life is filtered through a happy lens . . . start with that, and let the rest of your day unfold naturally.

AFFIRMATION FOR THE DAY:
The gifts that I give myself are
small reflections of the gift that I am.

BIG SPINS OF THE DAY:
None

○◑◐●

THURSDAY

July 26

MOON IN SAGITTARIUS/CAPRICORN
SUCCESS RATING: ★★

Get all your important work done in the daytime hours, because the Moon will be shifting positions later. Your intuition should be right on target if you can keep yourself focused on your center, not on *being* the center of everything. Use today to listen and be guided, for the astrological winds are changing . . . it would be in your best interest to prepare by trying your hardest not to leave a lot of unfinished business.

If you can, plan an evening that's restful and peaceful. The Void of Course Moon will be with you well into the night, so keep things light and uncomplicated, and don't try to wrestle with serious issues—there will be time for that tomorrow.

Venus has come almost to a standstill in preparation for her backward motion. Counter her initial effects by verbally (or otherwise) embracing the people who mean something to you. Let your colleagues, boss, friends, partner, and anyone else who's been supportive to you know your appreciation . . . this blessing will come back to you manyfold.

AFFIRMATION FOR THE DAY:
In those around me, I see the
part of me that welcomes love.

BIG SPINS OF THE DAY:
Moon Void of Course: 5:14 P.M. PDT / 8:14 P.M. EDT until
Moon enters Capricorn: 11:23 P.M. PDT / 2:23 A.M. EDT (Friday)

○◑◐●

FRIDAY

July 27

VENUS GOES RETROGRADE
MOON IN CAPRICORN
SUCCESS RATING: ★

Retrograde is a term used in astrology when a planet appears to be moving in reverse. Today Venus—the planet of love, appreciation, creativity, and charm—does the honors and begins a backward motion until the first week in September. If you recall, on June 23 I suggested that you take notes because Venus would return to that time period to help you clean up and resolve issues that have arisen since that date.

Most of this planet's issues are about love and appreciation, which easily translate into relationships and raises (the kind that increase your pay). However, I don't want to trivialize the Venus Retrograde at the risk of your missing the importance of the cycle. This event rules your self-worth, and during the next month or so, you'll be examining what it is that keeps yours low. You can't hug yourself if you secretly think that you aren't valuable . . . the good news is that Venus is around to help everyone clear away the cobwebs surrounding that idea.

AFFIRMATION FOR THE DAY:
I am willing to release my judgments of myself and replace them with loving acceptance.

BIG SPINS OF THE DAY:
Venus goes Retrograde 3° Virgo: 10:26 A.M. PDT / 1:26 P.M. EDT

○◑◐●

SATURDAY

July 28

MOON IN CAPRICORN
SUCCESS RATING: ★★★

The all-day Capricorn Moon goes Void of Course in the early evening and remains so until tomorrow morning. You're clearly receiving a lot of support today, not only to feel accomplished, but also to get the rest that you need in order to absorb all of the changes that are occurring. This is the first full day of the Venus Retrograde, which starts out in Virgo and ends in Leo. While it's in Virgo, your critical mind could be out of control and might make *you* its target.

With the Moon planted in the stoic sign of Capricorn, you're not going to be able to rally yourself out of any slumps with words alone. This Moon is just too serious for that, but it *will* give you the security that you need to bravely look at your *in*securities, and to ignore them if they're baseless.

Mercury is making a wonderful connection to Uranus—so think outside the box; color outside the lines; don't keep your path straight and narrow; and, by all means, avoid using clichés for the rest of the day! Tomorrow holds the Full Moon, and things are about to change.

AFFIRMATION FOR THE DAY:
There can be only One, and we are all a part of It.

BIG SPINS OF THE DAY:
Moon Void of Course: 7:24 P.M. PDT / 10:24 P.M. EDT until tomorrow
Mercury trines Uranus: 8:26 P.M. PDT / 11:26 P.M. EDT

○◑◐●

SUNDAY

July 29

FULL MOON IN AQUARIUS
MOON IN CAPRICORN/AQUARIUS
SUCCESS RATING: ★★

The day of the Full Moon is often filled with a mixed bag of intense emotions. Not only will you leave the traditional energies of Capricorn early this morning, but you'll also be inviting the rebellious spirit of Aquarius into the mix, as if to raise your thumbs to your temples, extend your wagging fingers, and say, "Nah, nah, nah, nah, nah!"

This Full Moon is a welcome relief from the rather brutal and serious tone of the previous few days. Although you aren't out of the fire yet, you're at least being given a chance to lighten up a bit and release some of the heaviness that you've been carrying around.

A Full Moon is great for letting go and entering the flow of the tide, which is high today. Keep yourself grounded, and remember that doing some small ritual under the Full Moon can help you set your focus for the next two weeks. Please rest tonight—July is leaving with a bang, and you'll want to be in good mental spirits for the shift.

AFFIRMATION FOR THE DAY:
I have the wisdom that I need to be happy,
and I willingly share it with the world.

BIG SPINS OF THE DAY:
Moon Void of Course: until 6:14 A.M. PDT / 9:14 A.M. EDT
Moon enters Aquarius: 6:14 A.M. PDT / 9:14 A.M. EDT
Full Moon at 7° Aquarius: 5:48 P.M. PDT / 8:48 P.M. EDT

○◑◐●

MONDAY

July 30

MOON IN AQUARIUS
SUCCESS RATING: ★

An all-day Aquarius Moon allows you to get your bearings by remaining (for the most part) quiet. You should be able to accomplish much today, and you may notice that your mind has a ruthless need for order, a valuable asset for starting a workweek.

The condition of the world may grab your attention—perhaps you're concerned about the homeless, or something more newsworthy. Try lending *yourself* that same compassion, and use it to appreciate your surroundings. Then, from a place of well-being, extend yourself outward. How are your colleagues and family members weathering this cycle? Find out by touching base with them.

This Moon can detach you from the issues closest to your heart, so put a little effort into tuning in to them as well. Friends from your past may be reaching out to you, and nostalgia could dominate your evening. It's a great night for bringing out an old movie or photo album to help you adjust to the upcoming Pisces Moon. I'd avoid important new beginnings for the next three days.

AFFIRMATION FOR THE DAY:
I am in harmony with what I think, do, and say.

BIG SPINS OF THE DAY:
None

○◑◐●

TUESDAY
July 31

MOON IN AQUARIUS/PISCES
SUCCESS RATING: ★

The last day of July is very interesting, to say the least. The high-minded nature of Aquarius is yielding to the soft and watery spirit of Pisces. Friends and family may call upon you for your support today, and it's okay to give it to them—but only after you see to your own needs.

Mars is clashing with Saturn today. The last time this happened was during Hurricane Katrina in 2005, when gasoline prices also skyrocketed. Keep an eye on weather patterns, both in the world and within yourself. This aspect can cause frustration, but this time around it will be lighter and faster moving.

It's a good idea to keep your temper in check and not push too hard in any one direction. There will be a tendency for you to meet resistance wherever you apply the most pressure . . . no signings or launchings today!

AFFIRMATION FOR THE DAY:
I love my world and the opportunities that it provides me for growth.

BIG SPINS OF THE DAY:
Moon Void of Course: 4:56 A.M. PDT / 7:56 A.M. EDT until
Moon enters Pisces: 10:41 A.M. PDT / 1:41 P.M. EDT
Mars squares Saturn: 4:59 P.M. PDT / 7:59 P.M. EDT

Thought for the Month

On Humility

Whenever life strikes me with more than my typical dose of problems, I usually assume that I must be doing something wrong. I conclude that I'm receiving some kind of signal from the Universe that I'm not heeding, and often it will lead me to cry out: "Okay, what do you want me to understand that I'm not getting?!"

It occurred to me that every time I explained away a difficulty as some warning from "the Universe," I was placing myself in a subordinate position, arrogantly refusing any responsibility for my own part in creating the problem. I'd think, *It's not me causing my life challenges—it's the Universe wagging its holy finger at me because I'm somehow stepping out of line.* This kind of thinking makes us seem less like children of a Divine source and more like slaves to it, living in the terror and fear (our favorite emotions) that if we mess up, we'll have to answer to our higher authority.

This Thought for the Month isn't challenging the existence of the Divine; it's challenging our *relationship* to it. We're extensions of something magnificent, yet we often allow ourselves to feel victimized and punished . . . as if that's how an all-loving Essence would operate (not that *I'm* an expert)! We should now push to remember that we're all one big extension of something wonderful and are just trying to pretend that we aren't. When something doesn't go our way, we need to ask ourselves, *Why did I really want this to happen?* rather than chalking it up to a big flip of "the bird" by the Universe. We're completely whole, forever loved, and utterly Divine—regardless of how much evidence we try to provide to the contrary.

AUGUST 2007
SUMMARY

You can see August's friendly intent in the amount of activity that occurs early in the month. Mercury enters the optimistic sign of Leo on the 4th, letting you know that it's time to quit worrying and start building confidence and hope. Jupiter stops moving backward on the 6th, the same day that Mars moves into Gemini—an alignment that greatly enhances your ability to do more than one thing at a time. The fact that Mars will eventually place itself opposite Jupiter is indicative of the enormous energy that's going to be available to you. In addition, Venus enters Leo on the 8th (she's still moving backward) and remains there for the duration of the month.

The only outer-planet involvement in August is Saturn's formation of a supportive aspect (Trine) to Pluto. On August 6, these two mighty celestial bodies will forge an alliance of fire, holding the potential to offer great hope. It should be newsworthy, so tune in to understand the global impact. This event has great implications, not only because it was these planets' *opposition* in 2001 that assisted in the era of terrorism, but also because it's happening on the tail of the Jupiter-Saturn connection from March and May.

Finally, on the 29th you'll welcome a Full Moon Eclipse in Pisces and will be showered with psychic rays. Under this Eclipse, as the boundaries that we use to identify everything around us dissolve, the past comes to the present, as if it never left. Compassion is possible, but sometimes the opposite occurs, and you could erect a wall to protect yourself from the vulnerability that you may feel. See if you can make your own choice between having empathy and defending yourself.

August highlights:

August 4: Mercury enters Leo

August 6: Jupiter Retrograde ends; Mars enters Gemini; Saturn trines Pluto

August 8: Venus enters Leo (moving retrograde)

August 12: New Moon 20° Leo

August 19: Mercury enters Virgo

August 23: Sun enters Virgo

August 28: Full Moon Eclipse 4° Pisces

◐

○◑◐●

W E D N E S D A Y

August 1

Moon in Pisces
Success Rating: ★★

In order to compensate for the wide-open, expansive nature of the Pisces Moon, you may have to develop a tough exterior—at least, that's how *some* of you deal with it. Others might be perceptive enough to recognize that such an outer shell is simply a defense, noting that the tougher the exterior, the more sensitive the interior. Try to play the part of one of the astute observers and perceive that tough demeanor as nothing more than a protective mask being worn by the childlike participants who are feeling a little vulnerable today. You can then become a mirror reflecting back the image of comfort, safety, and nondefensiveness.

That could very well be your biggest gift today—except for the one that may show up this evening, thanks to the Moon's connection to Uranus, the planet of surprises. It's a great way for you to welcome August, and a wonderful opportunity for you to remain at peace on a day when not everyone will be feeling the same.

Affirmation for the Day:
I remain whole and connected to
my source, regardless of my behavior.

BIG SPINS OF THE DAY:
None

THURSDAY

August 2

MOON IN PISCES/ARIES
SUCCESS RATING: ★★

A long Void of Course Moon in the morning doesn't do much to slow you down today, thanks to a wonderful connection between the Sun and Jupiter. Twice a year these two optimistic orbs hold hands in such a way that you feel empowered, bigger than life, and able to look obstacles of all sizes square in the face and laugh.

These are the Moon's final hours in Pisces, so it's wise to bring closure to issues from yesterday that were left open. Under the Aries Moon that arrives this afternoon, you won't have the patience or compassion to address any unresolved concerns, so wrap up unfinished things early on, and get ready for a terrific day.

One word of caution: Since Jupiter tends toward excesses, watch your intake of food and beverages and your output of words. Don't share things that you promised to hold secret.

AFFIRMATION FOR THE DAY:
I embrace peace, regardless of
what the world around me is doing.

BIG SPINS OF THE DAY:
Sun trines Jupiter: 8:13 A.M. PDT / 11:13 A.M. EDT
Moon Void of Course: 8:37 A.M. PDT / 11:37 A.M. EDT until
Moon enters Aries: 1:43 P.M. PDT / 4:43 P.M. EDT

○◑◐●

FRIDAY

August 3

MOON IN ARIES
SUCCESS RATING: ★★★★

Every once in a while, a day comes along that reflects just how cooperative this family of planets can be, and this is one of them. What makes today smooth isn't so much that the planets are favorably aligned; it's that they aren't remarkably *mis*aligned—and that has big implications for you. For most of the day, you should be able to put yourself first with little effort and make the choices that *you* desire. It's a healthy form of being selfish, and it's easier today because almost everyone around you will be doing the same thing.

Even if you think that you're excessively dependent on someone else, you'll still find it easier to make decisions that serve you. You already know that one of the biggest gifts you can give others is to be happy yourself, so take your leaps forward with an open heart. You don't have to be pushy on any level because the path is already open.

Today is the last day for Mercury to be in Cancer, making it easy to keep the people you love close to your heart—even if you're prancing around with reckless abandon.

AFFIRMATION FOR THE DAY:
I am powerful and fearless, and my heart is full of love.

BIG SPINS OF THE DAY:
Mercury sextiles Mars: 2:53 A.M. PDT / 5:53 A.M. EDT

○◑◐●

SATURDAY

August 4

MOON IN ARIES/TAURUS
SUCCESS RATING: ★★

When two or more planets shift signs in a day, it's not unusual for you to need a bit of time to psychologically adjust to the change. Today the Moon will slip into Taurus, and Mercury will enter the regal sign of Leo, suggesting that the aforementioned adjustment period could be useful. While you're resting, you can observe as your thoughts expand from money and security concerns to wonderment and hope—an effect brought to you by Mercury's entrance into Taurus.

The Void of Course Moon takes most of the day, so why not let this be a time when you can immerse yourself in the energetic song of the planets? Notice how your mood changes through each phase of the morning, giving way to a pleasurable evening.

If you have projects that you want or need to complete, do them . . . but don't forget to plan something social for the nighttime. You may not feel like it at first, but as the evening rolls around, there will be strong urges to be near friends (and food!).

AFFIRMATION FOR THE DAY:
My enthusiasm for living fully never diminishes.

BIG SPINS OF THE DAY:
Mercury enters Leo: 10:15 A.M. PDT / 1:15 P.M. EDT
Moon Void of Course: 10:31 A.M. PDT / 1:31 P.M. EDT until
Moon enters Taurus: 4:16 P.M. PDT / 7:16 P.M. EDT

○◑◐●

SUNDAY

August 5

LAST QUARTER MOON IN TAURUS
SUCCESS RATING: ★★

The Sun and Moon are fighting—because, like good parents, they want to make sure that you, their child, are being given the right guidance. One parent (the Sun) wants you to be proud and trusting and to allow everyone else to bring you what you need, yet the other (the Moon) believes that you should be shielded and comforted and ought to do everything it takes to assure your security. They each have your best interest at heart, but differ in their ideas on how to get there. Of course, the solution is for you to follow both sets of instructions . . . just not at the same time.

Today begin with the belief that you deserve to have all you want (honoring the Sun), and then make a list of those desires. Look around and notice what makes you uncomfortable or insecure so that you can ensure that those things are released (in recognition of the Moon). Any obstacles that appear today are designed to help you with your list, so accept them and attend to them as needed.

Be sure to do something wonderful for your body as a reward for your courage: New clothes, a hot bath, or a massage are great ways to top off the day!

AFFIRMATION FOR THE DAY:
Strife occurs only when I refuse
to accept my natural state of peace.

BIG SPINS OF THE DAY:
Last Quarter Moon 13° Taurus: 2:20 P.M. PDT / 5:20 P.M. EDT

○◑◐●

MONDAY

August 6

MOON IN TAURUS/GEMINI
SUCCESS RATING: ★★★

Lots of exciting planetary activity is in store for today. Move slowly as the Moon ends its time in Taurus, and use it to stay grounded. Aspirations are about to return in a big way as Jupiter stops moving backward and begins its forward motion again. However, like a train that's been traveling in reverse, it must first stop before going ahead—and that can feel a little strange initially.

The big news of the day is the Saturn-Pluto Trine that activates a very powerful energy. The last time this occurred was in November 2006, so this is the follow-up hit, and it will strike again in 2008. This is an extremely important aspect with respect to world events, as it suggests that the truth is guiding you, and foundations built on truth will prosper. If you entered into a business or investment in March or May, you will very likely see a tremendous opportunity for growth under this alignment, so stay your course.

All of you will probably begin to feel the return of your inner adventurer like a revival of hope, but Sagittarians will feel this effect the most. Late tonight Mars will leave Taurus and enter the flexible and multitasking sign of Gemini. And since it's clearly a big day of change—one that would be best absorbed at a slow pace—I wouldn't sign or buy big today unless your intuition tells you differently.

AFFIRMATION FOR THE DAY:
At my slightest request, help is always there.

BIG SPINS OF THE DAY:
Saturn trines Pluto: 3:08 A.M. PDT / 6:08 A.M. EDT
Jupiter goes Direct: 5:42 P.M. PDT / 8:42 P.M. EDT
Moon Void of Course: 6:50 P.M. PDT / 9:50 P.M. EDT until
Moon enters Gemini: 7:02 P.M. PDT / 10:02 P.M. EDT
Mars enters Gemini: 11:01 P.M. PDT / 2:01 A.M. EDT (Tuesday)

○◑◐●

TUESDAY

August 7

MOON IN GEMINI
SUCCESS RATING: ★★

Get out your telephones, magazines, and Internet-ready computers! You're under the influence of a Moon that wants you to get connected in the myriad ways available to you, and with Mars also hanging out in Gemini, there's nothing stopping you from being in multitasking heaven!

Go ahead and grab your cell phone: Make dinner reservations, check your appointments, and hold a conference call—all while driving with your elbows. You can do it! And what you *can't* accomplish today probably isn't worth doing.

Stay lighthearted in the rays of the Gemini Moon, but be warned: A clash with Venus and Mars may send you to the doghouse if you aren't cautious. Don't be negligent with regard to someone's feelings . . . with an active day in the mix, it's easy to forget that other people exist. Quick—while you're thinking of it, pick up the phone and send a message of love and support (your conference callees won't even notice that you've left them!).

AFFIRMATION FOR THE DAY:
I am a resounding success!

BIG SPINS OF THE DAY:
Venus squares Mars: 4:37 P.M. PDT / 7:37 P.M. EDT

○◑◐●

WEDNESDAY

August 8

MOON IN GEMINI/CANCER
SUCCESS RATING: ★★

You may have tossed and turned last night as your mind found a million things to think about—it's part of the package when a preponderance of planets are in mentally active signs (those would be Virgo and Gemini). However, there's still hope for those of you who'd like a cognitive respite: Retrograde Venus is about to leave Virgo and enter Leo, a placement that shifts your focus from the head to the heart.

Along the way, you'll get more help from the Moon, which is slipping into the watery sign of Cancer. In short, it's a day where the merry-go-round stops, and you can safely touch solid ground. Naturally, there will be a little swaying as you find your balance, but that won't take long—you'll soon find yourself centered and ready to do some work directed by your feelings, not your mind.

Don't be surprised if you encounter a little squabble along the way today—it's what I like to call a "welcome-home conflict." This means that someone unwittingly helps you come back from wherever it is you've been by causing trouble. It's really a very kind gesture, one that I'm sure you'll appreciate . . . if you can refrain from trying to get that person fired!

AFFIRMATION FOR THE DAY:
My courage is astounding.

BIG SPINS OF THE DAY:
Venus enters Leo: 6:10 P.M. PDT / 9:10 P.M. EDT
Moon Void of Course: 10:28 P.M. PDT / 1:28 A.M. EDT (Thursday) until
Moon enters Cancer: 10:37 P.M. PDT / 1:37 A.M. EDT (Thursday)

○◑◐●

THURSDAY

August 9

Moon in Cancer
Success Rating: ★★★

If you don't mind playing the caregiver, then this day is certainly meant for you. Cancer Moons have a delightful way of bringing out the hugger in everyone ("delightful," that is, if you don't mind hugging). There appears to be an obvious dissolution of boundaries under this Moon, and it seems that people are getting personal. Some may ask you directly why you look down, or colleagues might sneak in and bring you the paper because they thought it would "perk you up." It's not that you're likely to be depressed today . . . it's just that whatever you're feeling seems to be everybody's business.

Be careful of how you deal with this situation of intrusion. There *is* a reason why Cancer is given the moniker of the "Crab"—if you recall, crabs have pinchers. If someone crosses your boundaries, be polite yet firm, since even the nicest people with the best intentions can be aggressive under this Moon's spell. Use your shell as a shield if you have to, but don't yield to the inevitable guilt if you're forced to push back a pusher. A wonderful Mercury aspect will help you say what you mean, something that isn't usually easy when Cancer Moons hit.

Affirmation for the Day:
All people I see are my reflection: I treat them lovingly because I treat *myself* lovingly.

BIG SPINS OF THE DAY:
Mercury trines Jupiter: 8:37 A.M. PDT / 11:37 A.M. EDT

○◑◐●

FRIDAY

August 10

AUGUST

MOON IN CANCER
SUCCESS RATING: ★

Before you shrug your shoulders in disgust when I tell you that it's an all-day Void of Course Moon, listen for the unseen benefit (aka the "silver lining"). The Moon is the astrological ruler of Cancer, so when the Moon is *in* Cancer, you tend to feel as if the sign's energies are twice as strong. While there's nothing wrong with feeling all emotional and cuddly, two full days of it can be overwhelming, especially if you aren't a "watery" type. A Void of Course Moon actually helps you unhook from the intensity of this Moon, and can aid you in staying focused by diminishing any excess emotion. Now, emotions are fine—but sometimes work is done more efficiently when you can remain objective about it. Picture how hard it is to get something accomplished when you feel a strong sense of dread surrounding it.

Today's advice is to pick a project that you've been avoiding and finish it . . . you might be surprised by how easy it is to do so when you've successfully achieved partial dissociation! Finally, please note that this is not a great day for big business deals or large purchases.

AFFIRMATION FOR THE DAY:
My emotions are a loved and supported part of me.

BIG SPINS OF THE DAY:
Moon Void of Course: 5:58 A.M. PDT / 8:58 A.M. EDT until tomorrow

○◑◐●

SATURDAY

August 11

MOON IN CANCER/LEO
SUCCESS RATING: ★★★

The Leo Moon helps you melt away any leftover Cancer moodiness and replace it with dramatic optimism, so use this day to reenergize yourself. Let people wait on you with an unashamed sense of entitlement while you fan yourself with detached disinterest, and shoo them away when they've accomplished your requests. That's a sure way to win friends today, especially since they will all be in a good mood, thanks to the Leo Moon's royal call. If you're one of those people who isn't very likely to play out the aforementioned scenario, then you might settle for just appreciating the incredible things in your life (surely you have them).

This day may bring a wonderful wash of memories to the forefront. People from your past could emerge as if out of nowhere, especially if you've been thinking of them. That's right, your psychic abilities are enhanced—so use them to your advantage. This would also be a great evening for inspired conversation, which you can take with you into sleep.

AFFIRMATION FOR THE DAY:
My essence stretches into infinity.

BIG SPINS OF THE DAY:
Moon Void of Course: until 3:42 A.M. PDT / 6:42 A.M. EDT
Moon enters Leo: 3:42 A.M. PDT / 6:42 A.M. EDT

○◑◐●

SUNDAY

August 12

NEW MOON IN LEO
SUCCESS RATING: ★★★

It's time to work on everything that is Leo under this wonderful New Moon. Once a year, the Moon meets the Sun in this sign, filling you with dramatic flair and a deep desire to proudly bring forth your inner child. Use this day to make big wishes. . . . Find the part of you that wants the approval of certain people, and then see yourself as already having acceptance—not from them, but from *yourself.*

The Leo New Moon activates your heart and allows you to dream big. This is the Moon that reminds you that you can indeed have anything you want, so recognize yourself as someone who deserves more. Write down your desires, and burn them in a candle flame, as if you were sending them off to be taken care of by the Universe. Also, everything is bigger under this Moon, so make your intentions count, and don't forget that depression can be a small, but usually brief and unintrusive, part of this cycle.

AFFIRMATION FOR THE DAY:
What I desire, I deserve.

BIG SPINS OF THE DAY:
New Moon at 20° Leo: 4:03 P.M. PDT / 7:03 P.M. EDT

MONDAY

August 13

MOON IN LEO/VIRGO
SUCCESS RATING: ★

An all-day Void of Course Moon combined with a couple of serious Saturn aspects makes today much more somber than its predecessor. Venus is bringing a serious component to the mix by moving in so closely with Saturn that you can almost see yesterday's balloon of expansion deflate before your eyes. . . . Okay, I'm being a bit dramatic here, but I'm taking an astrologer's license under the last moments of the Leo Moon to make a point.

Your issues are likely to go from trusting in Divine intervention to relying on pure hard work. It's not that you lose faith—you just develop the urge to give assistance to your circumstances. Saturn tends to squelch the appreciation factor that Venus carries, which could lead you to feel a bit taken for granted.

The Sun and Neptune are also in today's mix, and like the couple who drinks too much at a party, they'll be causing a little more chaos than was expected. Don't sign anything today if you can help it, since there isn't enough clarity in your space to make that kind of decision.

AFFIRMATION FOR THE DAY:
My job feeds my soul completely.

BIG SPINS OF THE DAY:
Moon Void of Course: 6:35 A.M. PDT / 9:35 A.M. EDT until
Moon enters Virgo: 11:04 A.M. PDT / 2:04 P.M. EDT
Sun opposes Neptune: 11:26 A.M. PDT / 2:26 P.M. EDT
Venus conjuncts Saturn: 12:16 P.M. PDT / 3:16 P.M. EDT

○◑◐●

TUESDAY

August 14

MOON IN VIRGO
SUCCESS RATING: ★★★

The (sometimes) anal Virgo Moon would normally have you chasing all the little dust bunnies that are lying around your home or office with a vacuum cleaner—but something is amiss. It seems that your inner Virgo neat freak is being softened today by a planetary twist brought to you by Mercury and Neptune. Although it may get you off the hook from cleaning, this Mercury-Neptune combination can make you feel a bit detached and disoriented. The effects are short-lived, but they can cause trouble if you believe everything you hear. It's a great day for car salespeople and other savvy sellers, but don't be duped . . . just say "No!"

There's a surprise in the air tonight that could get your adrenaline flowing, so avoid late gulps of caffeine.

(**Note:** Neptune will be closest in its approach to Earth today. If you're a sky watcher, this is the best time to view the planet, although it will only appear as a tiny blue dot in all but the most powerful telescopes.)

AFFIRMATION FOR THE DAY:
I am part of a perfect order.

BIG SPINS OF THE DAY:
Mercury opposes Neptune: 1:09 P.M. PDT / 4:09 P.M. EDT

○◑◐●

WEDNESDAY

August 15

MOON IN VIRGO/LIBRA
SUCCESS RATING: ★★★★

Astrologers refer to this as the "Superior Conjunction of Mercury," but you can think of it as the end of confusion and the beginning of focusing on your future. To this point, you've been cleaning up the past . . . I know that you've heard that a lot, but most of your time up until now really has been spent sculpting past decisions and events into a shape that met your needs. Today is calling for the start of fresh material—a new canvas, so to speak—that allows you to take off in a new direction, or simply redefine the old one, and you're getting lots of help.

Venus is holding hands with Pluto, reflecting an increase in your desires and your ability to manifest them with little effort. Romance also figures big today, and friends prove invaluable. Keep an eye on the window of the Void of Course Moon, which will signal that the time has come to rest and regroup until tomorrow.

AFFIRMATION FOR THE DAY:
I am in charge of my physical world and all that I see in it.

BIG SPINS OF THE DAY:
Venus trines Pluto: 6:49 A.M. PDT / 9:49 A.M. EDT
Mercury conjuncts Sun: 12:57 P.M. PDT / 3:57 P.M. EDT
Moon Void of Course: 2:03 P.M. PDT / 5:03 P.M. EDT until
Moon enters Libra: 9:05 P.M. PDT / 12:05 A.M. EDT (Thursday)

○◑◐●

THURSDAY

August 16

MOON IN LIBRA
SUCCESS RATING: ★★★★

The planets continue to reflect ease and many opportunities today, so unless you *like* the feel of your head in a vice, this cycle should be one that you enjoy. Compared with the last few weeks, today is considerably more gracious and allows for far more worry-free choices. And speaking of choices, the Moon is in Libra (the sign that abhors making a decision), and it beckons you to look toward the brighter side of the day. Friends, family, work, and colleagues can all be considered for their gifts, rather than for the problems that they can create (sometimes you have to squint to *find* those gifts, but you can do it).

A wonderful aspect between Mercury and Venus allows you to speak eloquently today—draw on it to give verbal strokes of kindness. You can also use this aspect to your advantage by realizing that everyone will be susceptible to a little flattery, especially since the planet of appreciation is still moving backward. Your words have power, so use them wisely.

AFFIRMATION FOR THE DAY:
I speak from my heart, which is connected to all that is Divine.

BIG SPINS OF THE DAY:
Mercury conjuncts Venus: 10:27 P.M. PDT / 1:27 A.M. EDT (Friday)

○◑◐●

FRIDAY

August 17

MOON IN LIBRA
SUCCESS RATING: ★★★★★

It might be time to completely transform yourself today: New clothes, a new hairstyle, and that new something you've had your eye on are all great ways to treat yourself. Venus's backward journey has denied you long enough, and this is the day to rebel against feeling unworthy, unattractive, or any other "un" that you've been experiencing.

The potential for breakthroughs abound everywhere you look, and there's a resonating call to remember that you work hard just to make it through each day. It's time to celebrate with friends and loved ones, but be sure to give what you most want to receive just to keep things in balance (a favorite Libra word).

Launching projects or businesses, signing contracts, and making big purchases are all getting a green light now. Don't let this day pass without taking a moment to remember gratitude, the single most important form of expression you have.

AFFIRMATION FOR THE DAY:
I am filled with the light of love
and blessed by its reflection everywhere.

BIG SPINS OF THE DAY:
Mercury trines Pluto: 10:21 A.M. PDT / 1:21 P.M. EDT
Venus conjuncts Sun: 8:41 P.M. PDT / 11:41 P.M. EDT

○◑◐●

SATURDAY

August 18

MOON IN LIBRA/SCORPIO
SUCCESS RATING: ★★★★

Today encourages you to bring a little bit of sobriety to your weeklong party. The planets are getting ready to change signs, and Saturn—the planet of discipline—is starting to reemerge into your consciousness. You may notice a slight shift in your energy, especially when contrasted with the last few days. Don't confuse depression with coming down from a high, since every now and then it's good to remember that the guardrails on a winding road are useful boundaries, not the bars of a cage.

The morning Void of Course Moon suggests that you take things slowly today and review the progress that you've made. Mercury is contacting Saturn, and whenever these two get together, things become a little more serious, causing you to look realistically at your circumstances. "Realistic," though, in no way implies "without magic."

Use tonight's Scorpio Moon to gently look at your fears, which are merely shadows that vanish in any light.

AFFIRMATION FOR THE DAY:
I release my judgments today and replace them with the unconditional love of the Divine.

BIG SPINS OF THE DAY:
Moon Void of Course: 5:22 A.M. PDT / 8:22 A.M. EDT until
Moon enters Scorpio: 9:14 A.M. PDT / 12:14 P.M. EDT
Mercury conjuncts Saturn: 6:45 A.M. PDT / 9:45 A.M. EDT

○◑◐●

SUNDAY

August 19

MOON IN SCORPIO
SUCCESS RATING: ★★★

Mercury's entrance into Virgo is a crowd-pleaser, especially if you've missed having extreme clarity. While the planet is in the sign that loves order, it will turn your attention to your life and expose the big, fat mess that you've made of things (just kidding). Actually, you could initially feel that you've created a mess, but that just happens on the first day. As you acclimate to your new awareness, you'll see exactly what needs to be done, and you'll do it with surprising ease.

So, if you or those around you are being unduly critical, remind yourself that this is just Mercury making a big entrance, and it won't be long before things settle down. The planet is the natural ruler of Virgo, so this adjustment should be pretty quick.

The Sun is holding hands with Pluto, so it looks as though secrets are going to be exposed. In fact, today is about coming clean in more ways than one, so go with it . . . a little air on an old wound can do wonders.

AFFIRMATION FOR THE DAY:
Who I am is more important than what I do.

BIG SPINS OF THE DAY:
Mercury enters Virgo: 6:01 A.M. PDT / 9:01 A.M. EDT
Sun trines Pluto: 11:11 A.M. PDT / 2:11 P.M. EDT

○ ◑ ◐ ●

MONDAY

August 20

FIRST QUARTER MOON IN SCORPIO
SUCCESS RATING: ★★

The Scorpio Moon leads the way for most of today, and it helps you keep your focus on what lies beneath the surface. As you're guided back to your work, you might feel that today's ride is a bit bumpy. *Grumpy* may actually be the primary emotion that you see around you, but keeping a good sense of humor will help tremendously.

I was going to offer you the joke about the Virgo standing in front of a firing squad, making his last request that the soldiers swab their bullets with alcohol before firing—but by the looks of things today, there's a good chance that your propensity for grouchiness would prevail. So in lieu of listening to my humor, why not take a colleague to lunch and commiserate about the state of the world? After all, remember the saying "Two grumps in a bar are better than fifteen in the office." And with that, I'm outta here!

AFFIRMATION FOR THE DAY:
I am surrounded by overwhelming reasons to feel gratitude for my life.

BIG SPINS OF THE DAY:
First Quarter Moon 27° of Scorpio: 4:55 P.M. PDT / 7:55 P.M. EDT
Moon Void of Course: 6:35 P.M. PDT / 9:35 P.M. EDT until
Moon enters Sagittarius: 9:45 P.M. PDT / 12:45 A.M. EDT (Tuesday)

○◐◑●

TUESDAY

August 21

MOON IN SAGITTARIUS
SUCCESS RATING: ★

The Sagittarius Moon dominates the sky today, bringing you the opportunity to shoot your "arrows of wonder" into the sky. However, with today's alignment of Saturn and the Sun, you may have to aim carefully. When these two celestial orbs come together, you'll often prefer to view things without the frills of emotional coloring: You'll want to see if your goals are realistic or altruistic, and if you're heading in the direction that you really want.

Under the Sagittarius Moon, it's hard for you to give up your hope and wonderment, and although it may feel as if you're being asked to do so, you're not. Saturn just wants you to feel safe enough to fly, and sometimes that means grounding the airplane for a full inspection.

I wouldn't launch a business on this day, unless you want it to be built on a motto of "All work and no play."

AFFIRMATION FOR THE DAY:
I see the Divine child in you that is also within me.

BIG SPINS OF THE DAY:
Sun conjuncts Saturn: 4:29 P.M. PDT / 7:29 P.M. EDT

○◑◐●

WEDNESDAY

August 22

MOON IN SAGITTARIUS
SUCCESS RATING: ★★

Whoa! Slow down a bit! I know that you're eager to shake off the shackles of Saturn, but you have to do it properly . . . there's nothing worse than carefully calculating your escape and then missing the mark. Energies are changing—that's for sure—and now is the time to introduce your higher wishes into the mix. Take a minute today to reach into your world of dreams (the idealistic kind), and see yourself in your personal kingdom, where all that you desire comes true. While you're there, send a bolt of creative magic to the mortal part of you, and then come back and play.

You'll be guided flawlessly, thanks to the lovely aspects that the Moon is making. Also, this is the last full day of Leo—so if you've forgotten to wish your Lion friends a happy birthday, you'll have some sucking up to do!

AFFIRMATION FOR THE DAY:
I am the beauty in the word *beautiful*.

BIG SPINS OF THE DAY:
None

Happy Birthday, Virgo!

AUGUST 23–SEPTEMBER 23

Virgo is arguably the most stereotyped of all the Zodiac signs. There aren't many of you who haven't heard that people born under this sign are picky, neat, prudish, or perfectionistic. And there's some truth to this characterization, as Virgos do tend to focus their attention on things that are "of the Earth" (such as the house, the car, people, germs, and so forth). However, that's just their secondary concern . . . the primary motivation of this unique sign is finding *stillness,* which Virgos absolutely crave.

To achieve tranquility, Virgos must first take care of the all tasks surrounding them (after all, *someone* has to keep track of the multitude of things to do that exist in the world!), and then—once the list is completed—maybe the Virgins of the Zodiac can finally rest. Mother Teresa was an extreme Virgo and exhibited this trait in her last years of work with the poor and sick.

Virgos want to help, but not necessarily because they're benevolent. You see, lending a hand also allows their minds to rest, knowing that things are in order. Then after *your* needs are taken care of, Virgos can retreat into their own private world, where they're able to unwind, make a mess, and release their outside duties. People of this sign who are forced to live with others should always have a room that belongs only to them; and they must also avoid martyrdom, which is a technique they use to push others away in order to have time alone.

AFFIRMATIONS FOR VIRGO:

I trust the intelligence within me.
I trust the perfect order of things.
I am perfect exactly as I am.

○◑◐●

THURSDAY

August 23

SUN IN VIRGO
MOON IN SAGITTARIUS/CAPRICORN
SUCCESS RATING: ★★

The morning Void of Course Moon counsels you to move slowly until you feel grounded and ready to take on the day. It's going to be full of adjustments as the Sun leaves Leo and enters the precise and earthy sign of Virgo. However, the Moon will be in Capricorn (also an Earth sign) for most of the day, so you'll get help in keeping your focus on the physical world around you. It may be hard to find your balance at first, thanks to the many distractions that you seem to magnetically attract—in fact, it's almost as if there's a bus waiting to unload a million little things on your already-full to-do list.

So this is the perfect day to organize but not take action, as there will be plenty of time for that tomorrow. Confrontations are a waste of energy, so if someone is begging you to give him or her boundaries, set the rules firmly, but don't issue more instructions than are necessary.

AFFIRMATION FOR THE DAY:
My world is in perfect order because it reflects me.

BIG SPINS OF THE DAY:
Sun enters Virgo: 5:08 A.M. PDT / 8:08 A.M. EDT
Moon Void of Course: 5:55 A.M. PDT / 8:55 A.M. EDT until
Moon enters Capricorn: 8:20 A.M. PDT / 11:20 A.M. EDT
Mars opposes Jupiter: 9:03 A.M. PDT / 12:03 P.M. EDT

○◑◐●

FRIDAY

August 24

MOON IN CAPRICORN
SUCCESS RATING: ★★

Use the productive Capricorn Moon to get your work done early, because the afternoon introduces a very long Void of Course Moon that lasts until tomorrow evening. Don't worry—you'll be given the energy to accomplish everything that you need to.

I do have to caution you that the temptation to talk is going to be very strong. Mercury is making a connection with Jupiter, and that spells *c-h-a-t-t-y* in a big way. The only thing that's really negative about this is that you may have the tendency to tell more than you should (think *secrets*), so be observant of your words and remain respectful, as doing so will pay off in a big way.

This placement also suggests a very active mind, one that could have a hard time falling asleep. Do what you can during the day, then go on a raging drinking binge later tonight . . . well, okay, try some responsible, social sipping.

AFFIRMATION FOR THE DAY:
I accept intimacy with effortless desire.

BIG SPINS OF THE DAY:
Moon Void of Course: 4:41 P.M. PDT / 7:41 P.M. EDT until tomorrow
Mercury squares Jupiter: 6:04 P.M. PDT / 9:04 P.M. EDT

○◐◑●

SATURDAY

August 25

MOON IN CAPRICORN/AQUARIUS
SUCCESS RATING: ★★

The big problem with today isn't that you could lose your temper; it's that you might use your mouth to express it. Mercury is now battling with Mars, and this usually creates the effect of quick judgments and harsh words. Knowing about this planetary squabble in advance could help you stay in check if you happen to be caught up in its wave.

Later today, Venus will be bickering with Neptune and will go on to issue a warning: Don't leave room on your forehead for the word *sucker* to be stamped on it. In other words, it could be easy for you to fall for flattery that's meant to manipulate you. If you find yourself getting "worked," I'm giving you special permission not to follow the Mercury suggestion I just made. That is, go ahead and blow your top—sometimes anger is the perfect antidote to help you snap out of a slippery situation.

AFFIRMATION FOR THE DAY:
I am the Sun, Moon, and solar system, and they are me.

BIG SPINS OF THE DAY:
Mercury squares Mars: 8:59 A.M. PDT / 11:59 A.M. EDT
Venus opposes Neptune: 2:48 P.M. PDT / 5:48 P.M. EDT
Moon Void of Course: until 3:35 P.M. PDT / 6:35 P.M. EDT
Moon enters Aquarius: 3:35 P.M. PDT / 6:35 P.M. EDT

○◑◐●

SUNDAY

August 26

MOON IN AQUARIUS
SUCCESS RATING: ★★★

Leave it to the rebellious Aquarius Moon to break with tradition and bring you a day that *isn't* filled with clashes and tension. Although you may very well still feel some of yesterday's "erratica" (I invented that word), for the most part you're entering a wonderful cycle.

See if you can feel the change in attitude emerging. The Aquarius Moon likes to lift you above the norm and give you the overview that's often lacking when things get stressful. Be careful not to go too far up there, though, since Aquarius is also known to be judged as aloof. When you get a little time today, let someone you love know how you feel.

AFFIRMATION FOR THE DAY:
I am always young enough to learn more.

BIG SPINS OF THE DAY:
None

○◑◐●

MONDAY

August 27

MOON IN AQUARIUS/PISCES
SUCCESS RATING: ★★

Oh, did I mention that tomorrow is a Total Lunar Eclipse? Well, I, too, can get wrapped up in the planetary chaos and forget to bring things up, but I'm big enough to know not to blame the Mercury clash with Mars. . . . Nope, I take full responsibility for being able to point the finger at Mercury and *Uranus* for my negligence—they just shouldn't be so hostile!

Seriously, though, there's a Full Moon Eclipse tomorrow in the wee hours of the morning, and it might be a supportive gesture to light a candle with the intention of staying open to receive the gifts that it represents. This very same Eclipse happened 19 years ago to the day at the exact same degree. If you're familiar with your birth chart, the area that Pisces rules will get special attention. However, if you don't know your chart, then be aware that this event will illuminate your *urge to merge,* your *abuse of substances,* your *passion for compassion,* and your *obsession with possession.*

This is the dreamer's Moon, so think big tonight, and open yourself up to releasing your past and embracing the gifts that are about to come. This Eclipse will be visible over the Americas, the Pacific, eastern Asia, and Australia, and the best time for viewing is 3:35 A.M. PDT / 6:35 A.M. EDT (10:35 P.M. UT tonight).

AFFIRMATION FOR THE DAY:
I forgive everyone for all perceived wrongs and release them with love.

BIG SPINS OF THE DAY:
Moon Void of Course: 6:24 P.M. PDT / 9:24 P.M. EDT until
Moon enters Pisces: 7:35 P.M. PDT / 10:35 P.M. EDT

○◑◐●

TUESDAY

August 28

FULL MOON LUNAR ECLIPSE IN PISCES
SUCCESS RATING: ★★★

Happy Full Moon Eclipse! This is the day when you can see the shadow of the Earth on the Moon, and it will be visible to most of the world (see yesterday). This Eclipse is in early Pisces and will bring your focus to music, movies, creativity, compassion, and issues from your past.

There will be lots of excitement, thanks to an electrifying placement of Mercury and Uranus, and you'll be able to feel the elevated energy all around. Because this is an enhanced Full Moon, emotions could be wildly erratic, so I doubt that there's much point in trying to focus on anything else. It's a wonderful day to send out the intention for your desires.

Pisces Moons allow you to show great compassion for people you don't even know. Sometimes the deep feelings that emerge can make you feel sad or even isolated. Because this is an Eclipse, remember that things are magnified, but this won't last that long. Ride the emotional wave to shore . . . and may it bring you all that you desire!

AFFIRMATION FOR THE DAY:
Life supports me in every way.

BIG SPINS OF THE DAY:
Full Moon Lunar Eclipse at 5° Pisces: 3:35 A.M. PDT / 6:35 A.M. EDT
Mercury opposes Uranus: 12:39 P.M. PDT / 3:39 P.M. EDT

○◑◐●

WEDNESDAY

August 29

MOON IN PISCES/ARIES
SUCCESS RATING: ★★

The Pisces Moon will be finishing its run for most of the day, but it will go Void of Course in the afternoon. If you can still walk after yesterday's Eclipse, then try to focus on your work while some semblance of clarity exists. You've officially entered a new cycle—while simultaneously ending a 19-year-old one—so there are many reasons to carry an optimistic attitude.

The energy of the Pisces Moon guides you to a softer place where nostalgia and intense feelings live. Don't worry if you feel less energetic than usual, as this is part of the Pisces cycle. Let yourself flow effortlessly with the day, and try to find a quiet place, if only for five minutes, where no one else can find you (think *bathroom*), so you can release accumulated energy and find your center. . . . And be sure to spend the evening quietly as well.

AFFIRMATION FOR THE DAY:
My thoughts are clear, and I express myself with ease.

BIG SPINS OF THE DAY:
Moon Void of Course: 3:22 P.M. PDT / 6:22 P.M. EDT until
Moon enters Aries: 9:25 P.M. PDT / 12:25 A.M. EDT (Thursday)

○◑◐●

THURSDAY

August 30

MOON IN ARIES
SUCCESS RATING: ★★★

You have a wonderful Aries Moon fueling your day and helping you release the often-heavy aftereffects of the Pisces Moon. Welcome challenges with open arms, and push forward with any project that you have in the works. Sometimes the Aries Moon urges you to look for difficulties, and if you can't find them, you may be tempted to create them.

Don't be a troublemaker today, but rather, use the upside of Aries to be a cheerleader. Many people are still recovering from the Pisces Eclipse and could use a helping hand, which means that you have to look around you and take notice. You can be the voice of inspiration if you want to be.

AFFIRMATION FOR THE DAY:
Everyone I meet has my best interests at heart.

BIG SPINS OF THE DAY:
None

○◑◐●

FRIDAY

August 31

MOON IN ARIES/TAURUS
SUCCESS RATING: ★★★

The Moon doesn't change signs until very late tonight, so you've got another full day of fiery Aries to get you through life. If it's sunny out, you can forget about being cooped up indoors, so you might want to think of your excuse to escape.

This is the end of the powerful month of August, which brought you an Eclipse and several strong Success Ratings. Take a moment to review your journey and learn something from where you've been. It's okay to do this under tomorrow's Taurus Moon, since I know how hard it is to stop yourself when you're under the influence of the Ram!

This evening provides the perfect time to have that intimate and honest chat. Try to remember that relationships aren't about keeping score (at least, *pretend* that you remember)—you can catch more flies with honey than with vinegar.

AFFIRMATION FOR THE DAY:
I am surrounded by solutions.

BIG SPINS OF THE DAY:
Moon Void of Course: 10:19 P.M. PDT / 1:19 A.M. EDT (Saturday) until
Moon enters Taurus: 10:36 P.M. PDT / 1:36 A.M. EDT (Saturday)

Thought for the Month

The Reflection of Kindness

There are many times during the day when I notice that I'm looking for a positive reflection of myself from someone else. At the grocery store, when I greet the cashier and she doesn't reply (or even continues to look away throughout the whole checkout process), I get uncomfortable and self-critical. I notice this same impact when I greet my own customers. Some appreciate my hello and sincerely return it, while others see my greeting as an attempt to try to sell them something, and they ignore me. The latter response, like that of the cashier, distresses me.

I began noticing that I spend an enormous amount of time looking for and evaluating my own reflection, as given to me by others. Nice responses would make me feel good, and not-so-nice ones sent me into my self-critical mode. But in all the years of getting feedback from the outside world, I never thought to ask myself what *I* might be reflecting back to others. It made perfect sense that I responded kindly to people who smiled when they greeted me—but I was always the reactor, rarely the initiator. I decided to spend one whole day just paying attention to the reflection that I was offering to others, and as you may have guessed, the results were remarkable.

This month's thought is suggesting that we try being interest*ed* instead of interest*ing,* extend kindness in lieu of demanding it, and become ourselves the reflection of acceptance rather than looking for it in others.

SEPTEMBER 2007
SUMMARY

SEPTEMBER

September plays host to some big celestial events. First, Saturn enters Virgo quite early in the month (September 2). This hasn't occurred since 1978, and it suggests a marked change in how you'll seek security. The world may see an increase in the demand for environmental conservation and good common sense. Critics will emerge, and leaders will face the scrutiny that's eluded them up to this point.

But September has more to offer than Saturn's move into Virgo—it also brings you to the end of the Venus Retrograde on the 8th. Finally, you'll be able to feel appreciated again, and you'll even have the ability to sprinkle some gratitude of your own and recognize the support you've received from those around you.

The first day of fall, which is also the first day of Libra, occurs on the 23rd of the month. It's called the Autumnal Equinox because night and day are of equal length—but from that moment on, the days will begin to get shorter and the nights longer until the first day of winter in December.

The New Moon of September is an Eclipse in Virgo on the 11th. As if to say, "Let me help you prepare for this cycle of Saturn in Virgo," the Eclipse supports you in looking at the details of your life. Notice the important shifts that occur in your mind: You'll probably look at your surroundings with a different eye, one that sees the flaws and knows the steps required to correct them. This Eclipse opposes Uranus and promises to bring sudden change . . . not just to your life, but to the world.

Main events:

September 2: Saturn enters Virgo
September 5: Mercury enters Libra
September 7: Pluto Retrograde ends

September 8: Venus Retrograde ends
September 11: New Moon Eclipse 18° Virgo
September 23: Autumnal Equinox (Sun enters Libra)
September 26: Full Moon at 3° Aries
September 27: Mercury enters Scorpio
September 28: Mars in Cancer

◐

○◑◐●

SATURDAY

September 1

MOON IN TAURUS
SUCCESS RATING: ★★★

September is launching with a nice Taurus-type blanket of security, which you're able to wrap around yourself for the whole day. Try to enjoy this date without the push to understand that seemed so prevalent in August, since this month brings big changes initiated by Saturn's shift in signs. This planet only moves into a new sign every two and a half years, so it's not a small event . . . it's a change in consciousness that affects everyone.

Most Leos you know understand what those changes mean, because Saturn has just been in their sign, supporting the Lions in getting serious about their work, duties, and responsibilities. The rest of you discovered the meaning of true pride, and what you had to do to achieve it.

Now, as Saturn enters Virgo, you learn about order and humility as if you were given a giant, cosmic vacuum cleaner to serve as one hand and a magnifying glass as the other. You can now become focused on the minutiae of your life, since that's what all foundations begin with: the tiny details.

So be the couch potato that you've always wanted to be, soak in your tub, and break your diet today. There's a new perspective coming, and getting everything in order should be the first item on the list.

AFFIRMATION FOR THE DAY:
My life becomes more wonderful every day.

BIG SPINS OF THE DAY:
None

○◑◐●

SUNDAY

September 2

MOON IN TAURUS
SUCCESS RATING: ★★

You may not notice the effects of Saturn's move into Virgo, at least not right away. The Taurus Moon has a way of keeping you focused on your comfort, so you may get to sleep in a bit before the day's activities force you out of bed. You could start noticing little twinges of change: Perhaps you'll see an increase in your mind's activity, or maybe you'll note tiny irritations that start to appear. It's all part of the adjustment that occurs when a new cycle is at hand.

Today Saturn changes into Virgo for a one-year stay, and all Virgos will eventually hear the planet's message of purpose resonating within them. This alignment last took place from 1978 until 1980—a time when the world's first woman head of state was democratically elected, and nuclear-reactor breakdowns brought awareness to the environment.

Move slowly and let the day guide you. Annoyances may be more prevalent, so be in contact with the part of you that's a rock of support, and know that balance will be struck soon.

SEPTEMBER

AFFIRMATION FOR THE DAY:
At this very moment, phenomenal encouragement and support embrace me.

BIG SPINS OF THE DAY:

Saturn enters Virgo: 6:43 A.M. PDT / 9:43 A.M. EDT
Moon Void of Course: 5:48 P.M. PDT / 8:48 P.M. EDT until tomorrow
Mercury squares Pluto: 10:02 P.M. PDT / 1:02 A.M. EDT (Monday)

○◑◐●

MONDAY

September 3

LAST QUARTER MOON IN GEMINI
SUCCESS RATING: ★

No matter how much energy you think you have today, you must approach every activity with grounded common sense and awareness. A clash between Mars and Uranus could result in accidents due to overstimulation and carelessness. On the positive side, this aspect does provide a lot of energy that you can use to accomplish anything . . . but it's very powerful and should be directed consciously.

The Sun and Jupiter are providing supportive backup, but everything today points toward a tendency to overdo. Make this date successful by taking a breath before jumping into any project, and especially before hopping into your car. As my mother used to say when I was driving, "It's not *you* I'm worried about—it's everyone else!" (Of course, her credibility *was* diminished by the fact that she was a woman who refused to use her turn signals because she thought she'd wear them out!)

It's Labor Day in the United States, so no working allowed!

AFFIRMATION FOR THE DAY:
I am clear and thoughtful.

BIG SPINS OF THE DAY:
Moon enters Gemini: 12:31 A.M. PDT / 3:31 A.M. EDT
Mars squares Uranus: 1:09 P.M. PDT / 4:09 P.M. EDT
Venus sextiles Mars: 4:37 P.M. PDT / 7:37 P.M. EDT
Sun squares Jupiter: 5:05 P.M. PDT / 8:05 P.M. EDT
Last Quarter Moon at 11° Gemini: 7:33 P.M. PDT / 10:33 P.M. EDT

○◐◑●

TUESDAY

September 4

MOON IN GEMINI
SUCCESS RATING: ★★

SEPTEMBER

Yesterday's warning about moving slowly still applies, but it should be easier to maneuver with awareness and balance now. The Moon is securely resting in Gemini, the sign that never quits learning, and the urge to connect with others will likely keep you in verbal exchanges for most of the day. Keep your cell phone charged, since you don't want your battery dying in the middle of your big deal!

Your mood will probably remain on the lighter side, but there's always a chance that Gemini's "other twin" could emerge, coloring the day a smidgeon darker than it really is. Nevertheless, there's enough for you to do to keep your active mind engaged today. If you do happen to meet those feelings of hopelessness, pick up the phone and make dinner plans immediately. Tonight is a perfect time to exchange concerns with a friend.

AFFIRMATION FOR THE DAY:
I feel empowered when I express my feelings.

BIG SPINS OF THE DAY:
None

○◑◐●

WEDNESDAY

September 5

MOON IN GEMINI/CANCER
SUCCESS RATING: ★★

Another day of change is ahead, only this time you'll very likely discover that Mercury moving into Libra has some added benefits that you couldn't find when the planet was in Virgo. You may have found it difficult to sleep while Mercury was activated in Virgo, but that should now change.

Your attention is moving toward the Libran concerns—relationships, justice, and the all-important issue of fashion! That's right: It's time to see what you can do to reward yourself for all the dieting you did last month (you *did* go on a diet, right?).

The Cancer Moon will help bring focus to your loved ones, who may be calling for your attention in some way. You have plenty of it to give today, so do so generously . . . there's nothing better for removing your own pain than helping remove the hurt from someone else.

AFFIRMATION FOR THE DAY:
I am a money magnet, and my powers of attraction get stronger every day.

BIG SPINS OF THE DAY:
Moon Void of Course: 4:02 A.M. PDT / 7:02 A.M. EDT until
Moon enters Cancer: 4:09 A.M. PDT / 7:09 A.M. EDT
Mercury enters Libra: 5:03 A.M. PDT / 8:03 A.M. EDT

○◐◑●

THURSDAY

September 6

MOON IN CANCER
SUCCESS RATING: ★

It should be easy for you to unhook yourself from undue worries today when the Moon goes Void of Course this morning, until tomorrow. While that does suggest that big purchases be taken off your list (along with the signing of important documents), it doesn't mean that you can't be productive. On the contrary, Void of Course Moons have proved to be highly active cycles, especially when aimed toward the completion of something that was started previously.

If you feel as if you were in a bubble looking out at the world, you aren't alone, and you should know that this sensation will pass as the day moves forward. Nostalgic memories may take over your mind, along with a flood of colorful ideas, and creativity is definitely high today. Try to use it to your advantage, as sometimes the best solutions are born from totally unrelated activities.

AFFIRMATION FOR THE DAY:
I release all resistance to my full self-expression.

BIG SPINS OF THE DAY:
Moon Void of Course: 10:05 A.M. PDT / 1:05 P.M. EDT until tomorrow

○◑◐●

FRIDAY

September 7

MOON IN CANCER/LEO
SUCCESS RATING: ★

The Void of Course Moon that started yesterday will end by midmorning and enter the royal sign of Leo. The big news of the day is that Pluto, the planet of true transformation, has stopped moving in reverse and is ready to go forward. That's a good thing for everyone, and it's particularly positive for Scorpios. You see, Pluto rules their sign, and last April the planet began to spin backward (something it does every year), taking their attention with it.

Today the ability to see progress with regard to your personal, inward explorations will begin to emerge. It also helps that the Moon is in Leo, shining an optimistic light on your current conditions. You may have noticed that September is playing the role of getting things back on track—a process that isn't always comfortable, but *is* ultimately extremely helpful. Move at your own intuitive pace today, as tomorrow brings yet another big shift.

AFFIRMATION FOR THE DAY:
I breathe deeply and nourish
myself with the healing life force.

BIG SPINS OF THE DAY:
Pluto goes Direct: 7:55 A.M. PDT / 10:55 A.M. EDT
Moon Void of Course: until 10:00 A.M. PDT / 1:00 P.M. EDT
Moon enters Leo: 10:00 A.M. PDT / 1:00 P.M. EDT

○◑◐●

SATURDAY

September 8

MOON IN LEO
SUCCESS RATING: ★★★

SEPTEMBER

The end of the Venus Retrograde starts today, and you'll now have the ability to recognize and appreciate yourself—and others—with renewed clarity. There's still work to do since Venus must *re*-traverse the terrain that she just traveled through, but she'll help you bring closure to unfinished relationship issues. With the help of the Leo Moon, you can start spreading a bit of sunshine to areas of your life that have been dreary and overcast.

Mars is holding hands with Neptune, bringing forth a healing energy that can be directed toward anything you choose. Be the healer today: Tend to those in your life who aren't quite feeling the magic that this cycle has to offer.

If you've been struggling with a physical or emotional ailment, open yourself up to receive a dose of healing comfort . . . you'll be much more tuned in to it. This has been a very tough week of changes, so you're not only advised, you're *encouraged,* to treat yourself to something wonderful. This is a great way to start the weekend, since purchases can be made more confidently and with less chance of your changing your mind.

AFFIRMATION FOR THE DAY:
I am whole, well, and full of love, and I extend this feeling to all those around me.

BIG SPINS OF THE DAY:
Venus goes Direct: 9:18 A.M. PDT / 12:18 P.M. EDT
Mars trines Neptune: 9:06 P.M. PDT / 12:06 A.M. EDT (Sunday)

○◑◐●

SUNDAY

September 9

MOON IN LEO/VIRGO
SUCCESS RATING: ★★

Get your most important work done in the morning before the Moon goes Void of Course for the rest of the day. There's an intensity to the air, as the Sun and Uranus are struggling with each other in a cosmic tug-of-war. Your energy may be high, but you might have to use your focus in short, quick bursts before you feel a need to move on to the next project.

This day will be far from frivolous, especially if you have the opportunity to renew your connection with friends, or even with your spiritual side. Although the energies today are mostly positive and supportive, you're cautioned to act consciously. It's very easy to overestimate your abilities, which can cause you to overextend and possibly injure yourself.

Tonight may be underwhelming in contrast to the day, so plan some kind of entertainment for yourself. Don't let your mind start spinning about tomorrow—and do what you can to keep your focus on what *is* working in your life, not what's broken.

SEPTEMBER

AFFIRMATION FOR THE DAY:
I keep my thoughts positive, and
the world around me follows suit.

BIG SPINS OF THE DAY:
Moon Void of Course: 11:08 A.M. PDT / 2:08 P.M. EDT until
Moon enters Virgo: 6:11 P.M. PDT / 9:11 P.M. EDT
Sun opposes Uranus: 11:46 A.M. PDT / 2:46 P.M. EDT

○◑◐●

MONDAY

September 10

MOON IN VIRGO
SUCCESS RATING: ★★★

This is the day before a Partial Solar Eclipse in Virgo. Only a very small phase will be seen in parts of Australia, New Zealand, and most of central and southern South America, but its effects will be felt by everyone. (I'm talking about it today because it happens early tomorrow morning for most of you.)

You may want to take some time to write out your desires. The Virgo Moon loves lists (it's part of the sign's desire for order) and adores fulfilling them (part of the desire for service). This Eclipse is a New Moon—where the face of the Sun will be blocked by the Moon—and it's powerful for starting something. This Eclipse occurred 19 years ago (in 1988) during the same month, so see if you can recall the tenor of that year (I was . . . 13—yeah, that's it, *13!*). This Eclipse will mark the end of that 19-year cycle, starting it all over again.

Because the Moon's energy is overmagnified during these cycles, I'd refrain from launching new projects on the day of the Eclipse; instead, I recommend that you give it time to settle. Of course, your own will and intuition always trump my suggestions, so tune in and follow your hunches.

(**Note:** Neptune will be at its closest approach to Earth. This is the best time to view the planet, although it will only appear as a tiny blue-green dot in all but the most powerful telescopes.)

AFFIRMATION FOR THE DAY:
I have unlimited choices, because opportunities surround my life.

BIG SPINS OF THE DAY:
None

○◑◐●

TUESDAY

September 11

NEW MOON ECLIPSE IN VIRGO
SUCCESS RATING: ★★

This Solar Eclipse highlights the events of the day and starts you on a new path that most of you will actually be able to feel. Since the Eclipse comes during a New Moon, you may have felt a looming depression just below the surface of your consciousness. Once it hits exactly, though, things start to change: The once-black Moon almost instantly begins to receive the light of the Sun, and your moods will follow suit. Hope finds its way back into your awareness as you begin your journey back to your day-to-day reality.

The interesting thing about this Eclipse is that it lies opposite Uranus (the planet of excitement and sudden change), so this would be a good time to keep an eye on world events. Uranus usually brings a surprise, and since this is such a powerful alignment, it's likely to be newsworthy.

In your own life, things could get hectic . . . but only if you let them. You can stay centered in the midst of anything, especially if you're prepared. Don't overextend yourself, and give your assistance only if it's appropriate to do so. You may not feel like working at your full pace today because you want time to acclimate to the power of this event. Virgo issues will be an important focus for the next two weeks and will include things such as organization, service, taking care of small animals, hibernating, and cleaning up.

Your mind will be active, so make sure to have something for it to put its attention on. Keep an eye on yourself today, and honor the fluctuating moods that may appear. . . . Congratulations! You made it through the last Eclipse of the year.

AFFIRMATION FOR THE DAY:
I accept myself as a perfect reflection
of the love that surrounds me.

BIG SPINS OF THE DAY:

New Moon Solar Eclipse 18° Virgo: 5:45 A.M. PDT / 8:45 A.M. EDT
Moon Void of Course: 9:14 P.M. PDT / 12:14 A.M. EDT (Wednesday) until tomorrow

○◑◐●

W E D N E S D A Y

September 12

MOON IN VIRGO/LIBRA
SUCCESS RATING: ★★

People from your past got you down? Well, you may get your chance to clear things up with the help of today's alignment. The Libra Moon will dominate most of the day, giving you extraordinary skill at telling someone the worst news in such a way that he or she will thank you—it's an ability that you'll have lots of use for when asked how you like someone's awful new hairstyle, or an outfit that's really more *out* than a *fit*. It's one of the charming gifts of the Libra Moon, and it's yours for the entire day. You won't be the only one playing this game, though, so you're just going to have to take people and their comments at face value.

Aside from your intuition being a little lopsided, this date is fine for making purchases that you've previously researched. If you keep your attitude pleasant, a loving exchange could highlight your evening. Get to bed early . . . tomorrow's energy rumbles.

SEPTEMBER

AFFIRMATION FOR THE DAY:
I speak honestly second and lovingly first.

BIG SPINS OF THE DAY:
Moon enters Libra: 4:32 A.M. PDT / 7:32 A.M. EDT

○◑◐●

THURSDAY

September 13

MOON IN LIBRA
SUCCESS RATING: ★★★

Like a baby bird fresh from its egg, your mouth may be flapping today without much control. It could be that the Libra Moon has finally taken hold, and you feel left out of the loop of your social connections. Phones may be working overtime today, and your urge for a shopping experience might overwhelm you if you're usually part of the non-shopping crowd.

Mercury is the star player today, and—if you haven't already deduced—it's the planet that rules your communication. Not only is it a chatty planet, it's a trickster, too, so get out and have fun today. Play hard and follow your heart . . . you've earned a frivolous day, and you should take full advantage of it.

There's nothing that's likely to come back to haunt you for your choices today, so put this book down and get going!

AFFIRMATION FOR THE DAY:
I embrace my lighthearted, playful side and celebrate its emergence.

BIG SPINS OF THE DAY:
Mercury sextiles Jupiter: 3:44 A.M. PDT / 6:44 A.M. EDT

○◑◐●

FRIDAY

September 14

MOON IN LIBRA/SCORPIO
SUCCESS RATING: ★★★

SEPTEMBER

A long Void of Course awaits you now, an omen of support while you find your balance. If you find that you have a lower energy level than usual, you're right on target with the tone of this date. The Moon goes Void of Course when it's resting before entering another sign, as if to say, "Hey, why don't you take a break with me?" Of course, you can always decline the offer and buzz right through the day, but it might not be as much fun. By now, it may have become clear that I was the kid who ditched school at the drop of a hat, so heed my words with full knowledge that the choice is yours, and your decisions will always be supported.

Tonight's Scorpio Moon will encourage depth and exploration. It may be fun to pull out a good mystery to read, or get together with a friend to solve a real one. (And Happy Birthday, Mom!)

AFFIRMATION FOR THE DAY:
I am perfectly tuned in to the Divine Source that surrounds me, and I need do nothing to have it.

BIG SPINS OF THE DAY:
Moon Void of Course: 9:10 A.M. PDT / 12:10 P.M. EDT until
Moon enters Scorpio: 4:37 P.M. PDT / 7:37 P.M. EDT

○◑◐●

SATURDAY

September 15

MOON IN SCORPIO
SUCCESS RATING: ★★★

In a rare move, the Moon is floating through space, not making a connection to any other planet for the entire day, so it's pure Scorpio today. This means that if you like the feeling of looking below the surface of everything, enjoy the feeling of power, and prefer staying in the shadows while others absorb the limelight, then this day is for you. Use it to deepen your awareness of yourself by listening to the inner world of your friends or family. The Scorpio Moon loves sharing secrets because it knows that they will be kept safe while under its domain.

The sky's the limit for doing what you want today. You can trust your intuition fully and take the leaps that you desire. Don't be too critical of others until you've had a chance to understand their motives—it's easy to assume that people are as in tune as you are, but that's usually not the case. Passions run high during these Moons, so check in with your desires . . . and run with them!

AFFIRMATION FOR THE DAY:
I love and accept all the people in my world.

BIG SPINS OF THE DAY:
None

SUNDAY

September 16

MOON IN SCORPIO
SUCCESS RATING: ★★★

More Scorpio Moon adventures are on the way! The Moon finds plenty of planets to play with, and that usually translates into an active day in your life. Be aware, though, that there may be some problems with communication due to a Mercury squabble . . . it's almost as if you're speaking another language when you try to express a point or make a request. But it does lighten up as the day progresses, so don't cause a brouhaha.

This day is about you getting in touch with your peace of mind, which could be easily disrupted. Honoring the Scorpio Moon's suggestion to be still, look below the surface, follow your passion, and remain just under the radar should give you a tremendous edge—in other words, be successful by being conscious. The Moon goes Void of Course this evening until tomorrow, so have a lighthearted, unplanned evening that indulges you.

AFFIRMATION FOR THE DAY:
I receive far more when I give, and I give generously.

BIG SPINS OF THE DAY:
Moon Void of Course: 4:41 P.M. PDT / 7:41 P.M. EDT until tomorrow

○◑◐●

MONDAY

September 17

MOON IN SCORPIO/SAGITTARIUS
SUCCESS RATING: ★

The Moon enters Sagittarius in the early part of the day and begins to call forth your inner mystic. This Moon has a way of letting your ego soar to the mountaintops—and then dropping it like a water balloon, as if to keep you in check.

Most of today's commotion is due to a biannual squabble between the Sun and Mars—tempers are loose and patience is nonexistent when these two get together. Sometimes biting your tongue is just not enough, so tape might come in handy. However, if you have an encounter that makes you so angry that you can't contain yourself, just walk away.

The upside of this alignment is an incredible rush of energy, but it can also make you careless. Most of the intensity will settle down by the afternoon . . . if you need to talk something out, do so toward the end of the day. Launching a business on this date will probably produce an aggressive enterprise that's constantly in the battlefield, so unless you're embarking on a wrestling or boxing endeavor, lie low for a while.

SEPTEMBER

AFFIRMATION FOR THE DAY:
My finances reflect my shift from money worries to money flurries!

BIG SPINS OF THE DAY:
Moon Void of Course: until 5:21 A.M. PDT / 8:21 A.M. EDT
Moon enters Sagittarius: 5:21 A.M. PDT / 8:21 A.M. EDT
Sun squares Mars: 1:50 P.M. PDT / 4:50 P.M. EDT
Mercury sextiles Venus: 2:28 P.M. PDT / 5:28 P.M. EDT

○◑◐●

TUESDAY

September 18

MOON IN SAGITTARIUS
SUCCESS RATING: ★★

SEPTEMBER

The fiery Sagittarius Moon has had time to stabilize, and so, in turn, have you. This is a day filled with activity and exciting possibilities, but you may have to work it to your advantage. The first thing to realize is that you have the "smooth-operator" aspect available to you if you want it, which means that if you desire something, you'll know exactly what to say to get it. People will trust you more readily today, and flattery will seem to have remarkable strength. Understand that this sweet-talking aspect is available to everyone—you might just as easily be on the receiving end—and the old rule of astrology remains "Use it or lose it." In other words, not everyone is actually going to realize that this quality is theirs for the taking . . . another great advantage of having some astrological know-how!

(**Note:** Mars returns to this point during its Retrograde later in the year, so take notes now.)

AFFIRMATION FOR THE DAY:
I intuitively know the best action to take to further my life in a loving direction.

BIG SPINS OF THE DAY:
Mercury trines Neptune: 7:01 P.M. PDT / 10:01 P.M. EDT

○◑◐●

WEDNESDAY

September 19

FIRST QUARTER MOON IN SAGITTARIUS
SUCCESS RATING: ★

Okay, you don't get to hide under the bed, even though during parts of this day you may actually find yourself considering this option. A clash between the Sun and Pluto could place you in the middle of a battle of wills, and there are a few indicators in today's sky that point to a conflict that can't be resolved without compromise. The harder you push for your point, the further away you drive the possibility of resolution. Remember that winning doesn't necessary make everything all right, since you still have to live or work with the losers.

It's best to let today unfold on its own until you have a clear idea of what you need to do. Sometimes silence is the best option, while other times standing up for yourself is more important. Whatever you decide to do, don't burn bridges, since a battle that's started today is just going to get worse.

AFFIRMATION FOR THE DAY:
I never have to prove myself to win approval,
for I completely respect my work and abilities.

BIG SPINS OF THE DAY:
Sun squares Pluto: 8:56 A.M. PDT / 11:56 A.M. EDT
First Quarter Moon at 26° Sagittarius: 9:48 A.M. PDT / 12:48 P.M. EDT
Moon Void of Course: 9:48 A.M. PDT / 12:48 P.M. EDT until
Moon enters Capricorn: 4:52 P.M. PDT / 7:52 P.M. EDT

○◑◐●

THURSDAY

September 20

MOON IN CAPRICORN
SUCCESS RATING: ★★

An all-day Capricorn Moon will help bring some stability to this rather tumultuous cycle. Keep your eyes on world news to see if the recent power struggles are being translated into current events through a battle or controversy.

In your personal life, it won't be hard to stir up trouble if that's what you're looking for. However, if that isn't on your list of preferences, then bite your tongue and be the neutral force in volatile surroundings. This is a tough but short-lived cycle that can produce amazing clarity for you if you don't dissipate your energy through anger or drama.

Use the stoic nature inherent in the Capricorn Moon to shut out any issues that aren't worth your time. Let any conflict be someone else's, and allow your own day to unfold powerfully.

AFFIRMATION FOR THE DAY:
The changes that I bring into my
life are always for my highest good.

BIG SPINS OF THE DAY:
None

○◐◑●

FRIDAY

September 21

MOON IN CAPRICORN
SUCCESS RATING: ★

Are you having troubles with your partner or friend? Do your loved ones slink away when you attempt to hug them? Are you feeling lost, alone, and frightened? . . . *Well, snap out of it!* This is not the time to play the victim, and you're certainly not going to get any sympathy. The all-day Capricorn Moon works best when you're strong, and you're probably going to need to be today. The planets of love are taking a hit, and if you can work with them in a reflective way, you'll find a lot more incentive to give yourself the affection you need rather than waiting for it from outside of you.

Most of the day may have you feeling a bit out of touch with reality, but you must remember that these are fast-moving aspects that will be gone by the weekend. Don't make them more real by trying to control everyone around you. Instead, go rent a movie, sit back, and munch on some popcorn until the ride is through. For those of you who are having a pleasant time, good for you (you're probably the type of person who feels comfortable in a crisis).

AFFIRMATION FOR THE DAY:
The only love I want is the love I already have.

BIG SPINS OF THE DAY:
Mars opposes Pluto: 1:34 A.M. PDT / 4:34 A.M. EDT
Venus opposes Neptune: 1:03 P.M. PDT / 4:03 P.M. EDT
Moon Void of Course: 11:16 P.M. PDT / 2:16 A.M. EDT (Saturday)

○◑◐●

SATURDAY

September 22

MOON IN CAPRICORN/AQUARIUS
SUCCESS RATING: ★★

The detached yet supportive perspective of the Aquarius Moon will be with you all day. This will very likely be a breath of fresh air, considering all the turmoil that's been blowing through. Since this is the last day for the Sun to be in Virgo, you may find yourself being supervigilant about getting things in order.

This is no ordinary cleaning day—rather, you find yourself yearning to be under the bed and beneath the baseboards, hunting innocent dust bunnies. Use this energy fully, since you'll want things neat and tidy when the Sun goes into Libra. How else are you going to have a party that's the envy of all your friends?

If you have a Virgo friend or colleague whom you didn't wish a happy birthday, it's probably too late. Luckily, though, people born under this sign don't usually mind the lack of attention.

(**Note:** Mercury will return to this date when it spins retrograde next month. It's a good idea to start taking notes from this day forward until October 11. During the Retrograde, you'll be clearer on the issues that Mercury will be supporting you in reviewing, which causes much less stress and worry and gives you a visible edge in moving forward.)

AFFIRMATION FOR THE DAY:
Peace is always with me and
appears at my slightest request.

BIG SPINS OF THE DAY:
Moon enters Aquarius: 1:18 A.M. PDT / 4:18 A.M. EDT

Happy Birthday, Libra!

September 23–October 23

Libra is the only sign on the Zodiac wheel that's represented by an inanimate object. Perhaps one of this sign's greatest gifts—as represented by the impartiality of the Scales—is the ability to judge without prejudice and with a complete lack of bias. Libras have a fascination with people . . . it's an Air thing, really. Those born under this sign can find the good in anyone merely by focusing on what's remarkable and complex about them. That's what makes Libras so charming, and it's also why relationships are their main mission.

There are many identifying features that will give this Venus-ruled sign away. Libras often have dimples, a great smile, and a signature attractiveness (inward or outward) that makes it feel safe for most people to approach them. They usually love interactions, parties, or gatherings of any kind where they can be free to participate in an array of conversations, as long as things don't get too heavy or restrictive. Remember, their motive is to engage you, explore you, and get you to exchange your ideas and thoughts about anything with them—whatever allows them to feel *connected* to you.

Libras will surprise you with their aggressive rejection of feeling tied to anything. As a matter of balance, just when you expect them to be nice, they'll show you their *not*-nice side; and when you think that they'll take your side, their inner impartial judge may emerge. The Libra quest for new relationships (of all kinds) makes it the most sought-after sign of the Zodiac . . . and the most elusive.

Affirmations for Libra:

All feelings are beautiful.

As I see the good in others, I see the good in myself.

My clothes, my body, and my hair
have nothing to do with my essence.

○◑◐●

SUNDAY

September 23

AUTUMNAL EQUINOX
SUN IN LIBRA
MOON IN AQUARIUS
SUCCESS RATING: ★★★

SEPTEMBER

Today the Sun enters the sign of the Zodiac symbolized by the Scales, which represent Libra's true objectivity. While the Sun is traveling through, you'll have access to this sign's wonderful charm (which is a quality of Libras—at least until you've made them angry).

Being charismatic may be more difficult today than usual, due to a weird Mercury alignment. You may know exactly what you want to say, but have trouble formulating the words. Your ability to focus, however, shouldn't be a problem at all . . . so put your mind toward any desire today, and it's yours.

The start of the Libra cycle is synonymous with the first day of fall, when you gracefully begin your harvest in preparation for winter. (Although it's springtime for your friends Down Under, they're still following the autumn cycle of the harvest.) The energies today should have an almost romantic feel to them. Remember that "Libra" and "conflict" don't mix well, so it's best to practice gentle ways of resolving problems if you expect to make headway.

AFFIRMATION FOR THE DAY:
I adore my relationships.

BIG SPINS OF THE DAY:
Sun enters Libra (Autumnal Equinox): 2:52 A.M. PDT / 5:52 A.M. EDT

○◑◐●

MONDAY

September 24

MOON IN AQUARIUS/PISCES
SUCCESS RATING: ★★★

Your words are very powerful today, so use them wisely. Be conscious of what you think, say, and write, because it all has an impact. Now I'm not saying that you must phrase everything perfectly or else bad things will happen. I'm not one of those "careful-what-you-wish-for" hysterical types, since I'm certain that the Universal Energy is neither stupid nor spiteful and knows exactly what you mean. I'm talking about the power of your words to unwittingly hurt yourself or others today through negative comments.

Your supportive words, on the other hand, can change lives, including your own—so consciously apply them throughout your day. The Pisces Moon will help keep your heart open . . . what you do from there is your choice.

AFFIRMATION FOR THE DAY:
Miracles are everywhere in my life.

BIG SPINS OF THE DAY:
Mercury sextiles Pluto: 3:53 A.M. PST / 6:53 A.M. EST
Moon Void of Course: 2:15 A.M. PDT / 5:15 A.M. EDT until
Moon enters Pisces: 5:56 A.M. PDT / 8:56 A.M. EDT

○◑◐●

TUESDAY

September 25

MOON IN PISCES
SUCCESS RATING: ★★★

Everybody really is beautiful when viewed from a certain perspective. Today's Pisces Moon helps you remember that underneath, all hearts are the same, but some people have an easier time getting there than others. You don't have to be a saint to make it through this day, but it would be very useful at least to act as if you saw everyone through a filter of compassion. It's difficult to remember that the meanest person you know is very scared and lonely, and the nicest person may actually be equally so.

Use this date as an experiment that helps you gain a perspective of just how alike everyone is. The objective behind the game is to practice forgiving yourself by releasing your judgments of at least one person around you. It's not easy, but the rewards are incomparable.

People from your past may make an appearance now, so afford them the same compassion discussed above . . . it can change history.

SEPTEMBER

AFFIRMATION FOR THE DAY:
I extend the love that is a part
of me outward to all that I see.

BIG SPINS OF THE DAY:
None

○◑◐●

WEDNESDAY

September 26

FULL MOON IN ARIES
MOON IN PISCES/ARIES
SUCCESS RATING: ★★

SEPTEMBER

Wouldn't it be nice if suddenly a swift and bold jolt of energy swooped down and electrified you? Well, the next best thing would be to have a Full Moon in Aries, and that's exactly what you've got today! Gone are the bleeding hearts and wimpy softies from under Pisces's rule, replaced by the Ram's armies of strength and valor! Yes, I'm being facetious, but sometimes under the Aries influence, you tend to see being gentle as a weakness. After all, this is the warrior Moon . . . nothing snaps you out of a sympathetic attitude the way that anger does, and the Aries Moon is rife with it.

Anger, when controlled and directed, is a powerful force that can help you achieve your goals. Of course, it's never okay to direct it toward another being in a physical or verbal way, but when used to overcome fear, it's amazing. Use this Full Moon to take charge of your life, and be ready to pioneer new territories and explore new possibilities. Evaluate your successes and admit your failures, and then commit to moving on. A candle lit tonight might help you solidify your intentions.

AFFIRMATION FOR THE DAY:
I am courageous and strong, and I reflect what is possible to everyone I meet.

BIG SPINS OF THE DAY:
Moon Void of Course: 5:32 A.M. PDT / 8:32 A.M. EDT until
Moon enters Aries: 7:23 A.M. PDT / 10:23 A.M. EDT
Mercury trines Mars: 10:53 A.M. PDT / 1:53 P.M. EDT
Full Moon at 3° Aries: 12:46 P.M. PDT / 3:46 P.M. EDT

○◑◐●

THURSDAY

September 27

MOON IN ARIES

SUCCESS RATING: ★★

Get ready for deep conversations and powerful insights as Mercury, the planet ruling your thoughts, moves into Scorpio. Use this day to affirm your ability to see the truth behind any exterior as you honor the profound depths that you're capable of reaching. Don't worry about going too far, since the Aries Moon doesn't have time to bother with heavy analysis . . . unless it's juicy and useful, that is.

There's a lot of magic in the air today, the kind that likes the smell of flowers and the sweet memories of a first kiss. You'll probably have a fearless approach to the adventures of the day, which may range from opportunities for growth to superficial and fleeting dialogues. One thing is for sure: The planetary alignments give you a strong reminder that you can—at any moment—invite peace into your life.

AFFIRMATION FOR THE DAY:
I cannot separate myself by word or deed from my connection to the Divine.

BIG SPINS OF THE DAY:

Mercury enters Scorpio: 10:18 A.M. PDT / 1:18 P.M. EDT

○◑◐●

FRIDAY

September 28

MOON IN ARIES/TAURUS
SUCCESS RATING: ★★

Moving from Aries to Taurus is like coming home to a home-cooked meal after a day in the trenches. The Taurus Moon certainly loves to remind you how good it feels to have a body, and how it's even better to get it pampered. If you follow the guidance of Venus—the planet that rules Taurus—you just might get more than merely catered to physically . . . you could get some good news.

Tonight Mars enters the homey sign of Cancer, giving you an edge in the art of emotional manipulation. No one will be able to say no to the childlike innocence that you'll be able to portray if you embrace this planet's energy as your own. Don't be surprised if you have to take a nostalgic trip back in time, since old toys and childhood experiences can be fondly revisited in your mind while Mars resides here. Sharing would be a nice thing to practice!

AFFIRMATION FOR THE DAY:
I am in balance with my spiritual,
mental, physical, and emotional sides.

BIG SPINS OF THE DAY:
Moon Void of Course: 7:00 A.M. PDT / 10:00 A.M. EDT until
Moon enters Taurus: 7:18 A.M. PDT / 10:18 A.M. EDT
Mars enters Cancer: 4:53 P.M. PDT / 7:53 P.M. EDT

○◑◐●

SATURDAY

September 29

MOON IN TAURUS
SUCCESS RATING: ★★★

SEPTEMBER

There's nothing in the way of your having a wonderful day—unless, of course, other people exist on the planet. . . . *Oh, wait!* I think that they do. Your desire for a comfortable existence today could be interrupted by the needs of others, and by certain events that seemingly crop up out of nowhere.

It would be best not to fight the tug from the outside world. You may find yourself growing roots on the couch, with a remote control stuck firmly to your hand, but you should detach yourself under today's earthy Moon. You'll have plenty of time to chill tomorrow. And remember that meals just seem to taste better under a Taurus Moon, so plan an evening out at a restaurant that has many rich choices—preferably with a separate menu for desserts!

AFFIRMATION FOR THE DAY:
I am worth my weight in love.

BIG SPINS OF THE DAY:
Moon Void of Course: 10:11 P.M. PDT / 1:11 A.M. EDT (Sunday) until tomorrow

○◑◐●

SUNDAY

September 30

MOON IN TAURUS/GEMINI
SUCCESS RATING: ★★★

Wow! Another month is over, and you're all the richer for it. Take a moment today and review your journey over the last 30 days. Remember, this is the month that brought you an Eclipse in Virgo, the forward motion of both Venus and Pluto, and a Full Aries Moon. You were accelerating during the course of September, and it helps to collect all the experiences that you're grateful for on a sheet (or two) of paper.

The Moon will enter Gemini today and ignite the communicator in you. Don't waste the date completely on the phone or by watching television—get out into the world and make your connections in person. I'm not just suggesting this because it's a good idea; I'm saying it because you have a better chance at being in the right place at the right time if you leave your home.

Good-bye, September, and thanks for all your gifts. . . .

AFFIRMATION FOR THE DAY:
I do look good!

BIG SPINS OF THE DAY:
Moon Void of Course: until 7:35 A.M. PDT / 10:35 A.M. EDT
Moon enters Gemini: 7:35 A.M. PDT / 10:35 A.M. EDT
Mercury sextiles Saturn: 11:16 P.M. PDT / 2:16 A.M. EDT (Monday)

Thought for the Month

YOUR POWER

Look at the areas of life where you've criticized yourself for what you don't have or for some quality that you feel you lack. (One way to know where you're judging yourself is to notice how you're judging others.) Pay attention to what you long for and to any statements that imply, "I can only be happy when this or that happens." Note how this kind of thinking keeps you powerless: a victim of circumstances and at the mercy of random events.

Now pick a moment to see yourself as completely satisfied. Picture what it would be like to have received everything your heart desires, and bring that feeling into the present. Imagine how it would feel to love everything about yourself—to wake up grateful that you have your body and mind, with an awareness of yourself as your own best friend, who will never turn on or hurt you. Imagine that you could walk away from any circumstance in your life and that you'd survive happily.

Feel the freedom of identifying only with your essence for just a few minutes, and then try it for a whole month. . . . *Change your mind!*

OCTOBER 2007

SUMMARY

There's something honest about October. Perhaps it's the fact that it doesn't introduce a new season, but allows you to bask uninterrupted in autumn's glow. Or maybe it's that the month holds such opposite signs within its domain that it stretches your awareness. It opens with the charm of Libra, the sign that sees the good in everyone, and finishes in the brooding sign of Scorpio, which identifies everyone's flaws. October juxtaposes these two seemingly opposite energies with an effortless display of beauty and death, depicted by the falling leaves. The month also fearlessly hosts Halloween, a day where gifts are given in exchange for a threat—quite a different approach from typical holiday celebrations.

October's theme of honesty carries on astrologically throughout the month, openly displaying big events that are conveniently kept grouped together, as if to prevent a stressful hunt for them. For example, Jupiter and Uranus are making their final difficult aspect to each other on the 9th, which is an important event because the last connection of the year between two planets means that a decision has been made. In addition, there's a New Moon on the 10th and a Mercury Retrograde on the 11th, and then it's fairly quiet until the 23rd, when the Sun enters Scorpio.

The Full Moon of October is on the 25th, in the sign of Taurus. This allows you to bring the beauty of the month into a sensual experience, where you can appreciate all the colors around you as you prepare for winter. There are many opportunities for romance in the air this month as well . . . so if you're looking for it, it's likely to find you.

Main Events:

October 7:	Venus enters Virgo
October 9:	Jupiter squares Uranus
October 10:	New Moon 18° of Libra
October 11:	Mercury Retrograde begins
October 23:	Sun enters Scorpio
October 25:	Full Moon 2° Taurus

○◑◐●

MONDAY

October 1

MOON IN GEMINI
SUCCESS RATING: ★★★★

October rolls in like the high evening tide: full of hope, power, and excitement. With the Moon planted firmly in the verbally responsive sign of Gemini, you have a chance to spread your enthusiasm to everyone you meet.

The early part of the day may seem active—if not overstimulating—as the Moon connects with Uranus, the planet of surprises. This date carries the promise of change, and allows you to grasp an overview of your life without judgment or worry. Desires are obtainable, and the path to achieving them is clear.

The second half of your day is dreamy and creative, like a well of magic that you have at your disposal—so use your imagination to sculpt what you desire. Make your plans, sign your contracts, and negotiate your deals . . . this is a wonderful cycle if you choose to take advantage of it.

AFFIRMATION FOR THE DAY:
I feel alive, open, and supported in all areas of my life.

BIG SPINS OF THE DAY:
None

○◑◐●

TUESDAY

October 2

MOON IN GEMINI/CANCER
SUCCESS RATING: ★★★

October remains a steady beacon for you as you head into the Cancer Moon. The ideas that you've been developing can now be explored through your feelings. Today you navigate the world through your senses and know the difference between a fleeting, bad idea and one that has staying power.

Under the rule of the Cancer Moon, security is your primary goal, and the welfare of your family and loved ones helps you weigh the realities of any future plans. This is a day that will help you weed out the probable from the improbable, since it will be clear what you will and won't do.

The underlying feeling of hope and good fortune is getting stronger, so tune in to it as you make the choices for your day. Take advantage of this cycle, since it seems that the entire year has had you waiting for this very fortunate turn. (Be sure to check the time of the Void of Course Moon, however, before signing important papers.)

AFFIRMATION FOR THE DAY:
Starting now, I choose to see the
unlimited choices placed before me.

BIG SPINS OF THE DAY:
Moon Void of Course: 3:52 A.M. PDT / 6:52 A.M. EDT until
Moon enters Cancer: 9:58 A.M. PDT / 12:58 P.M. EDT

○◑◐●

WEDNESDAY

October 3

LAST QUARTER MOON IN CANCER
SUCCESS RATING: ★★★

Each day after the Moon is full, it loses light—which it metaphorically sends to you for support as it approaches New Moon status. Midway through its journey, the Moon is half dark and half light, suggesting that you're at a crossroads and you get a chance to regroup before it enters its new cycle.

The Last Quarter Moon reminds you that the halfway point is here, and it wants to help you prepare for the upcoming New Moon cycle. Be on the lookout for obstacles that appear, since they're guideposts that support you in staying the course. Deal with them consciously, as they hold the key to your successful navigation of the week.

Venus is forming a powerful connection with Pluto today. Big successes in the romance and business departments, along with high passions, are awaiting your direction. Most of the solid foundations that you need to move forward will be built in the morning, making it the best time to be productive. There's a very long Void of Course Moon ahead that starts in the afternoon today and continues through that time tomorrow.

AFFIRMATION FOR THE DAY:
I am the extension of all that is Divine and perfect.

BIG SPINS OF THE DAY:
Last Quarter Moon at 10° Cancer: 3:07 A.M. PDT / 6:07 A.M. EDT
Venus trines Pluto: 6:12 A.M. PDT / 9:12 A.M. EDT
Moon Void of Course: 1:42 P.M. PDT / 4:42 P.M. EDT until tomorrow

○◑◐●

THURSDAY

October 4

MOON IN CANCER/LEO
SUCCESS RATING: ★★

Long Void of Course Moons affect people very differently. If you're a "lunar" person (one who primarily uses feelings and intuition for guidance), you'll probably feel somewhat detached or dissociated, and it's for your sake that pulling back and completing unfinished projects is strongly encouraged. Others who seem unaffected by the Moon's preparation for change can usually perform business as usual without much difficulty.

The problem lies in the fact that even if you aren't feeling the effects of the Void of Course Moon, people around you probably are. You're advised to move at a slower, more conscious pace than usual so that mistakes are less likely to happen and successful outcomes are assured. If you can, wait until tomorrow to formalize your agreements.

AFFIRMATION FOR THE DAY:
Every step that I take brings me closer
to my loving connection with the Divine.

BIG SPINS OF THE DAY:
Moon Void of Course: until 3:28 P.M. PDT / 6:28 P.M. EDT
Moon enters Leo: 3:28 P.M. PDT / 6:28 P.M. EDT

○◑◐●

FRIDAY

October 5

MOON IN LEO

SUCCESS RATING: ★★★★

The trend for success continues as the Moon grabs solid footing in Leo and shines promising hopes into your heart. Wedding plans this weekend create solid and successful foundations, and business agreements follow suit. The optimism available to you is useful not only for looking ahead with a positive vision, but also for examining your circumstances right now and seeing all of the things you have to be grateful for.

Extend a helping hand to those around you who may not be feeling as blessed. Remind people through your actions that by choosing a different window to look through, they, too, can be happy. Tonight is perfect for social gatherings and festivities—so be generous, tip big, and show your appreciation to others.

AFFIRMATION FOR THE DAY:
Thank you.

BIG SPINS OF THE DAY:
None

○◑◐●

SATURDAY

October 6

MOON IN LEO
SUCCESS RATING: ★★★★

Lush dreams were very likely dancing in your head last night, thanks to a rendezvous between the Moon and Neptune. The whole day is wide-open for your enjoyment—it's a perfect time to take a ride to enjoy the changing colors of autumn, and to ignore the messy closet that will probably be calling you loudly tomorrow.

Children figure prominently in today's forecast. If you have kids, this would be a great day to include them in a family outing; if you don't have any, the planets may be guiding you to *be* more childlike. Open your arms to a new experience or repeat a past one with fresh enthusiasm. The day is yours, so treat it as though *you* matter.

AFFIRMATION FOR THE DAY:
I am a revered child of the Divine.

BIG SPINS OF THE DAY:
Moon Void of Course: 10:29 P.M. PDT / 1:29 A.M. EDT (Sunday)

○◑◐●

SUNDAY

October 7

MOON IN LEO/VIRGO
SUCCESS RATING: ★★★

The Moon enters Virgo just after midnight on the Pacific coast and begins to fill you with a more serious tone. Virgo Moons tend to bring your attention out of the Leo clouds of pride and down to the details surrounding you. The messy closet that was just starting to nag at you is now audibly calling for your attention.

These Moons aren't *just* about cleaning, but there's nothing like using them for that purpose. The ability to see minute details is extraordinary now, but you may have to be careful not to go overboard. A critical eye on that closet can easily take the heat off of those around you, and that would be a positive thing. Be careful to contain the outward expression of your inner critic, known as "nit-picking," since it's not only unattractive—it can be hurtful.

AFFIRMATION FOR THE DAY:
My life and everything in it is in perfect order.

BIG SPINS OF THE DAY:
Moon Void of Course: until 12:04 A.M. PDT / 3:04 A.M. EDT
Moon enters Virgo: 12:04 A.M. PDT / 3:04 A.M. EDT
Venus enters Virgo: 11:53 P.M. PDT / 2:53 A.M. EDT (Monday)

○◑◐●

MONDAY

October 8

MOON IN VIRGO

SUCCESS RATING: ★★★

This day is made even more powerful by the entrance of Venus into Virgo. This is a helpful event for Virgos everywhere who have been feeling the oppressive nature of Saturn in their sign, since today's energy is electric.

The Moon, Jupiter, and Uranus all make strong aspects to each other (what astrologers call a "T-square"). You may experience a seemingly insurmountable number of distractions today, but they will ultimately be supportive in their content. There's no limit to what you can accomplish with Mars and Saturn in complementary positions, and the worst thing about this date is the possibility of becoming too obsessive.

Tonight a lovely (and lucky) aspect between the Sun and Jupiter promises magic, so do something fun that includes another person. Don't waste this evening living vicariously through the television . . . make your *own* reality show.

AFFIRMATION FOR THE DAY:
I embrace my preferences without judgment.

BIG SPINS OF THE DAY:

Mars sextiles Saturn: 8:45 P.M. PDT / 11:45 P.M. EDT

Sun sextiles Jupiter: 9:05 P.M. PDT / 12:05 A.M. EDT (Tuesday)

○◑◐●

TUESDAY

October 9

MOON IN VIRGO/LIBRA
SUCCESS RATING: ★★

Today begins with a long Void of Course Moon, giving you fair warning to start slowly. There's a buzz in the air that could turn to utter confusion if you don't remain grounded with some attention on your inner world. This is the day before the New Moon, and as I've mentioned before, you may feel slightly depressed as the Moon enters its dark phase (which is *only* a metaphor). Keep in mind that this period's duration is short-lived—but it's a useful time to begin to give attention to your feelings, regardless of your opinion of them.

A fairly rare clash between Jupiter and Uranus occurs today. Most astrologers would agree that any aspect involving Jupiter is generally fortuitous, but this particular clash (called a "Square") produces big, amazing results, usually after a struggle. (Please read more about this alignment in the January Summary.) This is the last of three connections that these planets make, and the results should be obvious.

The need for urgent decisions is an illusion: There's nothing that won't wait, so don't be fooled. As the Moon enters Libra this afternoon, you'll understand much more . . . so move easily.

AFFIRMATION FOR THE DAY:
The world around me reflects my inner condition—as I change, it changes.

BIG SPINS OF THE DAY:
Moon Void of Course: 4:08 A.M. PDT / 7:08 A.M. EDT until
Moon enters Libra: 10:58 A.M. PDT / 1:58 P.M. EDT
Jupiter squares Uranus: 11:19 A.M. PDT / 2:19 P.M. EDT

○◑◐●

WEDNESDAY

October 10

NEW MOON IN LIBRA
SUCCESS RATING: ★★★

The New Moon occurs late tonight (early tomorrow on the East Coast and in Europe), so you may feel the emotional mood of the day a little more intensely than usual. Usually these Moons can bring the desire for social connection with lots of friends, but this time you're toning things down dramatically, thanks to a Venus-Saturn connection.

Libra is as much about justice and fairness as it is about beauty and love. To understand the effects that this Moon is having, peek in on your favorite news channel and listen to the "new developments" section. Issues that are starting to emerge are reflections of the New Moon cycle, so use them to understand what energies are affecting you today.

Remember that New Moons mark the time to put a new set of goals in motion. Think outside of your normal perspective—reach to achieve objectives that you never thought could be accomplished. Write them down, and send them off tonight.

AFFIRMATION FOR THE DAY:
I have the courage to be happy, even when my circumstances are not going well.

BIG SPINS OF THE DAY:
New Moon 18° Libra: 10:01 P.M. PDT / 1:01 A.M. EDT (Thursday)

○◑◐●

THURSDAY

October 11

MERCURY RETROGRADE BEGINS
MOON IN LIBRA/SCORPIO
SUCCESS RATING: ★★

My longtime readers already know that I'm not going to send out warning flares because Mercury is starting its retrograde journey today. If I had my druthers, I'd actually throw a party in celebration, because I know what a gift this little planet can be. When you watch a movie twice, you get much more out of it, and the same is true of Mercury's backward motion through your lives.

Mercury allows you to review your choices: Sometimes you like them, while other times you wonder why you made particular ones. However, the more you learn about your reasoning, the stronger you become the next time a decision is required—that's one of the many Mercury Retrograde perks.

Use the morning and early afternoon to get your serious work done, and plan to relax this evening. You have to give yourself time to ready yourself for your new focus, so avoid high-end purchases and don't sign big deals today. Tonight an early bedtime makes a huge difference.

AFFIRMATION FOR THE DAY:
The absence or presence of material success does not change the utter contentment that I feel.

BIG SPINS OF THE DAY:
Moon Void of Course: 4:23 P.M. PDT / 7:23 P.M. EDT until
Moon enters Scorpio: 11:14 P.M. PDT / 2:14 A.M. EDT (Friday)
Mercury Retrograde 9° Scorpio: 8:52 P.M. PDT /11:52 P.M. EDT

○◑◐●

FRIDAY

October 12

MOON IN SCORPIO
SUCCESS RATING: ★★★

Scorpio Moons run deep, and they take you with them. This one is bringing Mercury along as well (I suppose the Scorpio Moon doesn't want to be alone). Since Mercury is often a chatterbox, and the Moon represents your emotions, you may end up sharing your feelings tonight . . . hopefully, when you're done, it will still be called "sharing," and not "ranting"!

If you have a propensity for alcohol or drug use, be warned that thanks to Neptune, tonight could give you the tendency to overindulge—so please keep an eye on your recreational choices. This is also a very creative aspect, but considering the combination of all the planets today, a strong drink is likely going to be what you desire most. If your vice of choice this evening is a good movie, choose one that will speak to your soul. Spiritual practices have more meaning under Neptune's reign.

Good dreams are awaiting your arrival tonight. . . .

AFFIRMATION FOR THE DAY:
I am my own greatest advocate.

BIG SPINS OF THE DAY:
Sun trines Neptune: 6:40 P.M. PDT / 9:40 P.M. EDT

○ ◑ ◐ ●

SATURDAY

October 13

MOON IN SCORPIO
SUCCESS RATING: ★★★

If you find yourself walking through this day thinking that you aren't as attractive as you'd like to be, you're reflecting the thoughts of millions. There's something that happens when Venus gets too close to Saturn that's akin to a brick hitting your ability to appreciate who you are.

When Saturn is in the picture, the only thing you feel confident enough to strip off is your sense of self-confidence. Perhaps I'm over-emphasizing the negative, since there's a good side to the connection of Venus and Saturn (other than the fact that they only stay together for a day or two): They bring maturity. Both planets are in the sign of Virgo, and together they help strengthen your discriminating palate, making it easier for you to choose the things you love and toss the things you don't. Don't be surprised if you find yourself attracted to older individuals—that's another Venus-Saturn gift, especially if you *are* an older individual!

Use today to weed out your undesirables (that doesn't include your kids!). You'll love feeling lighter once you've given your inner critic an outlet other than yourself.

AFFIRMATION FOR THE DAY:
My needs are met because I understand and accept them.

BIG SPINS OF THE DAY:
Moon Void of Course: 2:23 P.M. PDT / 5:23 P.M. EDT until tomorrow
Venus conjuncts Saturn: 9:29 P.M. PDT / 12:29 A.M. EDT (Sunday)

○◑◐●

SUNDAY

October 14

Moon in Scorpio/Sagittarius
Success Rating: ★★

A long Void of Course Moon beckons you to move slowly and let this day unfold of its own accord. If you use Sundays to rest, the alignment couldn't be more perfect, but relaxing isn't the only useful thing you can do right now.

Projects around the house that have been waiting for your attention will seem to go by much faster under a Void of Course Moon—as long as you aren't working on something electrical or mechanical. Clean out the garage or work on a crossword puzzle . . . it doesn't matter what you do, by midafternoon you'll be aiming your sights at bigger things!

Affirmation for the Day:
My circumstances do not define me;
they simply shape my character.

BIG SPINS OF THE DAY:
Moon Void of Course: until 11:58 A.M. PDT / 2:58 P.M. EDT
Moon enters Sagittarius: 11:58 A.M. PDT / 2:58 P.M. EDT

○◑◐●

M O N D A Y

October 15

MOON IN SAGITTARIUS
SUCCESS RATING: ★

The sign ruled by the largest planet in the solar system is beaming down on you today. A Sagittarius Moon activates the restless philosopher in everyone, and it injects you with the desire to frolic through the day with reckless abandon. Well, okay, I'm not a "frolicker" either, but it was fun to write that line, and this Moon makes *you* look for the joy in life in much the same way. Unfortunately, sometimes the act of seeking out fun brings you face-to-face with all the *un*-fun things around you. What I just described is the split that exists today between your inner magician and the demands of the world.

Today does indeed have its serious side, which is made more so when contrasted with the need for excitement inherent in the Sagittarius Moon. The best move today is not one of compromise, but of finding balance. For every hour of work you do, reward yourself with an hour of play. So, if you go to work from 9 A.M. until noon, make a note that you have three hours of amusement coming your way. You can take them whenever you'd like, but you have to use them before you go to bed. Now *that's* what I call "working with the Moon"!

AFFIRMATION FOR THE DAY:
Today I change the world by changing my perspective.

BIG SPINS OF THE DAY:
None

○◑◐●

TUESDAY

October 16

MOON IN SAGITTARIUS
SUCCESS RATING: ★★

You'll probably learn something new about someone today—not because you were sneaking around and investigating him or her, but because you were *listening*. Under the Sagittarius Moon influence, you usually like to talk about your adventures and philosophies to a sometimes-willing, and sometimes-*un*willing, audience. However, today there's an anomaly in the system: You actually care about what *others* have to say.

Venus and Mars are holding hands, the Moon is making a delightful connection with Jupiter, and you're recognizing that other people matter (I know for many of you that could be quite a revelation). Take advantage of this desire to connect . . . not only will today allow you to learn about those around you, but it will also let them see how terrific *you* are (and I'm not just blowing smoke here).

AFFIRMATION FOR THE DAY:
I say what needs to be said, and
I am always supported in doing so.

BIG SPINS OF THE DAY:
Venus sextiles Mars: 10:37 A.M. PDT / 1:37 P.M. EDT
Moon Void of Course: 5:33 P.M. PDT / 8:33 P.M. EDT until tomorrow
Mercury sextiles Venus: 8:18 P.M. PDT / 11:18 P.M. EDT

○◑◐●

WEDNESDAY

October 17

MOON IN SAGITTARIUS/CAPRICORN
SUCCESS RATING: ★★★

An active mind can keep you awake at night, as well as have you speaking before thinking. Today you'll want to remain conscious of your words—not just the ones you say aloud, but also those that you tell *yourself*.

The Moon's early entrance into Capricorn will be a great help in keeping you grounded and in control, while at the same time focusing you on your work and responsibilities. Speaking of work, get in a full day of it—that way, you'll be meeting the needs of the Capricorn Moon, *and* you'll feel in tune with things.

But when it's time to go home, don't take this work ethic with you. Tonight is about letting go and having quality (albeit *productive*) time with a loved one.

AFFIRMATION FOR THE DAY:
I effortlessly find everything that I need to know and learn.

BIG SPINS OF THE DAY:
Moon Void of Course: until 12:04 A.M. PDT / 3:04 A.M. EDT
Moon enters Capricorn: 12:04 A.M. PDT / 3:04 A.M. EDT
Mercury trines Mars: 1:37 A.M. PDT / 4:37 A.M. EDT

○◑◐●

THURSDAY

October 18

MOON IN CAPRICORN
SUCCESS RATING: ★★★

Ever wish that you had a day where everything on your list was handled effortlessly and interruptions were minimal? This might be one of those days—if you can just get through the early-morning hype and settle into your goals.

With the help of the Capricorn Moon, you could make some real progress in your life, from organizational enhancements to the completion of a project. With this nice balance of planetary energies, you should be able to focus on your desires and work toward making them a reality. Capricorn is ruled by the stern teacher Saturn, who supports strong effort and responsibility and puts the squeeze on laziness . . . so take the hint and do something productive today!

AFFIRMATION FOR THE DAY:
I raise my sense of self-esteem and realize that I am a child of the Divine.

BIG SPINS OF THE DAY:
None

○◑◐●

FRIDAY

October 19

FIRST QUARTER MOON IN CAPRICORN
SUCCESS RATING: ★★

Sometimes your mind is so clear and your thoughts are so solid that you wonder how you ever got through a month when you weren't feeling this way. Although today starts off slowly with an early Void of Course Moon, it eventually unfolds by lifting you above the horizon, where you can look at your life from the mountain's perspective.

This is the First Quarter Moon in Capricorn, a time to use your overview to guide you past any obstacles that may emerge. As the Aquarius Moon comes into your awareness, it will be easy to see the world as your reflection, and problems as tiny messengers that nudge you back to consciousness. Misunderstandings can be viewed as hints that you aren't quite connecting to your heart, while fear reminds you to be the light where darkness cannot exist.

AFFIRMATION FOR THE DAY:
I am deeply grateful for all that ever was and all that will ever be.

BIG SPINS OF THE DAY:

First Quarter Moon at 26° Capricorn: 1:34 A.M. PDT / 4:34 A.M. EDT
Moon Void of Course: 1:34 A.M. PDT / 4:34 A.M. EDT until
Moon enters Aquarius: 9:52 A.M. PDT / 12:52 P.M. EDT
Mercury sextiles Saturn: 6:54 A.M. PDT / 9:54 A.M. EDT

○ ◑ ◐ ●

SATURDAY

October 20

MOON IN AQUARIUS
SUCCESS RATING: ★★★

While in Aquarius, the Moon guides you to see all humanity as connected in some way. For many of you, it will bring an awareness of obvious global injustices; for others, it may direct your attention to your immediate world. Wherever your focus goes, however, it will be piercingly perceptive.

Today you get to recognize the strength of your convictions with quiet self-confidence. Relationships can be appreciated for their endurance and support, which are strong enough to weather any storm and powerful enough to be tender. This day carries wonderful possibilities that invite wisdom into your mind—use it to decide your course with confidence and grace. There's nothing that you can't accomplish where happiness is the goal. Expand your mind today, and share your insights with those around you who may need a gentle nudge.

AFFIRMATION FOR THE DAY:
My spirit is stirred as I choose to activate
my life with loving ambitions for happiness.

BIG SPINS OF THE DAY:
Sun sextiles Pluto: 6:36 A.M. PDT / 9:36 A.M. EDT

○◑◐●

SUNDAY

October 21

MOON IN AQUARIUS/PISCES
SUCCESS RATING: ★★★★

You'll probably feel a solid sense of clarity in the first part of the day. It seems that everything is as it should be in all areas of your life—even the part that you aren't completely at peace with. Use this awareness to affirm your decisions. Take a look at the choices you've made, and be willing to reevaluate them.

If you have a pressing issue that you're wrestling with, this is the day to sort it out. Let the objectivity of the Aquarius Moon activate your brilliance, while the acute perception of the Sun and Pluto help you stay honest.

The Moon turns Void of Course this afternoon, inviting you to unhook your mind and practice spontaneous "surfing" on the celestial tides. Tonight the Moon enters the watery world of Pisces, which washes away your thoughts like an eraser on a chalkboard. Early to bed ensures time in the realm of your dreams.

AFFIRMATION FOR THE DAY:
I am open to a new way of seeing, and I am willing to stretch myself to accommodate my new sight.

BIG SPINS OF THE DAY:
Moon Void of Course: 12:37 P.M. PDT / 3:37 P.M. EDT until
Moon enters Pisces: 4:04 P.M. PDT / 7:04 P.M. EDT

○◑◐●

MONDAY

October 22

MOON IN PISCES
SUCCESS RATING: ★★★

It's the final day of the Sun's journey through Libra; so, before you enter into the depths of Scorpio, it's a great time to review the last 30 days. Venus is bringing you an exciting surprise as she holds hands with Uranus and activates your sense of joy and appreciation. Creativity is high, and you're being given a blank canvas to paint on. Ideas and imagination are easily brought into physical form today, so it would serve you to be conscious of your thoughts. Notice what song is stuck in your head, and pay attention to the words: Is there a message for you within them?

If you find yourself thinking of someone, he or she will likely appear. If it's a person you don't want to see, then send out a psychic "Do not disturb!" message—he or she will get it. Good things are coming, but they're also already here. Urges to spend money may need to be reviewed for practicality.

AFFIRMATION FOR THE DAY:
I transform the most difficult tasks into ones of creative simplicity.

BIG SPINS OF THE DAY:
None

Happy Birthday, Scorpio!

OCTOBER 23–NOVEMBER 22

Imagine being immersed in the depths of the ocean . . . the *real* depths, those parts that have only been imagined by humans. This watery environment is black, still, and all-encompassing. Your mind can only speculate about what lurks around you, but here you are—alert, yet floating in a vastness that seems as infinite as outer space. Many things come to mind while drifting in these depths: You may wonder what demons are lurking in this unfathomable void; or you might find it peaceful, holy, and serene—a world where you are one of many, although your fellow travelers aren't visible.

The emotional world of Scorpio is very similar to these mysterious waters. People born under this sign seek the unseen and often imagine the worst. And yet they feel at home here within the enigma, alive and passionate, as adrenaline pumps through their bodies, preparing them for adventures on dry land.

Scorpios know that they're different, because they sense things that no one else seemingly can. They may hear your words, but they only really *believe* what their feelings are telling them. A Scorpio isn't very likely to miss much of the subtext during an interaction—if fact, catching lies is a pastime for people with this sign. It's not easy to shock them, either . . . in a way, they expect you to withhold some of the truth in order to protect yourself. After all, they understand the importance of being discriminating about one's disclosures more than anyone in the Zodiac.

AFFIRMATIONS FOR SCORPIO:
I am safe in every area of my life.
I am strong enough to allow support into my life.
I trust the flow of my life completely.

○◐◑●

TUESDAY

October 23

SUN IN SCORPIO
MOON IN PISCES/ARIES
SUCCESS RATING: ★★

It's a big day in many ways, which immediately indicates that you should slow down and tune in so that you can make the most of it. First, the Sun is changing from Libra to Scorpio and bringing your attention to your emotional inner world. For many of you, this change can incite depression (a natural response when moving from Libra to Scorpio), while in others, it may bring a sense of comfort and safety . . . it all depends on your natural inclination. Regardless, though, this cycle is encouraging you to collect your harvest of knowledge and store it as winter fuel.

Helping out today is a Mercury-Sun connection, which signifies the turning point of the Mercury Retrograde. Although the planet is still spinning backward, when it makes this connection to the Sun, you're encouraged to look ahead with new ideas rather than keeping your attention on the past.

The afternoon Void of Course Moon is suggesting that you take time to absorb the shift in your consciousness. Notice what your body is asking, and attend to its requests. I'd avoid making important decisions today, since there's just too much dust that has to settle.

AFFIRMATION FOR THE DAY:
Today I acknowledge how far I have come, and how much more I now have to give.

BIG SPINS OF THE DAY:

Sun enters Scorpio: 12:16 P.M. PDT / 3:16 P.M. EDT
Moon Void of Course: 1:18 P.M. PDT / 4:18 P.M. EDT until
Moon enters Aries: 6:25 P.M. PDT / 9:25 P.M. EDT
Mercury conjuncts Sun: 4:55 P.M. PDT / 7:55 P.M. EDT

○ ◑ ◐ ●

WEDNESDAY

October 24

MOON IN ARIES
SUCCESS RATING: ★★★

Sometimes a Herculean effort is required to achieve your goals, while other times you have immortal strength, but no objectives to accomplish. It's better to direct your power in the direction of those who need it, rather than creating a problem so big that it requires the use of force. Under the Aries Moon, you may feel as if your foot is on the gas pedal but the car is parked in the garage.

Don't let yourself stir up trouble today just to keep the buzz alive—if you've got a lot of energy and nowhere to put it, get to the gym. You'll want to use the Aries Moon to ignite the fire of inspiration, not the fury of anger. Find a place to put your motivation, and then *do* something motivational!

Start preparing for the Full Moon by chaining yourself to the basement walls . . . unless, of course, your neighborhood is werewolf friendly.

AFFIRMATION FOR THE DAY:
I am open and willing to receive the abundant inspiration surrounding me, and to use it for the highest good of all.

BIG SPINS OF THE DAY:
None

○◑◐●

THURSDAY

October 25

FULL MOON IN TAURUS
MOON IN ARIES/TAURUS
SUCCESS RATING: ★★

Your individual calendars may show the Full Moon on tomorrow's date, but it occurs tonight in the Pacific, mountain, and central time zones (early Friday for the East Coast and Europe). It's an exciting day with lots of energy, as the Moon finishes its journey in Aries. Try to avoid relationship conflicts brought on by a Venus-Uranus squabble—they just enjoy shaking things up so that you can have fun *making* up under the Full Moon.

Tensions do tend to mount on Full Moon days, so spend your morning focused on your duties. You'll be more peaceful knowing that you took care of yourself, regardless of what happens during the rest of the day. Use this Moon to focus on your desires and what's needed to bring them to fruition.

It's a Taurus Full Moon, so sensuality is high. Make a list of what you're most appreciative of, including people and events, and then write down the things you'd *like* to include but that haven't yet appeared in your life. Use that record of unfulfilled desires as your "Full Moon list," and save it so that you can check on your progress.

AFFIRMATION FOR THE DAY:
Every lofty trait that I admire is in me.

BIG SPINS OF THE DAY:
Venus opposes Uranus: 2:08 A.M. PDT / 5:08 A.M. EDT
Moon Void of Course: 2:47 P.M. PDT / 5:47 P.M. EDT until
Moon enters Taurus: 6:08 P.M. PDT / 9:08 P.M. EDT
Full Moon at 2° Taurus: 9:53 P.M. PDT / 12:53 A.M. EDT (Friday)

○◑◐●

FRIDAY

October 26

MOON IN TAURUS
SUCCESS RATING: ★★★

Satur**ate**. Medit**ate**. Marin**ate**. Procrastin**ate**. Do all the "**ate**" words you can think of, because the Moon in Taurus likes those transitive verbs (words where something is acted upon), especially when there's a "feel-good" component to the action. This is the day when you may have to reciproc**ate** a kindness or vener**ate** another person, because *not* doing so could implic**ate** you as being selfish. Duplic**ate** a pleasure, eradic**ate** a fear, emul**ate** a positive role model, and initi**ate** a friendship. Tell the truth to mitig**ate** a brewing tension, and exoner**ate** yourself from guilt. Commiser**ate** with those who need sympathy, and appreci**ate** the fact that you don't. Allevi**ate** your worries and doubts, and elimin**ate** self-loathing. Commemor**ate** your existence, and activ**ate** thoughts of love. . . .

Finally, mastic**ate** a delicious meal tonight—you've earned it!

AFFIRMATION FOR THE DAY:
I celebr**ate** the wonder of my life
and dissoci**ate** from what is not love.

BIG SPINS OF THE DAY:
Mercury sextiles Pluto: 10:55 A.M. PDT / 1:55 P.M. EDT

OCTOBER

○◑◐●

SATURDAY

October 27

MOON IN TAURUS/GEMINI
SUCCESS RATING: ★★

A really long Void of Course Moon guides you inward and suggests that you simply enjoy the day. When the Moon disconnects from its celestial neighbors, it fully expresses the sign that it's in without inhibition. It will be in earthy Taurus the first part of today, so you may experience a heightened awareness of your body's need for comfort . . . and respond with a trip to a clothing store, restaurant, or even the spa.

Later this evening, the Moon will transition into Gemini, activating your hunger for connections and information. Plan your social time in the evening so that you can be assured of meeting your need for "chatty" entertainment. (And don't forget about that stash of books or magazines that have gone unopened since you bought them!)

OCTOBER

AFFIRMATION FOR THE DAY:
I commit today's thoughts and actions
to the fulfillment of my deepest desires.

BIG SPINS OF THE DAY:
Moon Void of Course: 12:17 A.M. PDT / 3:17 A.M. EDT until
Moon enters Gemini: 5:12 P.M. PDT / 8:12 P.M. EDT

○◑◐●

SUNDAY

October 28

MOON IN GEMINI
SUCCESS RATING: ★★

The Gemini Moon activates your mind during the entire day. Due to the sign's dualistic nature, you may feel one way when you awaken, and another by the time you go to bed. Your mind might be mulling over everything from work to chess moves—getting you to think is what the Gemini Moon does best.

If you're swinging toward the other end of the Gemini polarity, you may find yourself depressed and without thought. That's a clear indication that the "emotional twin" is taking a turn at self-expression. Neither face of this Moon is long lasting, but rest assured that whichever side you're displaying is the one that needed to be asserted.

There's nothing getting in the way of your having what you want today—except that your overactive mind may actually have no clue as to what its real desire is. Ride the wave, for you'll get to shore soon enough.

AFFIRMATION FOR THE DAY:
Constancy is good for me . . . temporarily.

BIG SPINS OF THE DAY:
None

○◑◐●

MONDAY

October 29

MOON IN GEMINI/CANCER

SUCCESS RATING: ★★★

The morning gives you a green light for signing important documents and attending meetings, but a midafternoon Void of Course Moon cautions you to bring awareness to your choices. It's not that things have a tendency to fail when the Moon is Void of Course; it's that you're prone to disconnect from your own intuitive nature. Adding mindfulness to what you're doing ensures that you're conscious of your decisions, thereby increasing their chance of success.

The afternoon Moon enters Cancer, so it will probably heighten your drive for security and connection to your loved ones. Tonight your home could prove magical—but only if you make an effort to relax and radiate those good vibes. Plan for dreams with someone you care about, and watch what happens.

AFFIRMATION FOR THE DAY:
I am not this body, but I love it
for the exquisite vessel that it is.

BIG SPINS OF THE DAY:

Venus squares Jupiter: 2:09 A.M. PDT / 5:09 A.M. EDT
Moon Void of Course: 12:51 P.M. PDT / 3:51 P.M. EDT until
Moon enters Cancer: 5:50 P.M. PDT / 8:50 P.M. EDT
Sun sextiles Saturn: 8:43 P.M. PDT / 11:43 P.M. EDT
Jupiter sextiles Neptune: 8:59 P.M. PDT / 11:59 P.M. EDT

○◑◐●

TUESDAY

October 30

MOON IN CANCER
SUCCESS RATING: ★★★

It's a lovely day for surfing the celestial waves! The Moon is making gentle connections with many of the planets, and that translates into a feeling of ease. There's energy in the air today, and you should be able to use it to accomplish your list of things to do.

The world around you will very likely be reflecting the same harmonious feeling—although it's as if the next day were a holiday, what with all the preparations going on. Well, what do you know? Tomorrow is Halloween, and you *do* have much to accomplish. From getting the kids ready to solidifying your plans to hide out, use today to be well prepared.

Tomorrow presents a long Void of Course Moon, so you'll want to be of sound mind when making all of your arrangements.

AFFIRMATION FOR THE DAY:
I am not afraid to soar—in fact,
I revel in the very possibility.

BIG SPINS OF THE DAY:
None

○◑◐●

WEDNESDAY

October 31

MOON IN CANCER/LEO
SUCCESS RATING: ★

Most of the day will be spent within Cancer's cozy embrace during the long Void of Course Moon. Halloween gives the Cancer Moon a purpose, particularly surrounding the safety and comfort of small children. If you have a family or plan to dole out the treats tonight, make sure to extend a vibe of warmth and cheer. Moody Cancer Moons could create temperamental parents and children—so be one of the happy people on this magical night.

The big news for today is that Neptune is moving forward after a five-month retrograde. Pisceans may feel as if they've come back from a long voyage, and the rest of you may notice a surge in your psychic and intuitive abilities. Feel the magic of this day, and be sure to list your reasons to be grateful for October.

OCTOBER

AFFIRMATION FOR THE DAY:
I live and act as a teacher of love.

BIG SPINS OF THE DAY:
Neptune goes Direct: 9:59 A.M. PDT / 12:59 P.M. EDT
Moon Void of Course: 10:13 A.M. PDT / 1:13 P.M. EDT until
Moon enters Leo: 9:48 P.M. PDT / 12:48 A.M. EDT (Thursday)

Thought for the Month

THINKING AND FEELING

All of us have different ways of dealing with our feelings:

- Air signs (Gemini, Libra, and Aquarius) tend to "mentalize" them.
- Earth signs (Taurus, Virgo, and Capricorn) generally stew in them.
- Fire signs (Aries, Leo, and Sagittarius) are inclined to keep busy in order to dissipate them.
- Water signs (Cancer, Scorpio, and Pisces) are prone to react emotionally to them.

No matter what you do with your emotions, sometimes uncovering how you really feel first requires a discussion of what you *think* you feel. Verbalizing your thoughts, even if they aren't quite clear, allows you to peel away at the onion of your issue. At first, you might be adamant about something, but as you say it out loud, you may find that what you thought was the problem really wasn't it at all. Getting to the truth then becomes a process of talking through it—which isn't necessarily something that you know before starting your dialogue.

NOVEMBER 2007

SUMMARY

It may help to know that November 2007 brings you closer to your childhood fantasies than, say, the same month in previous years. For starters, almost like a goodwill gesture, this November ends the Mercury Retrograde on its first day, and then, exactly one week later, places Venus in her home of Libra.

Of course, no month can ever keep you smiling for its full duration, and by the 9th, the New Moon submerges you in Scorpio's watery depth. Now, I'm a big fan of this sign, but even I can see that bringing in such an intense Moon in the middle of a "Libra-fest" can be like dropping an elephant in the middle of a cocktail party—that is, it just seems out of place. However, the Scorpio New Moon *will* be quite useful in navigating the Mars Retrograde.

November introduces a series of relationship clashes. For example, Venus and Mars, the planets of love and passion, end up in a tangled web of lies and deceit that makes your favorite TV soap opera seem like a comedy show. The month also brings Thanksgiving on the 22nd, the same date that it introduces the inspired sign of Sagittarius—it's a double treat, and one that's sure to help the mood of the day. Then, two days later, you're showered with a sparkling Gemini Full Moon, which carries a message regarding the importance of connection.

This is the only month of the year that's free of big planetary squabbles and cosmic craziness. It's a period that holds to its promise that holidays can be fun . . . and dinner with the in-laws doesn't have to feel like a prison term.

Main Events:

November 1:	Mercury Retrograde ends
November 8:	Venus enters Libra
November 9:	New Moon 17° Scorpio
November 15:	Mars Retrograde begins
November 22:	Sun enters Sagittarius
November 24:	Full Moon 2° Gemini

◐

○◑◐●

THURSDAY

November 1

MERCURY RETROGRADE ENDS
LAST QUARTER MOON IN LEO
SUCCESS RATING: ★★

November starts off with a metaphorical peace offering: The unfairly maligned Mercury Retrograde ends today under the Last Quarter Moon in Leo. That's not to say that today is a bump-free zone, but Leo Moons like having minor reasons to overdramatize.

Often when Mercury changes course, there's a feeling of inertia—as if nothing is being done, or what was intended was driven off course. These are normal feelings reflecting the fact that before Mercury can begin to move forward, it must come to a complete halt, and it's the stopping that frequently creates the sensation of being stuck or unfocused. Luckily, this feeling is short-lived, and thanks to the Moon's bimonthly clash with the Sun, there will be enough fodder for whining. Of course, if you aren't into complaining, there are a few projects that could use your attention, too.

AFFIRMATION FOR THE DAY:
Unless I consciously change them, I willingly fulfill all agreements that I have made.

BIG SPINS OF THE DAY:
Last Quarter Moon at 9° Leo: 2:18 P.M. PDT / 5:18 P.M. EDT
Mercury Retrograde ends: 3:52 P.M. PDT / 6:52 P.M. EDT

○◑◐●

FRIDAY

November 2

MOON IN LEO
SUCCESS RATING: ★★

You should be sensing a return of your energy and focus today. Mercury is regaining its forward momentum, and the Moon is making some wonderful aspects to the outer planets. If you have a creative project to do, this is the day to tap in to your lush inner world and pull forth some ideas.

You know how some days are like swimming upstream, as if everything you aim for is met with resistance? . . . Well, this isn't one of those days. Whatever you approach seems to meet you halfway, almost as though it were telling you that you shouldn't have to work so hard. Under the brightly shining Leo Moon, you'll prosper by embracing this feeling of deserving, and the Moon is certainly trying to assist you. Unfortunately, it's not a great time for launching a new business or signing important documents, since those things are best done in the middle of the month.

AFFIRMATION FOR THE DAY:
I use my circumstances as instruments to make me wiser.

BIG SPINS OF THE DAY:
None

○ ◑ ◐ ●

SATURDAY

November 3

MOON IN LEO/VIRGO
SUCCESS RATING: ★★

Whatever hurdle you find in your path today, remember that it's a minor glitch designed to help make your next leap smoother. Anything that takes you off course from your original goal, even if it's just a phone call that takes more time than it should, can be considered to be such an obstacle.

The Moon slips into Virgo early today and gives you the eyes of an eagle. While it's true that you can now spot a mouse from miles away, you'll probably use this new vision to hunt bunnies—the dusty kind that live underneath your bed. This is one of those days where people may run from you if you grab the vacuum cleaner, not because of the noise, but because of the conviction with which you use it. But go right ahead . . . grab your arsenal of cleaning weapons, and fight the war on "error"! Dirt and grime, beware!

AFFIRMATION FOR THE DAY:
As I clean my environment, I erase my critical thoughts.

BIG SPINS OF THE DAY:
Moon Void of Course: 12:14 A.M. PDT / 3:14 A.M. EDT until
Moon enters Virgo: 5:45 A.M. PDT / 8:45 A.M. EDT

○◑◐●

SUNDAY

November 4

MOON IN VIRGO
SUCCESS RATING: ★★★

It's difficult to have a bad day when you get an extra hour of sleep, but with a Virgo Moon in your midst, it might just conjure up anger at why "they" mess with time in the first place. This Moon may have a little more spunk than yesterday's, so utilize it to your advantage. An unproductive use of the Virgo Moon would be to aim its critical eye at yourself or, secondarily, at others. Direct your ability to see flaws as inanimate objects, and avoid picking on the people around you.

Mars and Saturn are making a cozy connection, reinforcing the idea that productivity is high on the list of priorities. Whatever you put your mind to, you'll accomplish, since this aspect gives you great determination and will. Move at a steady pace . . . you'll have more of this energy available to you tomorrow.

AFFIRMATION FOR THE DAY:
I see all that is good around me.

BIG SPINS OF THE DAY:
Mars trines Saturn: 3:19 A.M. PST / 6:19 A.M. EST

○◑◐●

MONDAY

November 5

MOON IN VIRGO/LIBRA
SUCCESS RATING: ★★

If you managed yesterday without shredding yourself to pieces with undue criticisms, then you're halfway to the start of a good day. Venus is fighting with Pluto, and that can translate into struggles ranging from low self-esteem to feeling ousted from a close relationship in your life.

The surest way out of any conflict is to remain aware that balloons pop, volcanoes erupt, and tempers flare as ways to release energy that's been built up. Don't take rifts too seriously; instead, use them as opportunities to clear the air and lay healthy foundations for more growth. Power struggles should be avoided—you have nothing to prove to anyone, but others may want to prove something to *you.* Play the game if you wish, but don't forget that it *is* just a game.

The Moon goes Void of Course in the early afternoon, which is a time when you'll want to avoid signing those very important papers.

AFFIRMATION FOR THE DAY:
The only relationship I truly seek is with the Divine.

BIG SPINS OF THE DAY:
Moon Void of Course: 10:11 A.M. PST / 1:11 P.M. EST until
Moon enters Libra: 3:47 P.M. PST / 6:47 P.M. EST
Venus squares Pluto: 9:58 P.M. PST / 12:58 A.M. EST (Tuesday)

○◑◐●

TUESDAY

November 6

MOON IN LIBRA
SUCCESS RATING: ★★

There may be a little hangover effect from last night's Venus and Pluto clash. If you recognize an intense emotion lurking within you, you'll probably be given an opportunity to defuse it. Understand that this planetary alignment is not only about power struggles with other people . . . it's about trying to prove yourself in some way.

Observation is the quickest route to resolution. Once you're aware of what your true motives are, you can use your knowledge to guide you in making different choices. Conflicts are not well received under the Libra Moon, but bottling your feelings won't help either. Take some time today to center yourself by finding a place of inner calm—it's there that you can surrender your anger and ask to be guided to your highest good.

The Libra Moon does love a social gathering, so tonight may be your opportunity to surround yourself with loving people. Start making phone calls for an early dinner, as friends will prove to be invaluable tonight.

AFFIRMATION FOR THE DAY:
The guidance I need is always there—I choose to listen for it and trust the support that I am given.

BIG SPINS OF THE DAY:
None

○◑◐●

WEDNESDAY

November 7

MOON IN LIBRA
SUCCESS RATING: ★★★★

You should find that you're feeling better today and very likely more in tune with the lunar energy that's surrounding you with Libran grace. It's an exciting day, thanks to a wonderful connection between the Sun and Uranus—this is often considered to be a very success-promoting aspect, and it can bring good things if it's in the birth chart of any new venture. Sometimes, though, excitement can be distracting . . . after all, it's difficult to walk around calmly when you feel as if your finger is plugged into an electric socket. Try to stay grounded, and take a deep breath before working with anything mechanical.

This is the last day for Venus to be in the sign of Virgo, ending a 30-day plunge into self-evaluation with a critical eye. Soon all that will matter will be looking good enough to be on the cover of a fashion magazine (just kidding).

Whatever you do today, do it with consciousness. Remember that the Sun-Uranus connection can make you somewhat accident-prone due to its giant jolt of energy. Although this is usually benign, if you don't keep one foot on the ground, you could easily miss the brake pedal when you need it.

AFFIRMATION FOR THE DAY:
I trust my decisions and know that
I make choices that are good for me.

BIG SPINS OF THE DAY:
Sun trines Uranus: 8:49 A.M. PST / 11:49 A.M. EST
Moon Void of Course: 10:46 P.M. PST / 1:46 A.M. EST (Thursday) until tomorrow

○◑◐●

THURSDAY

November 8

MOON IN LIBRA/SCORPIO
SUCCESS RATING: ★★

Say good-bye to bad-hair days! Venus is leaving the hard-to-please sign of Virgo, and entering her home of Libra. Charm and grace will soon be yours again, because now you not only feel fantastic about who *you* are—you also feel the same way about everybody else!

Of course, it may take a while for this effect to kick in, so don't be too hard on yourself if you're still looking at the person next to you with a scrunched-up nose! You can blame that on the Scorpio Moon, which does have a way of finding everything that's wrong with everyone else. But don't sweat it: Sometimes it's just fun to laugh at your inner critic, because you know that eventually *all* people end up on its chopping block. Since both the Moon and Venus are in a state of flux, you can officially call this a day of change—so don't expect to feel too perky. But tomorrow . . . well, that's a different story.

AFFIRMATION FOR THE DAY:
I see my judgments of myself reflected
in my judgments of others, and
I bring them into my inner light.

NOVEMBER

BIG SPINS OF THE DAY:
Moon enters Scorpio: 4:19 A.M. PST / 7:19 A.M. EST
Venus enters Libra: 1:05 P.M. PST / 4:05 P.M. EST
Mercury sextiles Pluto: 2:24 P.M. PST / 5:24 P.M. EST

○◑◐●

FRIDAY

November 9

NEW MOON IN SCORPIO
SUCCESS RATING: ★★★

If you've been following this book from the beginning, then you know the New Moon drill: It's a time of renewal and regeneration because the Moon has symbolically given away all its light (when it "waned") and is now ready to start receiving it (as it "waxes").

The New Moon is a metaphor for your own journey into the light of awareness. Use the passion of Scorpio to ignite your desires, and focus your mind on what you truly want. Make a list of things you'd like to receive, and imagine yourself planting each item like a seed that will sprout by the Full Moon in two weeks. You don't have to wait for a New Moon to "plant" your desires, but when the current is flowing toward you, you may as well ride the wave and take advantage of its force.

Bring depth into your life today, either through a book or a conversation, since the Scorpio Moon loves to deepen your knowledge. It's best to sign contracts or make big purchases today, because tomorrow launches a very long Void of Course Moon.

AFFIRMATION FOR THE DAY:
As a child of the Divine, I deserve all that I desire.

BIG SPINS OF THE DAY:
New Moon at 17° Scorpio: 3:04 P.M. PST / 6:04 P.M. EST
Moon Void of Course: 7:20 P.M. PST /10:20 P.M. EST until tomorrow

○◑◐●

SATURDAY

November 10

MOON IN SCORPIO/SAGITTARIUS
SUCCESS RATING: ★★

A very long Void of Course Moon encourages you to slow down and bring your awareness to the present moment. This is a wonderful day for hanging around the house, repairing, cleaning, and organizing the projects that you've ignored—but it's not a great time to begin a new one. During the Void of Course Moon, things that are started tend not to interest you later and get thrown into the "unfinished-work" pile. However, this Moon *is* good for playing and having fun, so get out and take in the scenery around you (if you can). Visit a neighbor, or invite some friends over for some home cooking.

Many of you will feel a little disoriented or dissociated, but pay this no heed—just don't go and do something that requires your mind to be fully operational. That means that if you're buying a car or signing important documents, you'll want to make sure that you have a second opinion or someone there to supervise. . . . Overall, this day should be pleasant if you let the current drive your course.

AFFIRMATION FOR THE DAY:
There is nothing I can do that can
separate me from the love of the Divine.

BIG SPINS OF THE DAY:
Moon Void of Course: until 4:59 P.M. PST / 7:59 P.M. EST
Moon enters Sagittarius: 4:59 P.M. PST / 7:59 P.M. EST

○◑◐●

SUNDAY

November 11

MOON IN SAGITTARIUS
SUCCESS RATING: ★★

This is a perfect time for Veteran's Day, a holiday that honors the past. The Sun is clashing with Neptune, suggesting that you'll have an easy time remembering . . . but you may not like where your memories take you. Anchored by Mercury moving into Scorpio, this day promises to have depth of feeling—albeit of a mixed nature.

It's important to remember that the past doesn't exist. Rather, it's formed by brain cells recalling a moment that's long gone. This technique is useful in helping you appreciate the present, and it also serves as a reminder that no matter where you are now, eventually that, too, will become the past.

Mercury enters Scorpio today, giving you the fearlessness to confront and heal your personal history with great speed, if that's what you choose to do. Be gentle with yourself now, as well as with those around you who may have a hard time reconciling *their* past traumas.

This is an adjustment day, so it's okay to freely float—but do avoid verbal confrontations if you can. Everyone is dealing with this day in his or her own special way.

AFFIRMATION FOR THE DAY:
Peace is not a condition that I create;
it is a condition that I return to.

BIG SPINS OF THE DAY:
Mercury enters Scorpio: 12:41 A.M. PST / 3:41 A.M. EST
Sun squares Neptune: 5:42 P.M. PST / 8:42 P.M. EST

○ ◑ ◐ ●

MONDAY

November 12

MOON IN SAGITTARIUS
SUCCESS RATING: ★★

There may be some lingering effects from yesterday's Sun-Neptune clash, and you might feel that your mental or physical energy is not quite up to par. Yet as the day rolls on, you'll find it easier to get your momentum going. It may help you keep a serious eye on your work—not because something grave is happening, but because you'll be moving in the flow of the exuberant Sagittarius Moon cycle and could take on more than your fair share. Set a goal for yourself at work or school, and seek to achieve it.

Your mind is ready for a focus, and with Mercury in Scorpio, this will be easy to attain. The Sagittarius Moon reminds you that you can accomplish anything, and Mercury in Scorpio directs you how to get it. Bring in some of your inner powers to help you with the day . . . there's no point in being a magical child if you can't wave your wand around the workplace!

And finally, remember that there's still a little too much confusion to sign or buy big today.

AFFIRMATION FOR THE DAY:
I speak only kind words about the people around me, because I understand that I am talking about myself.

BIG SPINS OF THE DAY:

Moon Void of Course: 11:54 P.M. PST / 2:54 A.M. EST (Tuesday) until tomorrow

○◑◐●

TUESDAY

November 13

MOON IN SAGITTARIUS/CAPRICORN
SUCCESS RATING: ★★

"Help me, I'm melting!" If you're wondering where your energy is going, it's starting to slow down, thanks to the upcoming Mars Retrograde. The planet begins to spin backward about every two years or whenever Saturn changes signs (it shifted from Leo to Virgo in September). Mars regulates your energy, temper, and passions—so as it slows down, you do, too. This event begins on Thursday and lasts for about two months, but you'll only feel the sluggishness for the first few days while the Red Planet builds up speed in reverse.

Security and financial concerns will be the primary target of your activity, and you must understand that these issues are magnified—that is, you won't be seeing them on a true scale at first. Use today's Capricorn Moon to help you remain sober and clear about what's *really* going on in your life. Look at the truth without any drama or hype, and you'll find that this is one of the most progressive and important times of the year.

AFFIRMATION FOR THE DAY:
All is well, regardless of my mind's perception.

BIG SPINS OF THE DAY:
Moon Void of Course: until 5:01 A.M. PST / 8:01 A.M. EST
Moon enters Capricorn: 5:01 A.M. PST / 8:01 A.M. EST

○◑◐●

WEDNESDAY

November 14

MOON IN CAPRICORN
SUCCESS RATING: ★★

The world is not coming to an end, Armageddon is not nearby, and Earth is not going to explode. Honestly, people get so arrogant about their own power over some things . . . and so weak about it with regard to others! Mars is almost at a standstill, and you're feeling it—since the planet is in Cancer, worry is going to be prominent. If you take the ominous tone of the day *too* seriously, you'll forget that *you're* creating the hysteria.

Use today's wonderful Capricorn Moon for what it does best: staying sober and pragmatic. The Mars Retrograde is the only time that you'll stop long enough to examine just what it is you're really afraid of. Looking at your fears dissolves them, and running from them only sends you on a wild-goose chase, preventing you from knowing the kind of support you need. So, in a word, *relax* . . . and take the gentle ride that always leads you to your perfect destination.

AFFIRMATION FOR THE DAY:
I am a spiritual being who is having a dream that I am human and separate.

BIG SPINS OF THE DAY:
None

○◑◐●

THURSDAY

November 15

MARS RETROGRADE BEGINS
MOON IN CAPRICORN/AQUARIUS
SUCCESS RATING: ★

Early in the morning, Mars stopped moving forward, beginning a long journey back through Gemini that will last until January 2008. It starts off in the sign of Cancer, which could activate feelings of insecurity for some people, and a sense of great strength for others. It may take several days for you to find your balance.

Mars is the warrior planet, and while it's in retrograde, it may stir up strong desires. First, while it's in Cancer, those longings will be for security; and later, when it enters Gemini, they will be for understanding. In both phases, you'll be addressing all of the obstacles in the way of your desires . . . pretty cool, eh?

Use today's afternoon Void of Course to help you find your center. Don't push too hard in any one direction—and for goodness' sake, try not to take yourself or your circumstances too seriously.

AFFIRMATION FOR THE DAY:
I use my fears to gauge how far
I have veered from my center.

BIG SPINS OF THE DAY:
Mars Retrograde 12° Cancer: 12:22 A.M. PST / 3:22 A.M. EST
Moon Void of Course: 1:20 A.M. PST / 4:20 A.M. EST until
Moon enters Aquarius: 3:31 P.M. PST / 6:31 P.M. EST

○◑◐●

FRIDAY

November 16

MOON IN AQUARIUS
SUCCESS RATING: ★★★

The Moon is resting securely in the sign of Aquarius, allowing you to do the same. If you can focus your attention on the positive components of your life, you'll soar. The Aquarius Moon activates your mind and fills it with the power to hold on to any idea until it's manifested. Consider what thoughts you're allowing yourself to have and whether they're immersed in fear or trust, because they will create whatever they're focused on.

Most of this day is built to support you, even the little afternoon "bump" that could create a mini exchange of tempers. Don't confuse a stoic mind with a depressed one—you may be less in the mood for trivial dialogue, but that doesn't have to mean that you're sad.

Tonight try diving into some serious studies of the mind, and look upon affirmations as a way to counter any negative thinking. It's okay to buy big or sign contracts, as long as you've taken the time to consider all your options.

AFFIRMATION FOR THE DAY:
I gain strength by extending love to everyone I meet.

BIG SPINS OF THE DAY:
Mercury sextiles Saturn: 3:22 P.M. PST / 6:22 P.M. EST

○◑◐●

SATURDAY

November 17

FIRST QUARTER MOON IN AQUARIUS
SUCCESS RATING: ★★

More of yesterday's energy comes through today, and you'll be even better adjusted and ready to work with it. Hopefully, you've kept your mind in a positive state and are now seeing the results. The Aquarius Moon continues to fill you with the overview needed to see your life from a mountaintop, rather than from a ditch. Since the Moon is entering its First Quarter phase, you'll be able to clearly recognize the obstacles that are standing in the way of your desires. Emotions could be volatile today, depending on whom you talk to, so approach everyone with openness and respect. Under this Moon, you'll know pretty quickly who has work to do and who doesn't.

You'll have plenty of energy today to deal with whatever comes up, but you may find that you're not getting certain needs met. It's time to begin your commitment to acquiring whatever it is that will completely fulfill you. Keep in mind, though, that someone else shouldn't have to change in order for you to be okay.

AFFIRMATION FOR THE DAY:
My source of support speaks directly to me, without fear or judgment.

BIG SPINS OF THE DAY:

First Quarter Moon at 25° Aquarius: 2:33 P.M. PST / 5:33 P.M. EST
Moon Void of Course: 6:52 P.M. PST / 9:52 P.M. EST until
Moon enters Pisces: 11:15 P.M. PST / 2:15 A.M. EST (Sunday)

○◑◐●

SUNDAY

November 18

MOON IN PISCES
SUCCESS RATING: ★★

As the Moon shifted overnight into the imaginative sign of Pisces, you may have noticed that your dreams were more powerful than usual, since that sign rules the nocturnal world. There's also an interesting tension building between you and a friend or partner. There are two possible reasons why that is: (1) One of you is not listening to the other's advice, especially in areas related to mental or physical health; or (2) something is triggering jealousy. But don't worry, as both situations are symptomatic of the Moon's changing cycle today and will be easy to rectify.

The Pisces Moon is the doorway to your compassion, which should be extended toward others and yourself equally. Understanding will melt any strain, but don't yield so completely that you let yourself become a victim. You can stand up for what you believe in without attacking the other person—in fact, your integrity is likely to elicit their respect. People from your past may figure prominently, so keep your demeanor inviting, but with a sprinkling of boundaries. You're an easy target for the weak, so be discriminating.

AFFIRMATION FOR THE DAY:
I am strong; I am invincible; I am *me!*

BIG SPINS OF THE DAY:
None

○◑◐●

MONDAY

November 19

MOON IN PISCES
SUCCESS RATING: ★★

Mars and Venus are squabbling today. The planet representing your masculine side is taking issue with the one that symbolizes the feminine part of you, and the results could be reflected in your relationships. If you can remember last September, a similar issue emerged then—but the tables were turned, and it was Venus moving backward, not Mars.

If you're experiencing this passage as a love battle, the best recourse is to withdraw and keep your wits about you. Mars is in Cancer, enhancing your feelings of insecurity, which could be making everything seem worse than it is. If you aren't engaged in a relationship "war," then you may want to see if you're internalizing the same energy, which could show up as acute self-criticism or doubt. Again, the best response is to retreat until you can find your center.

Today it's important to take time to do nurturing things for yourself . . . consider anything from hot baths to massages. Stressful transits tend to place you in uncomfortable positions mentally, physically, and spiritually, so anything that you can do to bring peace to just one of those areas will make a world of difference.

AFFIRMATION FOR THE DAY:
I do not need anyone's approval to feel whole and loved.

BIG SPINS OF THE DAY:
Venus squares Mars: 6:19 P.M. PST / 9:19 P.M. EST
Mercury trines Mars: 6:53 P.M. PST / 9:53 P.M. EST
Moon Void of Course: 11:27 P.M. PST / 2:27 A.M. EST (Tuesday) until tomorrow

○◑◐●

TUESDAY

November 20

MOON IN PISCES/ARIES
SUCCESS RATING: ★★★★

The Moon leaves Pisces in the early morning, but it's around long enough to ensure that you have a lush night of dreaming. As the Aries Moon approaches, you'll feel your feisty spirit come back to life as you shake off the lingering fragments of emotional energy that you've absorbed over the last few days.

The sky is filled with wonderful happenings as Mercury, Mars, and Uranus all hold hands in what's called a "Grand Trine." This is a great aspect for moving ideas from your creative mind into action, so use it to act where you've previously encountered resistance. Go and get that checkup that you've been putting off, or support a friend in doing the same. News always tends to be better under a Grand Trine!

Plant positive thoughts about your life today, and let them take root. The most important thing to remember about Grand Trines is that they can create laziness, and if you don't act on them, nothing will happen—so use what you have. And just know that there's a Full Moon on the way that will help you reinforce your decisions.

AFFIRMATION FOR THE DAY:
I love my body and how it supports me fully.

BIG SPINS OF THE DAY:
Moon Void of Course: until 3:25 A.M. PST / 6:25 A.M. EST
Moon enters Aries: 3:25 A.M. PST / 6:25 A.M. EST

NOVEMBER

○◑◐●

WEDNESDAY

November 21

MOON IN ARIES
SUCCESS RATING: ★★★

Okay, so your relationships still require a little work—no big deal. The Aries Moon will help you find the courage to push people to consider what you want (I hope that you're bigger than they are!). It seems that more arguments occur under this Moon than when it's in any other sign, due to the aggressive nature of Aries. But the truth is that more *healing* actually takes place with the Moon in a Fire sign because of the permission you feel to spit it all out (or yell it all out, or hit the wall with a pillow, or what have you).

There are wonderful opportunities for breakthroughs today, thanks to that amazing connection of Mars, Mercury, and Uranus (remember the Grand Trine?). Use it to tell the truth, while staying in touch with your heart—in other words, speak your passions. Creativity is at an all-time high, so get out your palettes and paint (any form of self-expression will work). If you feel the need to lose your temper, scream in the car with your windows rolled up before confronting anyone head-on.

AFFIRMATION FOR THE DAY:
I believe in the amazing abilities of everyone I see, because I believe in my own.

BIG SPINS OF THE DAY:
Mercury trines Uranus: 9:58 A.M. PST / 12:58 P.M. EST

Happy Birthday, Sagittarius!

NOVEMBER 22–DECEMBER 21

At the heart of Sagittarius is the fire of spirituality. With heads up, shoulders back, and eyes aimed at far-off horizons, people born under this sign love the quest for truth—the kind that makes their adrenaline surge and takes their breath away. These are the Fire children, and they have an unquenchable thirst for knowledge. Sagittarians live in a magical realm of myths and knights, kings and queens, and it's imperative that they find a way to allow that world to mingle with the mundane reality of work and survival.

People of this sign are known for carrying a metaphorical bow with them, always ready to shoot their symbolic arrows of truth, and you can see this in action when they've decided to "share" their opinion about something. Regardless of their surroundings, Sagittarians may loudly avow that they "just can't stand" your hair. It's not that they're trying to be cruel . . . they're just seeing the world as one big family, and you as one of their siblings. Bigger is better, more is preferable, and boredom *must* be avoided at all costs! Jupiter, the planet of luck, is covering the Sagittarians' backs—a fact that would be hard not to boast about.

AFFIRMATIONS FOR SAGITTARIUS:

No matter which road I take,
I will be guided toward my highest good.

I am never stuck and am always free,
regardless of what it may look like.

All the knowledge that I need is within me—
learning is really just remembering.

○◑◐●

THURSDAY

November 22

SUN IN SAGITTARIUS
MOON IN ARIES/TAURUS
SUCCESS RATING: ★★

Today the Sun leaves the foreboding sign of Scorpio and lifts your head toward the sky in search of the truth—what a great gift to have on Thanksgiving Day! This is the season of magic, and you're a part of what makes it that way. So what if your relationship is falling apart? Who cares if you feel that this has been the hardest year you've ever faced in your life? Throw your worries onto the shaft of the Centaur's arrow, and shoot them away. Life is about more than those tiny details—it's about spreading your wings and reaching for the Sun!

Okay, I was kidding about the relationship part. I realize that when the Moon is in Taurus, the last thing that you want to hear is how your stability isn't guaranteed. Well, it *is* guaranteed . . . all you have to do is believe, and Sagittarius is here to help. Give yourself a day to get adjusted and you'll see what I mean.

By the way, this day was meant for you to eat—not just because of Thanksgiving, but also in honor of the Taurus Moon—so stuff yourself!

AFFIRMATION FOR THE DAY:
There is not enough paper in the world
to write down all that I am grateful for.

BIG SPINS OF THE DAY:
Moon Void of Course: 12:40 A.M. PST / 3:40 A.M. EST until
Moon enters Taurus: 4:19 A.M. PST / 7:19 A.M. EST
Sun enters Sagittarius: 8:50 A.M. PST / 11:50 A.M. EST

○◑◐●

FRIDAY

November 23

MOON IN TAURUS
SUCCESS RATING: ★★★

A full day of the Taurus Moon means a solid day of eating to your heart's content (didn't you do that yesterday?). Well, maybe that's not the whole significance, but food does taste better when the Moon is in the sign whose name can be partially found within the word "res*taur*ant"!

Use your body to feel your way through the day. If something makes you uncomfortable, then you shouldn't do it. Similarly, if you physically "light up" in response to something, then you probably ought to go for it. However, you should try to have some control over the Bull of desire during this Moon. I've known many people whose proverbial light went off for items that they really couldn't afford, so try to show good judgment today. Appreciate the people in your life who made a difference—that's an investment you not only *can* afford; it's one that you *should* spring for.

Avoid big purchases or legal contracts in the afternoon. It would serve you to light a candle tonight as a remembrance of the intentions that you sent out at the last New Moon, since there's a Full Moon in the morning.

AFFIRMATION FOR THE DAY:
My body is good to me, and I am good to it in return.

BIG SPINS OF THE DAY:
Moon Void of Course: 10:53 A.M. PST / 1:53 P.M. EST until tomorrow

○◑◐●

SATURDAY

November 24

FULL MOON IN GEMINI
MOON IN TAURUS/GEMINI
SUCCESS RATING: ★★

Communication is the theme as the Full Moon in Gemini lights up the night sky. This is a great day to establish contact with your spiritual side in order to hear the flawless guidance that's always being offered to you. It's also a perfect time to connect with friends of all different persuasions for the opportunity they provide to expand your knowledge.

This Full Moon beckons you to understand yourself *and* the world around you. Dive into books, magazines, or anything that can teach you something more than you already know. Aquarians are in for a special treat today, because the ruler of their sign, Uranus, is no longer moving backward. If you've been feeling a little overshadowed by your life, this date will turn that around: You can be heard, and your ideas can be understood—and that applies to everyone. Don't let misunderstandings hold too much meaning today. A fast-moving aspect between Mercury and Neptune is promoting inner dialogue and discouraging spontaneous purchases.

AFFIRMATION FOR THE DAY:
I accept that I am inextricably connected to all things.

BIG SPINS OF THE DAY:
Uranus Retrograde ends: 2:15 A.M. PST / 5:15 A.M. EST
Moon Void of Course: until 3:30 A.M. PST / 6:30 A.M. EST
Moon enters Gemini: 3:30 A.M. PST / 6:30 A.M. EST
Full Moon at 2° Gemini: 6:30 A.M. PST / 9:30 A.M. EST
Mercury squares Neptune: 9:50 A.M. PST / 12:50 P.M. EST

○◑◐●

SUNDAY

November 25

MOON IN GEMINI
SUCCESS RATING: ★★★★

Love is in the air. Well, love is *always* in the air, but today you have a better opportunity to feel it. An upcoming connection between Neptune and Venus (occurring tomorrow, to be exact) is helping you embrace your romantic side and toss out the analytical one, at least for a couple of days. What—or whom—would you like to romance? Perhaps a creative urge is about to be born, or maybe you've always adored long walks in the park. It doesn't have to involve a person, but it *will* be an experience.

Mercury is now giving you a chance to look below the surface of something in order to see its truth. Perhaps you'll recognize the reality of your essence and be so blown away by it that you ask for your own hand in marriage! Yes, I'm being silly, but when you think about it, if you liked yourself that much, there would be a lot more happiness in your life. So come on, grab a mirror . . . and fall in love.

AFFIRMATION FOR THE DAY:
I interpret all experiences today
through the filter of love and kindness.

BIG SPINS OF THE DAY:

Moon Void of Course: 11:38 P.M. PST / 2:38 A.M. EST (Monday) until tomorrow

○◑◐●

MONDAY

November 26

MOON IN GEMINI/CANCER
SUCCESS RATING: ★★★★

The Cancer Moon moves in early today, filling you with a feeling of warmth and a fondness for home and family. If you ever considered remodeling, this is the time to do so, as your taste will be impeccable, and your choices perfect. Venus and Neptune are now in a full embrace, so be sure to do something you love with a person you care about. If you don't have a special someone, today increases the odds that you can find him or her. You should have the energy you need to finish any project, although you may not really be in the mood for work (or school) of any kind.

A business that you start on this date will have an extra edge on the competition, because Venus and Neptune will be holding hands within its birth chart, and people will fall in love with whatever it is! It's also fine to make those extra-large purchases today and sign on any dotted lines. This window of opportunity will close again soon, so if you can, do it now.

AFFIRMATION FOR THE DAY:
Every moment in my life is the opportunity of a lifetime.

BIG SPINS OF THE DAY:
Moon Void of Course: until 3:07 A.M. PST / 6:07 A.M. EST
Moon enters Cancer: 3:07 A.M. PST / 6:07 A.M. EST
Venus trines Neptune: 1:55 A.M. PST / 4:55 A.M. EST

○◑◐●

TUESDAY

November 27

MOON IN CANCER
SUCCESS RATING: ★★★

Mars is going retrograde in Cancer, which means that every time the Moon goes into that sign, it will touch off a bit of Martian insecurity at some point. So if you find that you're a little more worried than usual today, you can rest assured, knowing that Mars is simply reminding you that you need to put attention on the things that make you feel safe. The Moon might also trigger your temper—or that of someone you know—but if you keep in mind that this is a fast-moving Moon, you may be more forgiving and let things slide until tomorrow.

In spite of all the potential worry that's in the air, if you listen closely, you'll hear a different tune: one that makes you smile. Two planets are coming together soon, and they spell *relief* in a very different way from the popular antacid. I'm not going to give it all away, because if Pluto and Jupiter knew that I couldn't keep a secret, they would tan my hide!

Go in peace (not *pieces*), and feel the foundation that's being built for you. It's okay to sign on the dotted line today.

AFFIRMATION FOR THE DAY:
Wonderful things happen in my life every day.

BIG SPINS OF THE DAY:
Moon Void of Course: 8:23 P.M. PST / 11:23 P.M. EST until tomorrow

○◑◐●

WEDNESDAY

November 28

MOON IN CANCER/LEO
SUCCESS RATING: ★★

You'll be able to enjoy most of this day under the Leo Moon, which enters early in the morning. Health-related topics may seem to appear now . . . perhaps someone you know will have something to tell you regarding his or her well-being, or you could learn something in a more general medical context.

It's a great time to get involved with your creative side: painting, sculpting, crafts, or any hobby that reminds you that you're more than your job or schoolwork. Children also seem to figure prominently today, perhaps as a reminder to get in touch with your childlike self.

Remember that it's good to be right, but it's better to be kind. In other words, if you aren't currently performing at the theater, don't create unnecessary dramas.

AFFIRMATION FOR THE DAY:
I take full responsibility for my actions, and I willingly and lovingly apologize when I recognize that this is needed.

BIG SPINS OF THE DAY:
Moon Void of Course: until 5:23 A.M. PST / 8:23 A.M. EST
Moon enters Leo: 5:23 A.M. PST / 8:23 A.M. EST

○◑◐●

THURSDAY

November 29

MOON IN LEO
SUCCESS RATING: ★★

You're on more solid footing now for the second day of the Leo Moon. There's a good chance that things will go relatively smoothly, but you may run out of steam earlier than usual. Take a moment at some point to remind yourself that you're your own best friend, and make a promise to stand by yourself through thick and thin. It may sound silly, but if you could just reassure yourself that the closest companion you'll ever have is *you* . . . well, you might be less willing to buy your friends all those wonderful gifts (just kidding). Seriously, though, remind your inner critic to ease up—it will make a difference.

Tomorrow gets interrupted by a Void of Course Moon, so use this date to get a chunk of work done. You can finish up later, but your best energy occurs right now. Leo Moons tend to keep you feeling optimistic, so tap in to your happy side and share it. Also, continue any artistic or creative endeavors, as they could easily pay off. Signing important documents isn't recommended, due to tomorrow's Sun-Saturn clash . . . you don't want that aspect in the birth chart of your new business or contract.

AFFIRMATION FOR THE DAY:
I may not like the cover, but I refrain from judgment until I have actually read the book.

BIG SPINS OF THE DAY:
None

○◑◐●

FRIDAY

November 30

MOON IN LEO/VIRGO
SUCCESS RATING: ★

It may seem that there's a choice you have to make between your duties and your desires today. The Sun is clashing with Saturn, and limitations usually abound. You might find that you're tired and need some rest, but your responsibilities just won't let up. The best solution is to compromise: Put some time into your work, then take a break and devote a few minutes to something completely selfish. You can't produce much if you aren't refueling. Keep your attitude positive, and avoid dwelling on anything that resembles being a victim. You do have many choices available to you, but they won't necessarily seem like the ones you want.

The Void of Course Moon lands right in the middle of the day (a good opportunity to be selfish), so this isn't one of your best contract-signing dates. Since this is the last day of November, it's a good idea to take some time out to review the wonders of the month. After all, you don't tend to forget the difficulties, but the magic and reasons to be grateful can get easily buried.

Say good-bye to November, the month that brought you the ultimate holiday for gratitude.

AFFIRMATION FOR THE DAY:
I am important and sweet to those around me, like honey is to bees.

BIG SPINS OF THE DAY:
Moon Void of Course: 9:25 A.M. PST/ 12:25 P.M. EST until
Moon enters Virgo: 11:45 A.M. PST / 2:45 P.M. EST
Sun squares Saturn: 12:23 P.M. PST / 3:23 P.M. EST

Thought for the Month

Gratitude Is an Experience

If you've ever had your breath taken away by a spectacular sunset or Eclipse, or by a person you fell in love with, then you know that there's a moment—however brief—that connects you with something wonderful. It's a feeling that transcends all your problems and moves you to what you might call a "spiritual high." Although the external event is usually short-lived, the feelings that result are priceless, because they offer you a glimpse into the essence of gratitude. And this experience is available anytime you choose. Below are some examples of my own moments of being thankful . . . you may have different ones.

I experience gratitude whenever I . . .

- . . . have the profound realization that I'm *in* this world, but not *of* it.
- . . . recognize the unyielding and ever-present messages of love and reassurance that surround me.
- . . . translate "acts of hate" as "cries for love."
- . . . ask for the impossible problem to be solved, and it is.
- . . . watch an unstoppable fear dissolve in seconds, just because I asked.
- . . . realize that my grievances with others are really attacks on myself, and I dispel them.
- . . . understand that no forgiveness is necessary, except that of myself for believing I've done something wrong.

- . . . remember that there is nothing I must do in order to have a true spiritual connection.

- . . . have the indescribable recognition that I haven't been left here to die—that, in fact, death is not real.

- . . . realize that I have been, and always will be, embraced by something so profoundly loving that it defies comparison with anything that I've ever experienced or believed.

- . . . know, without doubt, that I've never left the lap of the Divine, Who lovingly embraces me while I have this dream of separation.

○◑◐●

DECEMBER 2007

SUMMARY

Most of this month is filled with the inspired energy of Sagittarius. In fact, there are a couple of days in December that boast five planets in the sign at the same time, and understanding the motives of Sagittarius will help you ensure that time during these cycles is well spent. The sign is represented by the Archer, who is half immortal and half mortal: One part is mythological and larger than life, and the other is human and mundane. Sagittarians often feel a conflict between inhabiting the "real" world and living in the realm of imagination and magic. After all, once you experience yourself as a god or goddess, you don't revel in the idea of having to go to work and pay the bills!

With this abundance of Sagittarius in the December sky, you'll also feel the division between your Divine and mortal selves. Sometimes it can create a great deal of frustration, but there *is* an answer to the dilemma: You must bring your magic to support you in your everyday world. Affirmations are a great example of using the power of the mind to make magic, but there are many other tools also available.

The big news this month is the Conjunction (occurrence at the same point in space) of Jupiter and Pluto. Jupiter is the ruler of Sagittarius, and it will be in that sign, right next to Pluto, the planet of power and truth. This event occurs on December 11 and promises to be a lasting force through the rest of the year. Later, Jupiter will move into the stoic sign of Capricorn, as if to say, "Now that you have your power, let's put it to use."

This month is also host to the Winter Solstice, which begins when the Sun enters Capricorn, and we settle in for winter hibernation.

Highlights for the Month:

December 1:	Mercury enters Sagittarius
December 5:	Venus enters Scorpio
December 9:	New Moon at 17° of Sagittarius
December 11:	Jupiter conjuncts Pluto 27° Sagittarius
December 20:	Mercury enters Capricorn
December 21:	Sun enters Capricorn (Winter Solstice)
December 23:	Full Moon 2° Cancer

○◑◐●

SATURDAY

December 1

LAST QUARTER MOON IN VIRGO
MOON IN VIRGO
SUCCESS RATING: ★

Maybe it's the stress of the holidays, or perhaps there's global news that's heating up—whatever form events may take, Mars is positioning itself in such a way that things might seem a little more tense than usual. Awareness of this fact might help you divert any potential frustrations that may arise.

With the Last Quarter Moon in Virgo, your mind could be particularly sensitive to anything that disrupts your routine. Unfortunately, there's a very good chance that adhering to a strict regimen is almost impossible, thanks to Mercury's entrance into Sagittarius. Simply put, you'd do well to stay open-minded and let your day guide you. Sometimes the external world sets up circumstances in your life that must be attended to, and the more flexible you are, the less tension you'll see.

Remember to stop throughout the day just long enough to see how you're feeling. Stress has a funny way of hiding itself, and locating it is simply a matter of taking a breath.

AFFIRMATION FOR THE DAY:
I willingly give the steering wheel
of my life to my Divine guide.

BIG SPINS OF THE DAY:
Mercury enters Sagittarius: 4:21 A.M. PST / 7:21 A.M. EST
Last Quarter Moon at 9° Virgo: 4:45 A.M. PST / 7:45 A.M. EST

○◑◐●

SUNDAY

December 2

MOON IN VIRGO/LIBRA
SUCCESS RATING: ★★

Make the reduction of stress one of your main priorities today. Under an all-day Virgo Moon, it's very easy to override your own needs in lieu of others' (remember that the negative side of this sign is martyrdom).

Regardless of your own self-evaluation, take several moments at random throughout the day, and bring your attention to something peaceful. It could be a book, meditation, or even a simple bathroom break where you can be sure that no one will interrupt you.

Your mind should be open to a grander, more spiritual perspective . . . so call upon what soothes you, and keep those loving thoughts in close proximity. The evening beckons you to relax in the comfort of your own company, but if that's not possible, take yet another extended bathroom break before retiring.

AFFIRMATION FOR THE DAY:
At my slightest request, all the support I need appears instantly.

BIG SPINS OF THE DAY:

Venus sextiles Jupiter: 12:15 A.M. PST / 3:15 A.M. EST
Moon Void of Course: 6:12 P.M. PST / 9:12 P.M. EST until
Moon enters Libra: 10:02 P.M. PST / 1:02 A.M. EST (Monday)

○◑◐●

MONDAY

December 3

MOON IN LIBRA
SUCCESS RATING: ★★

You're starting today with the Moon planted firmly in the sign of Libra. Social connections call to you, whether you think you're in the mood for them or not. Libra encourages you to always look your best and recognize the beauty in those around you, although this can slide into superficiality if you aren't careful.

A sexy Venus-Pluto connection adds spice to the day, but your ability to make clear-cut choices still seems to be hampered. Quick, decisive action may not be as important as you think, so if you aren't getting a definite yes or no, then a good rule of thumb is to simply wait until you do—"Libra" and "clear decisions" is considered to be an oxymoron in the astrological world. Don't push against the grain today; instead, remain gracious and prudent in your actions.

Sleep might elude you tonight. Good preventive actions against insomnia could include laying off the caffeine earlier than usual, taking several deep breaths before retiring, or doing some mild exercise an hour before bedtime *(wink, wink)*.

AFFIRMATION FOR THE DAY:
I see the good in everyone around me, and I bring it to the surface.

BIG SPINS OF THE DAY:
Venus sextiles Pluto: 2:32 P.M. PST / 5:32 P.M. EST

○◑◐●

TUESDAY

December 4

MOON IN LIBRA
SUCCESS RATING: ★★★★

In sports, when one side has been losing and turns the game around, the fans shout, "Nice recovery!" . . . I suppose the same could be said for someone who was ill and is now well. If this month were an athletic team or sick friend who's bounced back, the phrase "Nice recovery, December!" would be more than appropriate, based on the alignments in the sky today. Thanks to a wonderful connection made by the Sun and Venus, you could easily call this a turning-point day.

You'll probably find it easier to appreciate yourself, your accomplishments, and the people around you. The more gratitude you can muster, the more elevated your mood becomes. I have no reservations about marking this day as a great one to launch something new—anything from a business to a friendship. And it's a perfect date for a holiday party, too!

AFFIRMATION FOR THE DAY:
Today I recognize the unconditional support that always surrounds me.

BIG SPINS OF THE DAY:
None

○◑◐●

WEDNESDAY

December 5

MOON IN LIBRA/SCORPIO
SUCCESS RATING: ★★★

Move slowly through the morning, and build up momentum at your own pace. Venus is leaving her home of Libra and diving into the deep waters of Scorpio, and wherever she goes, the planet leaves her mark of beauty and appreciation. As she enters the Scorpion's domain, she'll introduce you to a new way of looking at sexuality, passion, and—most important—your inner fears.

You may find today to be slightly undisciplined as you try to manage your affairs (that is, your *work*-related ones). This disarray is merely an adjustment, not only to Venus's new home, but to the Moon's as well.

Look forward to a more serious connection with another person, something other than a chat about the weather. You'd be surprised by how many people have been looking for an excuse to let down their guard. Business meetings and important papers can be processed today, although it would be wise to wait until after the Void of Course Moon.

AFFIRMATION FOR THE DAY:
I find more value in being interest*ed* than interest*ing*.

BIG SPINS OF THE DAY:
Venus enters Scorpio: 5:29 A.M. PST / 8:29 A.M. EST
Moon Void of Course: 6:49 A.M. PST / 9:49 A.M. EST until
Moon enters Scorpio: 10:32 A.M. PST / 1:32 P.M. EST

○◑◐●

THURSDAY

December 6

MOON IN SCORPIO
SUCCESS RATING: ★

Complaining about a problem without presenting a viable solution isn't helpful to anyone. Criticism does have a place when it's used to help improve something, but it needs the balance of supportive suggestions in order to make a difference.

Today Mercury is clashing with Saturn, and the result is often a battle with authority—don't get stuck on one side or the other. Recognize what *is,* and then propose what could be, without being self-righteous or lashing out at others. People will tend to listen to you if you're rational, but they'll dismiss you if you rant. While under the influence of Scorpio, try to remember that not everyone is as conscious as you, so what may look like an attack is often just an oversight.

Tonight pull out a mystery novel, and indulge your inner detective.

AFFIRMATION FOR THE DAY:
What I see on the outside is not necessarily the truth, but it is always only an inner glance away.

BIG SPINS OF THE DAY:
Mercury squares Saturn: 1:17 P.M. PST / 4:17 P.M. EST

○◑◐●

FRIDAY

December 7

MOON IN SCORPIO/SAGITTARIUS
SUCCESS RATING: ★

It's a long, long Void of Course Moon today, so the sky's the limit as to the possibilities. You might feel just slightly off balance, and if so, I recommend that you move slowly. However, you may appreciate the lack of interference that this Moon creates and find that much unfinished work can be completed. Don't take any feelings of depression or ambivalence seriously—they're just fleeting, and for some of you, this is a way to release the week's accumulation of energy.

The Sun is forming a connection with Uranus that could spell *accident-prone,* so be sure to pace yourself today, and avoid any spontaneous agreements or purchases that you might regret tomorrow. Do write down your ideas, however, as there is the potential for sheer genius to shine through you.

AFFIRMATION FOR THE DAY:
I am like a boat in the current of life's river: I trust the flow.

BIG SPINS OF THE DAY:
Sun squares Uranus: 12:35 A.M. PST / 3:35 A.M. EST
Moon Void of Course: 2:18 A.M. PST / 5:18 A.M. EST until
Moon enters Sagittarius: 11:12 P.M. PST / 2:12 A.M. EST (Saturday)

○◑◐●

SATURDAY

December 8

MOON IN SAGITTARIUS
SUCCESS RATING: ★★★★★

There's a very powerful New Moon coming tomorrow, so be sure to set some time aside to anchor your most personal aspirations and intentions. As you may have gathered by now, a day or two before the New Moon, a mild depression can be triggered—which is metaphorically related to the Moon's loss of light as it approaches the Sun.

On a subconscious level, you may feel that you've lost your light. Put a list together that reflects what you desire . . . remember that you don't have to be precise, as your higher self is neither stupid nor vindictive. Candles may help you focus and feel closer to the magic. Steal a quiet moment sometime tonight, and see yourself the way you really are: happy, fulfilled, and always connected to the light.

This is an incredible date for a wedding, for the bond will be indestructible.

AFFIRMATION FOR THE DAY:
The past and future are only illusions—
all I have is this very moment, where I am
whole and my needs are nonexistent.

BIG SPINS OF THE DAY:
Mars sextiles Saturn: 7:52 P.M. PST / 10:52 P.M. EST

○ ◐ ◑ ●

SUNDAY

December 9

NEW MOON IN SAGITTARIUS
SUCCESS RATING: ★★★

This inspiring New Moon stirs intense feelings today. At the height of their connection, the Sun and Moon will join three other planets in Sagittarius, which adds up to a total of five celestial bodies occupying the sign of the Archer.

While being showered by the Sagittarian arrows of enlightenment, you'll probably notice a strong desire to embrace your inner magic. Reach for the map, and pick a place that you've always wanted to visit—or reconnect with your favorite spiritual book. Today is all about excitement and hope.

The downside of this prevalence of Sagittarius is that you can fall prey to feeling disappointed that you have to do your mundane rituals. For some people, just going to work could be hard. Remember, though, that you're creating a new foundation today, and the walls and fixtures will come next. Don't forget to *believe*.

AFFIRMATION FOR THE DAY:
The world responds completely to my heart's desires.

BIG SPINS OF THE DAY:
New Moon at 17° Sagittarius: 9:42 A.M. PST / 12:42 P.M. EST

○ ◑ ◐ ●

MONDAY

December 10

Moon in Sagittarius/Capricorn
Success Rating: ★★★★

Enjoy your lofty Sagittarius fantasies in the early part of the day, because you'll be entering the more pragmatic world of Capricorn by midafternoon. Most of the morning occurs under the often-unproductive Void of Course Moon, so take your time getting your engines revved. And when you finally do, don't move faster than the speed limit.

Today has a Mercurial trap, one that could set your mind off in countless different directions. Too much input might disorient you, and squabbles could result. Bite your tongue if you feel that it's wagging out of control. This type of energy could make you regret your words, and the sad part is that if you aren't conscious, you won't even remember having uttered them in the first place.

Even though there's all that Mercury confusion, the power of the other planets could make this an outstanding day for contractual agreements. Use your intuition, and heed what your body is telling you.

Affirmation for the Day:
The guidance I follow is always presented in a loving and supportive manner, which is how I recognize it.

BIG SPINS OF THE DAY:
Moon Void of Course: 7:37 A.M. PST / 10:37 A.M. EST until
Moon enters Capricorn: 10:52 A.M. PST / 1:52 P.M. EST
Mercury squares Uranus: 4:25 P.M. PST / 7:25 P.M. EST

○◑◐●

TUESDAY

December 11

MOON IN CAPRICORN
SUCCESS RATING: ★★★★★

Jupiter and Pluto are meeting at the same point in Sagittarius, and their union is considered to be one of the most successful, powerful connections that you can have in the chart of any business or marriage. Jupiter is good fortune and Pluto is power—together they make an almost indestructible team. It will be interesting to see what the news is reporting over the next few days.

Venus and Mars are joining in the celebration, promising harmonious relationships and plenty of fun. If you happen to fall in love today, the two of you could conquer the world. Be aware, though, that this afternoon starts a Void of Course Moon that won't be over for 24 hours. It's as if the Universe knew that you'd need to rest tomorrow and assimilate the power that today ushered in.

AFFIRMATION FOR THE DAY:
Each day I find talents in myself that I never knew existed.

BIG SPINS OF THE DAY:

Jupiter conjuncts Pluto: 11:19 A.M. PST / 2:19 P.M. EST
Venus trines Mars: 3:16 P.M. PST / 6:16 P.M. EST
Moon Void of Course: 3:58 P.M. PST / 6:58 P.M. EST until tomorrow
Sun sextiles Neptune: 7:48 P.M. PST / 10:48 P.M. EST

○◑◐●

WEDNESDAY

December 12

MOON IN CAPRICORN/AQUARIUS
SUCCESS RATING: ★★

There's certainly no reason why you couldn't have an extremely productive and powerful day. Most of the big alignments that existed yesterday are still in place. My advice is to feel out the Void of Course Moon and make a personal decision regarding any big plans you'd like to launch. Some people are very clear and focused during this Moon, while others feel foggy and disoriented.

Usually these are days dedicated to unfinished work and projects that need some attention, but if you're moved to sign on a dotted line today, let your intuition be your guide. Venus and Saturn are commingling in a way that suggests you'll be pleased with almost any choice you make.

AFFIRMATION FOR THE DAY:
It is effortless for me to change any belief.

BIG SPINS OF THE DAY:
Venus sextiles Saturn: 11:33 A.M. PST / 2:33 P.M. EST
Moon Void of Course: until 9:02 P.M. PST / 12:02 A.M. EST (Thursday)
Moon enters Aquarius: 9:02 P.M. PST / 12:02 A.M. EST (Thursday)

○◑◐●

THURSDAY

December 13

MOON IN AQUARIUS
SUCCESS RATING: ★★★

Finally, some *stability*—it's a funny word coming under the Aquarius Moon, which is known for its desire to shake things up for sheer entertainment value. Hopefully, you'll set a whole new batch of aspirations into motion, but don't sweat it if you can't think of any . . . sometimes things happen even when your mind doesn't jump in and get involved.

Today may offer you a trip to the past: A memory, an old movie, or maybe even a longtime friend might pop in to say hello. You'll probably feel tired, the kind of "to-the-bone" exhaustion that makes you wonder why you aren't sleeping well. Don't fret—you're in a wonderful cycle that will embrace *you,* even if you're too exhausted to return the embrace. Rejuvenation will come readily if you so desire . . . try a sip of wine tonight before retiring.

AFFIRMATION FOR THE DAY:
I am always in the perfect place at the perfect time, because I am blessed.

BIG SPINS OF THE DAY:
Mercury sextiles Neptune: 7:02 P.M. PST / 10:02 P.M. EST

○ ◑ ◐ ●

FRIDAY

December 14

MOON IN AQUARIUS
SUCCESS RATING: ★★★★

There's luck in the air—a lot of it. This kind of good fortune might make you feel like taking a few risks that would normally be considered . . . well, too *risky.* You may find yourself floating on a feeling of optimism that's been lacking for way too long.

However it is that you experience this day, keep the thought deep within you that you can have whatever you desire. It may not show up in the exact way you picture it or in the precise moment that you want it to, but it *will* appear—just look at your record up to now. Chances are, you have an old wish list lying around that has everything checked off (except for the date with that no-good person you were strangely attracted to).

There's nothing in the way of your success, not even fear. So go for anything you want . . . and rest assured that the safety nets are deployed.

AFFIRMATION FOR THE DAY:
It is safe to let love in, and I am willing to receive it.

BIG SPINS OF THE DAY:
None

○◑◐●

SATURDAY

December 15

MOON IN AQUARIUS/PISCES
SUCCESS RATING: ★

The Moon enters imaginative Pisces early today and brings you into the watery den of illusions and dreams. A strain between Venus and the rogue comet Chiron makes this one of the worst days to launch a business or sign a contract.

Try to perceive your judgments not as reflections of who you are, but of how you view yourself. The Pisces Moon tends to help you see everything as a mirror, even the weather, so—rain or shine—remember that the world is serving you by making you aware of your oneness with all things.

Someone may try to exert some authority over you today. If you can meet his or her request without sacrificing yourself, then do so. Otherwise, politely decline and walk away, and then aim straight for the bathtub to have a good soak.

AFFIRMATION FOR THE DAY:
I am in a constant state of self-healing on all levels.

BIG SPINS OF THE DAY:
Moon Void of Course: 3:51 A.M. PST / 6:51 A.M. EST until
Moon enters Pisces: 5:15 A.M. PST / 8:15 A.M. EST
Venus squares Chiron: 2:06 P.M. PST / 5:06 P.M. EST

○◑◐●

S U N D A Y

December 16

MOON IN PISCES
SUCCESS RATING: ★★

Everything may still feel a little tentative in the relationship department. At first, things may seem to swing in one direction, and then—in an instant—they'll turn the other way. The idea is not to be attached to the outcome.

Under this Moon, you tend to merge with another person's perspective, often without knowing it. Try to separate yourself by taking a breath and imagining that each time you exhale, you're releasing anything that you've absorbed from those around you.

This is a perfect time to rest, but like yesterday, it's not great for the solidification of agreements. And if you're a flirtatious type, this date issues yet another warning: Affairs that occur today are happening under an aspect called the "marriage breaker." Be smart and stay in tonight—and read a wonderful book on turtles.

AFFIRMATION FOR THE DAY:
All of my relationships are embraced by a circle of love, including my relationship to *me*.

BIG SPINS OF THE DAY:
None

○◑◐●

MONDAY

December 17

LAST QUARTER MOON IN PISCES
SUCCESS RATING: ★★

After a seemingly turbulent few days, everything can now come to fruition. Today should hold a great deal of information for you in the areas where you've been stymied. This is a significant date, thanks to the Superior Conjunction between Mercury and the Sun, which heralds a new chapter of awareness and brings closure to past events that were hurtful or confusing.

There's an excess of change and activity in the air—too much for me to endorse this as a good time for successful launchings, but *you* can be the judge. This kind of electric energy is right up the alley of some more high-voltage types. However, if you'd prefer a nice, peaceful day, you might try booking a flight to your favorite island.

AFFIRMATION FOR THE DAY:
I offer others the love and acceptance that I want to receive.

BIG SPINS OF THE DAY:

Last Quarter Moon 25° Pisces: 2:18 A.M. PST / 5:18 A.M. EST
Mercury conjuncts Sun: 7:27 A.M. PST / 10:27 A.M. EST
Moon Void of Course: 10:27 A.M. PST / 1:27 P.M. EST until
Moon enters Aries: 10:53 A.M. PST / 1:53 P.M. EST
Venus trines Uranus: 10:43 P.M. PST / 1:43 A.M. EST (Tuesday)

○◑◐●

TUESDAY

December 18

MOON IN ARIES
SUCCESS RATING: ★★★

Your inner pioneer is screaming to get out from under this Aries Moon. Feisty and fiery, it activates your warrior spirit and sends you out into the world broadcasting a silent dare: *Get out of my way or I'll run you over.*

There's a major planetary shift as Jupiter leaves Sagittarius and enters Capricorn. This placement will last for all of next year and suggests that you're going to bring your focus toward rebuilding in a big way. The cycle last occurred in 1996, so you may want to look back to that period for some clues.

Capricorn is the sign of the corporation, and since Jupiter is the planet of expansion, it looks as if you're going to see an increase in mergers. Of course, all that means today is that you may need a little time to adjust. Move slowly and nurture a big idea.

AFFIRMATION FOR THE DAY:
I love my mind, and I use it to heal what is ailing.

BIG SPINS OF THE DAY:
Jupiter enters Capricorn: 12:13 P.M. PST / 3:13 P.M. EST

○ ◑ ◐ ●

WEDNESDAY

December 19

SATURN RETROGRADE
MOON IN ARIES/TAURUS
SUCCESS RATING: ★★★

Mind-bending insights are available to you today if you want them. The powerful connection of Mercury and Pluto is giving you the perception you need to see right to the heart of any issue. Used with gentle compassion, this could be very beneficial in helping others understand parts of themselves that they would otherwise reject. Don't be intimidated by your own fearlessness, but do make sure that you aren't being narrow-minded or unfair when engaging in a dialogue with someone who disagrees with you.

Saturn is going retrograde, and since it's in Virgo, you'll begin the next cycle with a serious examination of your life. Be warned: Saturn in Virgo makes you extremely sensitive to criticism, and self-scrutiny can be unduly harsh. So before you start a critical campaign against yourself, invite a friend over who can counter any slanted "microanalysis" that you might wage.

Capricorns are doubly affected by this backward spin, so if that's your sign, keep an eye out for the scales tipping too far in one direction.

AFFIRMATION FOR THE DAY:
I recognize my anger as an attack on myself, and I am now replacing it with compassion.

BIG SPINS OF THE DAY:
Saturn Retrograde 9° Virgo: 5:37 A.M. PST / 8:37 A.M. EST
Mercury conjuncts Pluto: 10:49 A.M. PST / 1:49 P.M. EST
Moon Void of Course: 11:33 A.M. PST / 2:33 P.M. EST until
Moon enters Taurus: 1:38 P.M. PST / 4:38 P.M. EST

○◑◐●

THURSDAY

December 20

MOON IN TAURUS
SUCCESS RATING: ★★

It's a seriously optimistic day—or maybe an "optimistically serious" day. Whichever way you frame it, Mercury is joining Jupiter in Capricorn, and it won't be long before the Sun gets there, too. Capricorn loves a purpose, and while Mercury is in that sign, your thought processes will probably become less like the aimless pursuit of just anything and more akin to a soldier's mission.

Discover what your objective is. Notice what ideas your mind is wrapping around, and be conscious of your choices. The Sun is joining Pluto today for a cup of truth and a sprinkle of passion, and you can easily see through any fog.

Capricorn uses depression as a way to clear out the old. So if you notice that this season is eliciting more than the usual holiday blues, remember that it's a useful process that's triggered symbolically by the planet's entrance into Capricorn. The best antidote is to be compassionately aware that your low spirits don't define the truth but are pathways to finding yourself. And once your moods are felt, they simply melt away.

AFFIRMATION FOR THE DAY:
I love all the forms of expression that emerge *from* me, but I never forget that they are not *me*.

BIG SPINS OF THE DAY:

Mercury enters Capricorn: 6:43 A.M. PST / 9:43 A.M. EST
Mercury conjuncts Jupiter: 1:54 P.M. PST / 4:54 P.M. EST
Sun conjuncts Pluto: 4:14 P.M. PST / 7:14 P.M. EST
Moon Void of Course: 10:06 P.M. PST / 1:06 A.M. EST (Friday) until tomorrow

Happy Birthday, Capricorn!

DECEMBER 21–JANUARY 20

No other sign deals with the world as instinctively as Capricorn does. It starts when people of this sign are young, and you can see it in their eyes—they have a mission, and no one is going to take them off course. It's almost as if they're finishing what they started in some other lifetime, although Capricorns are far too pragmatic to entertain such ideas.

Most Capricorns hide their age well. It's as if they're doing everything backward: They come into the world seeming much older than they are, and they get younger as they mature. There are few people born under this sign who will tell you that their early life was easy. Most of them started working as soon as they could talk—perhaps caring for an ill parent, completing long lists of chores, or watching over the other siblings. Whatever their tasks, they started them early, knowing that they'd have to rely on their inborn skills to perform them.

Capricorns follow an internal set of rules where there are no shortcuts, and there's something about their symbol (the mountain or sea goat) that captures their multifaceted ability to handle any situation. People born under this sign may present a tough exterior, but anyone who's allowed to enter their lives knows the depth of the embrace that they provide. If you listen closely to a Capricorn's story and watch his or her attitude, you'll see into the heart of someone you can truly rely on.

AFFIRMATIONS FOR CAPRICORN:

I am a whole, wonderful being regardless of what I *do.*

I accept support graciously and without strings attached.

I have everything I need right now to be happy and whole.

○◑◐●

FRIDAY

December 21

WINTER SOLSTICE (PST)
SUN IN CAPRICORN
MOON IN TAURUS/GEMINI
SUCCESS RATING: ★★

The Winter Solstice is the longest night of the year—the day when the Sun moves into the stoic sign of Capricorn. It's little wonder that candles are the main theme in many religions' ceremonies on this day, as it celebrates light. (Although friends Down Under are seeing an opposite lighting effect, they're still experiencing the internal pull.)

Remember that depression is the natural response to the reflection of longer nights, so don't start popping the antidepressants (unless prescribed to do so, of course). The Moon is Void of Course until the afternoon, so take the morning in slowly, and let the change of season find you.

Later, you'll feel the buzz of the Gemini Moon's desire for connection. It's the perfect night to celebrate winter . . . so light a candle, and send off your intention of peace and love, knowing that your blessing will come right back to you.

AFFIRMATION FOR THE DAY:
I celebrate the darkness as a reflection of the power of my light.

BIG SPINS OF THE DAY:
Moon Void of Course: until 2:14 P.M. PST / 5:14 P.M. EST
Moon enters Gemini: 2:14 P.M. PST / 5:14 P.M. EST
Sun enters Capricorn (Winter Solstice): 10:08 P.M. PST / 1:08 A.M. EST (Saturday)

○◑◐●

SATURDAY

December 22

MOON IN GEMINI
SUCCESS RATING: ★★★

It's a wonderful day on many levels as the Sun and Jupiter hold hands for their yearly rendezvous. Although this date may have undertones of seriousness, there's still a feeling of hope and inspiration just waiting to be embraced.

Venus and Mercury are clashing with some of the bigger guys, suggesting that sensitivities could be high and squabbles might erupt, but you have a choice as to how you want to play in today's energy. Try to remember that winning an argument may signify that you're the victor, but it doesn't mean that you're right. Err on the side of compassion today.

Let those who aren't feeling the magic of the season see what's possible through the twinkle in your eye. With so many planets in Capricorn, it's easy to forget that not everyone is able to tough it out as easily as you do. Make a wish tonight . . . the Sun-Jupiter alignment only happens once a year, so let it be useful!

AFFIRMATION FOR THE DAY:
Compassion is the first doorway I walk through.

BIG SPINS OF THE DAY:
Venus squares Neptune: 2:22 A.M. PST / 5:22 A.M. EST
Mercury opposes Mars: 10:29 A.M. PST / 1:29 P.M. EST
Sun conjuncts Jupiter: 9:56 P.M. PST / 12:56 A.M. EST (Sunday)

○◑◐●

SUNDAY

December 23

FULL MOON IN CANCER
MOON IN GEMINI/CANCER
SUCCESS RATING: ★

It's a day of reconciliation and compromises as the Moon challenges most of the planets. Emotions may seem volatile and edgy right now, which is very likely being translated into the pressure of the holidays. If you keep your focus on meeting people halfway, you'll probably find that this is actually a time of great accomplishments. Full Moons are generally emotional and erratic, but your awareness can change everything. Be helpful and supportive, allowing yourself to be the reflection of the balance that's possible regardless of circumstances.

Take a moment to light a special Full Moon candle and send out your kind intentions. Mars is staying active throughout the holiday season, so consider yourself duly warned that many people around you are feeling tightly wound. This is a great day to take a brisk walk, especially if you find that biting your tongue is starting to hurt.

Remember your family, and remind yourself that you can make all the difference in the world with one smile.

AFFIRMATION FOR THE DAY:
I extend love outwardly, even where it does not seem to be welcomed.

BIG SPINS OF THE DAY:
Moon Void of Course: 12:26 P.M. PST / 3:26 P.M. EST until
Moon enters Cancer: 2:19 P.M. PST / 5:19 P.M. EST
Full Moon at 2° Cancer: 5:16 P.M. PST / 8:16 P.M. EST

○ ◑ ◐ ●

MONDAY

December 24

MOON IN CANCER
SUCCESS RATING: ★

Your moods—and those of the people around you—will vary greatly today. Mars and the Sun are clashing, and that's a sure sign that tempers may very well flare and passions might get misdirected. Just stay conscious, and remember that all religions with celebrations during this cycle have love as their foundation.

If you're doing any last-minute shopping, you'll see the planetary clash in action. Please be mindful that this date can create accidents that are born of impulsive and thoughtless acts. On the upside, there's a lot of energy in the air today—so use it to feel accomplished. If you're attending any gatherings, be mindful of the time and your consumption of alcohol or drugs.

Dreams tonight could prove useful and lush, so try to retire early.

AFFIRMATION FOR THE DAY:
I reclaim the radiant and loving person that is me.

BIG SPINS OF THE DAY:
Sun opposes Mars: 11:47 A.M. PST / 2:47 P.M. EST

○◑◐●

TUESDAY

December 25

MOON IN CANCER/LEO
SUCCESS RATING: ★★

A warm and cozy Cancer Moon Christmas is here. The focus on family and the feeling of love may engulf you when the Moon touches Venus first thing in the morning—and as the hours pass, Mercury manages to rebuild burned bridges through honest and supportive communication.

The Moon is Void of Course for most of this date, suggesting that emotions will feel balanced and easy. There's a lot of room to move slowly and allow the day to define your course. Pushing to meet deadlines defeats the purpose of a peaceful holiday, but if you have to do so, give yourself plenty of time to get ready in order to avoid stress.

If you're not in the company of your family right now, you'll very likely find the restful tone to be a refreshing change of pace.

AFFIRMATION FOR THE DAY:
I am the reflection of Divine love.

BIG SPINS OF THE DAY:
Moon Void of Course: 5:18 A.M. PST / 8:18 A.M. EST until
Moon enters Leo: 3:53 P.M. PST / 6:53 P.M. EST
Mercury trines Saturn: 3:10 P.M. PST / 6:10 P.M. EST

○◑◐●

WEDNESDAY

December 26

MOON IN LEO
SUCCESS RATING: ★

The wonderful optimism of the Leo Moon carries the theme for today. In the first part of the morning, you may feel a little disconnected (or perhaps *wish* that you could be) from the people around you, but that will change.

Mars is returning with a jolt of power for you, suggesting that more plans are in the works. Perhaps you're using this day to return gifts or take advantage of after-Christmas specials—in either case, be ready to confront some supercharged energy out in the world.

Keep your spirits high and your outlook positive. Don't let someone's undisciplined demeanor upset you. Oh, and I have some great news: Romance is making a comeback!

AFFIRMATION FOR THE DAY:
My circumstances are never so difficult that they prevent me from finding the constant rock of peace within me.

BIG SPINS OF THE DAY:
Mars opposes Jupiter: 11:52 A.M. PST / 2:52 P.M. EST

○◑◐●

THURSDAY

December 27

MOON IN LEO/VIRGO
SUCCESS RATING: ★

This is the last Leo Moon of the year, so do your best to express its highest potential. Generosity, optimism, and courage come to mind as qualities that you can embrace while these royal lunar rays beam down. You may experience a loss of energy during the day due to the shift of the Moon into Virgo, but it shouldn't be diminished enough to put you in a slump. It could be difficult to muster up the will to work, but if you can, seize the day and enjoy it.

Later tonight the Virgo Moon will call your attention to the things that need to be organized. Keep your smile pasted on, even if you aren't feeling as perky as you could. If you're having a hard time remembering that everything is okay, just find someone who's having a worse day than you are, reassure him or her that all is well, and then see how you feel. Remember that giving is the same as receiving.

AFFIRMATION FOR THE DAY:
I willingly use my humor in a loving way to bring a smile to everyone I see.

BIG SPINS OF THE DAY:
Moon Void of Course: 6:55 P.M. PST / 9:55 P.M. EST until
Moon enters Virgo: 8:45 P.M. PST / 11:45 P.M. EST

○◑◐●

FRIDAY

December 28

MOON IN VIRGO
SUCCESS RATING: ★★★

Try to mute your inner critic today—there's just too much good stuff happening. The Moon is embracing you in a tender way, along with many of the planets, and that could make this day seem effortless. There's a moment when you could find yourself taking things *way* too seriously, though. Perhaps you made a mistake or found one that you believe could have been avoided. So what? Use the dry humor of Virgo to make a joke of it and move on.

You aren't likely to be in a social mood this evening, but if you are, you'll have lots of takers on an invitation to dinner. Your mind could be restless tonight . . . stop your caffeine consumption early so that you'll be able to fall asleep.

AFFIRMATION FOR THE DAY:
I reclaim my childhood innocence
and use it every chance I get.

BIG SPINS OF THE DAY:
None

○◑◐●

SATURDAY

December 29

MOON IN VIRGO
SUCCESS RATING: ★★

It's another all-day Moon in Virgo! When it lands on a weekend, this Moon definitely has a cleaning agenda. Maybe you're hosting a New Year's party, or perhaps there are decorations that just need to be put away . . . well, this is your day! Wrap everything up in an orderly fashion, label the outside of your boxes, and get ready for 2008. Your mind is likely to be plugged in and turned on, so if you find yourself on the verge of obsessing, you can intervene forcibly with a break for hot tea.

Phone conversations may help you focus your energy, but don't let the outside world distract you from your goals. This is still not a social Moon for most of you, but if you do feel compelled to gather with friends, you'll probably be in store for a good time. Increased mental activity suggests that you get to bed early for some restful sleep.

AFFIRMATION FOR THE DAY:
I love my imperfections, and
I understand that they do not define me.

BIG SPINS OF THE DAY:
Mercury sextiles Uranus: 8:10 P.M. PST / 11:10 P.M. EST

○◑◐●

SUNDAY

December 30

MOON IN VIRGO/LIBRA
SUCCESS RATING: ★★

A big day of change awaits you, kicked off by the Sun and Saturn holding hands. It's easy to work toward your goals and desires when these guys are in the material sign of Capricorn. Although their connection may add a itsy-bitsy, teeny little bit of seriousness to the day, Venus helps out by leaping into Sagittarius. I guess that means you can be "seriously" playful, but having two very different energies vying for your time might cause some anxiety.

Since this is a day when many of the planets are changing signs, you may feel a little disoriented. If that happens, just think about this: You're at the very end of a long year, and you survived! If you're at the bottom of the barrel, there's no where to go but up—and if you're feeling great, then there's nothing to worry about. Now get moving . . . there's a celebration to get ready for.

AFFIRMATION FOR THE DAY:
I look back on any part of my life and see an enormous number of reasons to be grateful.

BIG SPINS OF THE DAY:
Moon Void of Course: 5:10 A.M. PST / 8:10 A.M. EST until
Moon enters Libra: 5:38 A.M. PST / 8:38 A.M. EST
Sun trines Saturn: 5:24 A.M. PST / 8:24 A.M. EST
Venus enters Sagittarius: 10:02 A.M. PST / 1:02 P.M. EST

○◑◐●

MONDAY

December 31

MOON IN LIBRA
SUCCESS RATING: ★★

Well, you did it—not only were you able to survive a very intense year, but you also managed to make New Year's Eve fall on a light, social Libra Moon! For the most part, the planets are cooperating, as if to ensure that you get to have a night of fun. For those of you (like me) who participate in all celebrations via the television, make your evening enjoyable: Pop some corn (and the champagne cork, of course), enjoy a good movie, and wait for the ball to drop.

Thank you for riding through this year with me. I have good news for next year starting with a wonderful—*oops!* . . . I'll save that information for next year's book!

I sincerely hope that you have attained all that you desired this year. And, look out for *Mark's Power Peek 2008!*

AFFIRMATION FOR THE DAY:
I am love.

BIG SPINS OF THE DAY:
Mars enters Gemini: 8:02 A.M. PST / 11:02 A.M. EST

Thought for the Month

Before All This

Before there were these problems,
Before there were these bills,
Before there were these arguments,
Before there were these pills,
Before there were these mortgages or payments due for rent,
Before there were these headaches over how much cash I've spent,
Before there were these losses of so many of those I love,
Before there were these guilty thoughts that fit me like a glove,
Before there were these highs and lows,
Before there were these frights,
Before there were these worries to keep me up all night,
Before there were these wars that keep my fear on high,
Before there were these aches and pains that never say good-bye,
Before all those things that make the mountain look so steep—
Was me embraced in loving light, about to fall asleep.

May your awakening be gentle and your remembrance be full!

○ ☽ ☾ ●

AFTERWORD

Thank you for sharing the journey of 2007 with me. I hope that this book proved a worthy companion as you navigated each day throughout the year.

There's something to be said for sharing an experience—knowing that there were people out there facing issues similar to mine helped me feel safer and less afraid. May next year bring you even more peace and joy, because that's really what we're all striving for.

Until then, I'm with you on the quest. . . .

ACKNOWLEDGMENTS

Naming the people who helped make this book possible is a more daunting task than actually writing the entire thing. There were countless letters of support and words of encouragement, and the love that came my way was likewise immeasurable. All of it was like precious fuel that kept my fingers typing and my attitude optimistic. Of the many, there were also the few who lost sleep with me, fed me, yelled at me, and generally sacrificed so that *Mark's Power Peek 2007* could become a reality. They include:

Louise Hay; her assistant, Shelley Anderson; and the CEO of Hay House, Reid Tracy—the only reasons that the book could have ever been born.

Dee Rock, Kelly Crowther, and John Joseph—it took the three of you with Mars in Virgo to manage this Mars in Pisces. You were amazing!

Jill Kramer—my refreshingly honest Virgo editor.

Ernest and Mary Husson—my loving parents, who still fretted and worried and made sure that I was eating throughout the entire process.

Joy Hewitt-Kind and Marsha Pruett—my on-call nurses with herbs and needles!

Michael DeCamillis—for keeping my head turned in the right direction.

Christopher Matthews—for getting passing grades while keeping the Website content fresh so that I could write.

Monica Lockrem, Judy Greth, and Clarity MacKay—the Twelfth House staff, who kept the store afloat and barricaded me in so that the writing could continue.

Audra, Paula, Drueann, Catherine, Julia, Radliegh, and Mo—the Twelfth House psychics, who all lovingly predicted this moment.

Tom Strapp and Sam Larbi—my friends and the technicians of Powersource, who made the Website and the "Power Peek" available to the world.

The "Power Peek" members—the reason for it all.

PART III

APPENDICES

GETTING TO KNOW THE ZODIAC SIGNS BETTER

Elements and Modalities

Elements define the basic temperament of each sign, and are based on the four primary elements introduced in ancient Greece: *Earth, Air, Fire,* and *Water.* Each one rules three Zodiac signs, which share its same qualities. Here's a brief description of each:

<u>Fire</u>

Signs Ruled: Aries, Leo, Sagittarius

Highest Motive: Inspiration, transformation, spirituality, optimism, and exploration

Lowest Motive: Intrusiveness, self-aggrandizement, narcissism, and fear of monotony

<u>Earth</u>

Signs Ruled: Taurus, Virgo, Capricorn

Highest Motive: Security, sensuality, productivity, and practicality

Lowest Motive: Miserliness, laziness, outward focus, and stubbornness

Air

Signs Ruled: Gemini, Libra, Aquarius

Highest Motive: Connection, objectivity, understanding, and brilliance

Lowest Motive: Detachment, fear of commitment, coldness, and obsessiveness

Water

Signs Ruled: Cancer, Scorpio, Pisces

Highest Motive: Compassion, nurturing, empathy, and healing

Lowest Motive: Dependency, addiction, secretiveness, and meddling

Modalities define the behavior of each sign, and are determined by the division of each season into three parts. They are differentiated by the individual characteristics of each segment within the season: *cardinal, fixed,* and *mutable.* There are four signs in each modality—one for each season. Each sign in the Zodiac is specifically categorized by one of these properties, along with one of the previously described elements.

Cardinal: First of the Season

Cardinal Signs: Aries, Cancer, Libra, Capricorn

Highest Motive: Encouragement, initiative, and enthusiasm

Lowest Motive: Aggression, impatience, and the desire to start things but not to finish

Fixed: Middle of the Season

Fixed Signs: Taurus, Leo, Scorpio, Aquarius

Highest Motive: Stability, supportiveness, and consistency

Lowest Motive: Stubbornness, obsessiveness, and fixation

Mutable: End of the Season

Mutable Signs: Gemini, Virgo, Sagittarius, Pisces

Highest Motive: Flexibility, accommodation, and understanding

Lowest Motive: Unreliability, changing moods, and the fear of stability

BEING PREPARED: THE PRE- AND POST-RETROGRADE ZONES*

(*The *Pre- and Post-Retrograde Zones* are areas of space [translated into dates] that a retrograde planet will revisit before and after the actual retrograde period.)

Dates and Degrees for All of the Planets' Retrogrades

MERCURY RETROGRADE (First)

January 30: Mercury enters Pre-Retrograde Zone 25° Aquarius

February 13: Mercury Retrograde begins 10° Pisces

March 7: Mercury Retrograde ends 25° Aquarius

March 27: Mercury leaves Post-Retrograde Zone 10° Pisces

MERCURY RETROGRADE (Second)

May 30: Mercury enters the Pre-Retrograde Zone 2° Cancer

June 15: Mercury Retrograde begins 12° Cancer

July 9: Mercury Retrograde ends 2° Cancer

July 24: Mercury leaves the Post-Retrograde Zone 12° Cancer

MERCURY RETROGRADE (Third)

September 21: Mercury enters the Pre-Retrograde Zone 23° Libra

October 11: Mercury Retrograde begins 9° Scorpio

November 1: Mercury Retrograde ends 23° Libra

November 17: Mercury leaves the Post-Retrograde Zone 9° Scorpio

VENUS RETROGRADE

June 23: Venus enters the Pre-Retrograde Zone 17° Leo

July 27: Venus Retrograde begins 3° Virgo

September 8: Venus Retrograde ends 17° Leo

October 11: Venus leaves the Post-Retrograde Zone 3° Virgo

MARS RETROGRADE

September 16: Mars enters the Pre-Retrograde Zone 24° Gemini

November 15: Mars Retrograde begins 12° Cancer

January 30, 2008: Mars Retrograde ends 24° Gemini

April 4, 2008: Mars leaves the Post-Retrograde Zone 12° Cancer

JUPITER RETROGRADE

January 9: Jupiter enters the Pre-Retrograde Zone 10° Sagittarius

April 5: Jupiter Retrograde begins 20° Sagittarius

August 6: Jupiter Retrograde ends 10° Sagittarius

November 1: Jupiter leaves the Post-Retrograde Zone 20° Sagittarius

SATURN RETROGRADE

April 19: Saturn Retrograde ends 18° Leo

September 15: Saturn enters the Pre-Retrograde Zone 2° Virgo

December 19: Saturn Retrograde begins 9° Virgo

May 2, 2008: Saturn Retrograde ends 2° Virgo

August 7, 2008: Saturn leaves the Post-Retrograde Zone 9° Virgo

URANUS RETROGRADE

March 6: Uranus enters the Pre-Retrograde Zone 15° Pisces

June 23: Uranus Retrograde begins 19° Pisces

November 24: Uranus Retrograde ends 15° Pisces

March 15, 2008: Uranus leaves the Post-Retrograde Zone 19° Pisces

NEPTUNE RETROGRADE

February 1: Neptune enters the Pre-Retrograde Zone 19° Aquarius

May 24: Neptune Retrograde begins 22° Aquarius

October 31: Neptune Retrograde ends 19° Aquarius

February 18, 2008: Neptune leaves the Post-Retrograde Zone 22° Aquarius

PLUTO RETROGRADE

December 4, 2006: Pluto enters the Pre-Retrograde Zone 26° Sagittarius

March 31, 2007: Pluto Retrograde begins 29° Sagittarius

September 7: Pluto Retrograde ends 26° Sagittarius

December 27: Pluto leaves Post-Retrograde Zone 29° Sagittarius

○☽☾●

ABOUT THE AUTHOR

A man with a lifelong interest in the inner workings of the mind, **Mark Husson** received his undergraduate degree in psychology, and went on to receive his master's in counseling from West Virginia University. It wasn't until a copy of *Linda Goodman's Love Signs* fell into his hands in 1979 that it became clear to him that astrology had the potential to be the fastest and most definitive map of the psyche.

In 1982, that map became the focus of Mark's career when he moved to Denver and met Jungian astrologer John Joseph. The two opened Denver's premier astrological store, the Twelfth House, in 1989, which developed a reputation not only for its psychological approach to astrology, but also for its promotion of the ideal that spirituality is something that's guaranteed regardless of one's beliefs. Thus, the slogan "Inspiring the Human Adventure" became the store's trademark, and a mantra that Mark believes is an integral part of being a good astrologer.

Mark developed a training program for psychic readers, teaching them tools for dealing with people and respecting their roles, which made the Twelfth House readers among the most trusted in the world. Subsequently, Mark's astrological classes and workshops have enabled psychotherapists, psychiatrists, psychologists, and laypeople to become aware of astrology's ability to empower them and their clients. Those classes became the largest single gathering related to psychological astrology that Denver had ever seen, and they continue to be offered twice a year.

In July of 1998, Mark designed the Twelfth House Website (**www.12house.com**), which has been recognized for its psychological approach to astrology and for the "Power Peek" newsletter, which is sent to Website members each week.

○ ◑ ◐ ●

We hope you enjoyed this Hay House book.
If you'd like to receive a free catalog featuring additional
Hay House books and products, or if you'd like information
about the Hay Foundation, please contact: